TRUE STORIES
OF THE
GREAT WAR

TALES OF ADVENTURE—HEROIC DEEDS—EXPLOITS
TOLD BY THE SOLDIERS, OFFICERS, NURSES,
DIPLOMATS, EYE WITNESSES

Collected in Six Volumes
From Official and Authoritative Sources
(See Introductory to Volume I)

VOLUME III

Editor-in-Chief
FRANCIS TREVELYAN MILLER (Litt. D., LL.D.)
Editor of The Search-Light Library

1917
REVIEW OF REVIEWS COMPANY
NEW YORK

Copyright, 1917, by
REVIEW OF REVIEWS COMPANY

CONTENTS

The Board of Editors has selected for VOLUME III this group of stories told by Soldiers, Naval Officers, Nurses, Nuns, Refugees, Airmen, Spies, and other participants and eye-witnesses of the Great War. They have been collected from twenty-three of the most authentic sources in Europe and America, and include 143 personal adventures and episodes. The selections have been made according to the plan outlined in the Introductory to Volume I, for selecting from all sources the "Best Stories of the War." Full credit is given in every instance to the original source. All numerals are for the purpose of identifying the various episodes and do not relate to the chapters in the original volumes.—EDITORS.

VOLUME III—TWENTY-TWO STORY-TELLERS—143 EPISODES

WHAT I FOUND OUT IN THE HOUSE OF A GERMAN PRINCE   1
STORIES OF INTIMATE TALKS WITH THE HOHENZOLLERNS
Told by an English-American Governess
(Permission of Frederick A. Stokes Company, of New York)

"FROM CONVENT TO CONFLICT"—A VISION OF INFERNO .   18
A NUN'S ACCOUNT OF THE INVASION OF BELGIUM
Told by Sister Antonia, Convent des Filles de Marie
(Permission of John Murphy Company, of Baltimore)

"WAR LETTERS OF AN AMERICAN WOMAN"—IN BLEEDING FRANCE 30
EXPERIENCES IN THE SIEGE OF PARIS
Told by Marie Van Vorst, American Novelist
(Permission of John Lane Company, London and New York)

"A GERMAN DESERTER'S WAR EXPERIENCE"—HIS ESCAPE   48
"THE INSIDE STORY OF THE GERMAN ARMY"
Told by—(Name Withheld)
(Permission of B. W. Huebsch, of New York)

"THE SOUL OF THE WAR"—TALES OF THE HEROIC FRENCH   70
REVELATIONS OF A WAR CORRESPONDENT
Told by Philip Gibbs
(Permission of Robert M. McBride and Company, New York)

(Vol. III)

CONTENTS

"TRENCHING AT GALLIPOLI"—IN THE LAND OF THE TURKS 91
    ADVENTURES OF A NEWFOUNDLANDER
    Told by John Gallishaw
      (Permission of the Century Company, of New York)

SCENES "IN A FRENCH HOSPITAL" 106
    STORIES OF A NURSE
    Told by M. Eydoux-Demians
      (Permission of Duffield and Company, of New York)

"FLYING FOR FRANCE"—HERO TALES OF BATTLES IN THE AIR 126
    WITH THE AMERICAN ESCADRILLE AT VERDUN
    Told by James R. McConnell
      (Permission of Doubleday, Page and Company, of New York)

THE LOG OF THE "MOEWE"—TALES OF THE HIGH SEAS . . 166
    THE ADVENTURES OF A MODERN PIRATE
    Told by Count Dohna-Schlodien, her Commander
      (Permission of Wide-World Magazine)

PRISONER'S VOYAGE ON GERMAN U-BOAT UNDER THE SEA 196
    Told by—(Name Withheld by Request)
      (Permission of New York Times)

THE DARKEST HOUR—FLEEING FROM THE BULGARIANS . 208
    OUR EXPERIENCES IN THE GREAT SERBIAN RETREAT
    Told by Alice and Claude Askew
      (Permission of Wide World Magazine)

A MAGYAR PALADIN—A RITTMEISTER OF THE HUSSARS . 222
    ALONG THE ROAD FROM POLAND TO BUDAPEST
    Told by Franz Molnar
      (Permission of New York Tribune)

OUR ESCAPE FROM GERMAN SOUTH-WEST AFRICA . . . 231
    Told by Corporal H. J. McElnea
      (Permission of Wide World Magazine)

WHAT AN AMERICAN WOMAN SAW ON THE SERBIAN FRONT 261
    HOW I VIEWED A BATTLE FROM A PRECIPICE
    Told by Mrs. Charles H. Farnum of New York
      (Permission of New York Sun)

"KAMERADS!"—CAPTURING HUNS IN THE ALPS WITHOUT A FIGHT 270
    DIARY OF A LIEUTENANT OF ALPINE CHASSEURS
      (Permission of Wide World Magazine)

(Vol. III).

CONTENTS

LIFE ON A FRENCH CRUISER IN WAR TIME 282
"LES VAGABONDS DE LA GUERRE"
Told by René Milan
(Permission of Current History)

OVER THE TOP WITH THE AMERICANS IN THE FOREIGN LEGION 293
Told by Donald R. Thane
(Permission of New York Herald)

SECRET STORIES OF THE GERMAN SPY IN FRANCE . . . 306
HOW SIXTY THOUSAND SPIES PREPARED FOR THE WAR
(Permission of Wide World Magazine)

HOW STRONG MEN DIE—TALES OF THE WOUNDED . . . 329
EXPERIENCES OF A SCOTTISH MINISTER
Told by Rev. Lauchlan Maclean Watt
(Permission of The Scotsman)

THROUGH JAWS OF DEATH IN A SUNKEN SUBMARINE . . 336
Told by Emile Vedel in L'Illustration, Paris
(Permission of New York World)

ESCAPE OF THE RUSSIAN LEADER OF THE "TERRIBLE DIVISION" 343
TRUE STORY OF HOW GENERAL KORNILOFF ESCAPED ACROSS HUNGARY
Told by Ivan Novikoff
(Permission of Wide World Magazine)

THE AERIAL ATTACK ON RAVENNA 358
Told by Paoli Polettit in L'Illustrazione Italiana
(Permission of Current History)

(Vol. III)

Underwood & Underwood.

BRINGING IN A WOUNDED COMRADE

Some of the Most Heroic Acts of the War Have Been Performed as Part of the "Day's Work" of the Ambulance Corps. This French Ambulance Attendant is Risking His Own Life During the French Offensive at Verdun to Carry a Fellow Poilu Back Through the Woods Razed by German Gun Fire.

READING HOME NEWS BEFORE STARTING FOR THE TRENCHES

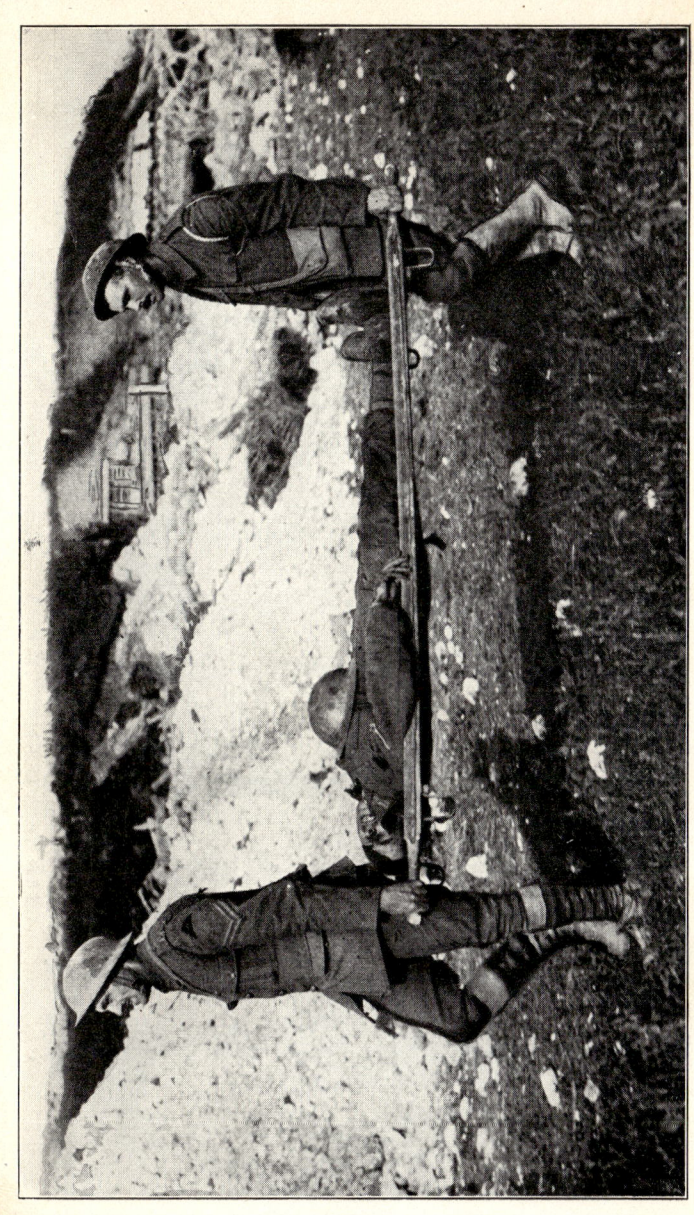

HE CHARGED WITH HIS BATTALION A FEW HOURS EARLIER

A FRIEND'S TURN YESTERDAY—HIS PERHAPS TODAY

WHAT I FOUND OUT IN THE HOUSE OF A GERMAN PRINCE

Stories of Intimate Talks with the Hohenzollerns

Told by an English-American Governess

These true stories reveal for the first time the "inside workings" of the German Court. They are told by a woman who overheard conversations between the members of the House of Hohenzollern and the military and diplomatic castes. She was governess in a German princely house at the outbreak of the war, having secured her position through Prince Henry of Prussia, whom she met in Washington, during his visit to the United States. Her grandfather was an admiral in the United States Navy. She tells frankly of her conversations with the Kaiser, the Crown Prince, General von Bernhardi, the Krupps, Count Zeppelin, General von Kluck, Herr Dernburg, and important secret service people, who took her into their confidences. These revelations (which have been published by *Frederick A. Stokes Co.*, of New York) are most absorbing reading. Here we are necessarily limited to a selection of but six anecdotes from the hundreds of entrancing stories in her book. The book is a valuable record of her experiences as governess of two young princes at their game, "destroying London before supper," to her final escape in disguise after the war began.

BY a coincidence, it was five years ago, on the day of my internment in a German castle last August (1914), that I undertook to teach English and other things to the children of that castle's owner. During four of those years I did my duty to my three little charges as well as I knew how. For the rest of the time, up to two days before the declaration of war between France and Germany, my conduct may have been questionable: but that was because I put duty to my country ahead of duty to the family of a

German prince. They were my employers; they trusted me, and I am not sure whether I decided rightly or wrongly. All I know is that I would do the same if I had to live through the experience again. . . .

As for the most important men who visited them, it is different. I owe those persons nothing, and see no reason for disguising their names. Most of them have now, of their own accord, thrown off their peace-masks, and revealed themselves as enemies of England, if not of humanity, outside German "kultur." What I have to tell will but show how long they have held their present sentiments. . . .

*I—A CONVERSATION WITH THE KAISER

My two Princes and their cousin were having an English lesson with me in a summer-house close to their earthworks. It had been raining.

I was reading aloud a boys' book by George Henty which I had brought among others from England for that purpose, and stopping at exciting parts to get the children to criticize it in English. We were having an animated discussion, and all three were clamoring for me to "go on—go on!" when I heard footsteps crunching on the gravel path which led to the summer-house. I did not look up, because I thought it might be Lieutenant von X—— who was coming, and my charges were too much excited to pay attention. But presently I realized that the crunching had ceased, close to us. My back was half turned to the doorway, and before beginning to read again, I looked round rather impatiently.

---

* All numerals throughout this volume relate to the stories herein told—not to the chapters in the original books.

In the House of a German Prince 3

Two gentlemen in uniform were standing in the path, one a step or two in advance of the other. Nobody who had seen any of the later photographs could have failed to recognize the foremost officer as the Kaiser, though the portraits were idealized. The face of the original was older, the nose heavier, and the figure shorter, stockier than I had expected. Nor had I been told about the scar high up on the left cheek. I was so taken by surprise that I lost my presence of mind. Jumping up, I dropped my book, and knocked over the light wicker chair which was supposed to be of British manufacture. I was so ashamed of my awkwardness—such a bad example to the children!—that I could have cried. To make matters worse the Emperor burst out laughing, a good-natured laugh, but embarrassing to me, as I was the object of his merriment.

"I have upset the United Kingdom and the United States of America!" his Imperial Majesty haw-hawed in good English, though in rather a harsh voice, making a gesture of the right hand toward the chair of alleged British make, and the fallen book with George Henty's name on its back, at the same time giving me one of the most direct looks I have ever had, full in the face. It seemed to challenge me, and I remembered having heard that a short cut to the Kaiser's favor was a smart repartee. The worst of it was that like a flash I thought of one which would be pat, if impertinent, but I dared not risk it.

Luckily my two Princes rushed past me to throw themselves upon their sovereign, and their cousin followed suit, more timidly. Perhaps she had discovered that his Imperial Majesty does not much care for little girls unless they are pretty.

The Kaiser was kind but short in his greeting of

the children, and did not seem to notice that they expected to be kissed. Probably he was not satisfied as to their state of health, as they had been sent out of an infected town, and he has never conquered his horror of contagious diseases. With his right hand (he seldom uses the left) on the dark head of the elder boy, he pivoted him round with rough playfulness. "Don't you see that Miss ——'s chair and book are on the floor?" inquired the "All Highest." "What is a gentleman's duty—I mean pleasure—when a lady drops anything?"

"To pick it up," replied the child, his face red as he hurried back into the summer-house and suited the action to the word.

"Very good, though late," said the Kaiser. Then, no doubt thinking that I had had time to recover myself, he turned to me, more quizzical than ever. "Perhaps according to present ideas in England I am old-fashioned? But I hope you are not English enough to be a suffragette, Miss ——?"

I recognized the great compliment of his knowing my name, as I am sure he expected. I had heard already that suffragettes were to the Emperor as red rags to a bull, and that he always brought up the subject with Englishwomen when he met them for the first time. I ventured to remark that to be English was not necessarily to be a suffragette.

He shook his finger at me like a schoolmaster, though he smiled.

"Ah, but you are not an Englishwoman, or you would not say that! All these modern Englishwomen are suffragettes. Well, we should show them what we think of them if they sent a deputation here. But while they confine themselves to their own soil we

In the House of a German Prince

can bless them. They are sowing good seed for us to reap."

I had no idea what his Majesty meant by the last sentences, though I could see that an innuendo was intended. His certainty that he was right about all modern Englishwomen was only what I had seen in visitors to Schloss ———, every one of whom, especially the Prussians, knew far more about English ideas and customs than the English knew about themselves. I had sometimes disputed their statements, though without effect, but I could not contradict the Emperor. All I could do was to wonder what he had meant by "sowing the good seed," and a glance he had thrown to his aide-de-camp (or "adjutant," as the officer might more Germanly be called), but it is only after these five years that I have perhaps guessed the riddle. The Kaiser must even then have begun to count on the weakening of England by its threatened "war of the sexes."

. . . .

The Emperor proceeded to introduce his officer attendant, who was a Count von H——— He informed me that he and his suite had travelled all night in the royal train, to inspect the nearby garrison and breakfast with the officers. Having a short time to spare, he had arranged to motor up to Schloss ——— and have a look at the children, in order that he might report on the Princes' health to their mother and father the next time they saw each other.

"No sign of the malady coming out in them?" he inquired. "And the youngest? He, too, is all right?"

On hearing that the baby was not as well as could be wished, he looked anxious, but cheered up when he heard that the feverishness was caused by cutting teeth.

"That is not contagious!" said he. "Though some of us might be glad to 'catch' a wisdom tooth."

When he made a "witticism," he laughed out aloud, opening his mouth, throwing back his head slightly with a little jerk, and looking one straight in the eyes to see if one had appreciated the fun of the saying. The more one laughed the better he seemed pleased, and the more lively he became, almost like a merry child. But when the subject was dismissed, and he began to think of something else, I noticed—not only on that day, but on others, later—that occasionally an odd, wandering, strained expression came into his eyes. For a moment he would appear older than his age; though when his mind was fixed upon himself, and he was "braced" by self-consciousness, he looked almost young and very vital, if fatter than his favorite photographs represented him.

That day at Schloss —— the Emperor did not stay with us longer than twenty minutes at most, but he managed to chat about many things in that time, the latter part of which was spent in talking with Lieutenant von X——, to find whom he sent the younger of my Princes.

. . . .

I have heard that the Kaiser is always anxious as to the first impression he makes, even upon the most insignificant middle-class person; and having delivered himself of this harangue, he set to work to smooth me down before departing. He asked questions about myself, and the family (his friends) with whom I had lived in England. With his head thrust forward and wagging slightly, he mentioned several advantages which an English governess had over a German one; and then he blurted out, sharply and suddenly, that, if my little Princes' parents had listened to his advice, they would have had an Englishwoman for their children two years sooner. "But the Princess —— is the most self-willed woman I know," he said. "You may think I am indiscreet! I am forever accused by newspapers of being indiscreet, because I speak what I think. But this is no secret. You will learn it for yourself if you are as intelligent as I suppose. She never was intended by nature to be a wife and mother, though she would be a charming person if she were neither. As it is she will do what she likes in spite of everything and everyone. There! I have said enough—or too much. Where is von X——?"

The Lieutenant was hovering in the background, ready for an auspicious moment: and the Emperor turned his attention to the governor of my elder Prince. It was not till he was ready to go that he had another word for me, and then it was only "Auf wiedersehen." He graciously put out his hand, palm down, for me to shake. I noticed how large it was in contrast with the left, which he kept out of the way. It was beautifully cared for, and there were more rings on it than an Englishman or American would wear, but it was not an attractive shape, and looked somehow unhealthy. As if in punishment to me for such a thought, the big hand gave mine a fearful grip. It was like the closing of a vise, and I could almost hear my bones crack. I wondered if the Emperor had cutlivated this trick to show how strong he was; but I should have been glad to take his strength on faith.

I could not help wincing, though I tried not to let my face change. If it did, he appeared to take no notice. He had finished with me, after a military salute; and letting the children run by his side, he and his attendant, with Lieutenant von X——, walked down the path. . . .

II—STORY OF BERNHARDI AND THE KRUPPS

One of the most interesting things that happened to me in my first year was a visit (with the Princess, of course) to Villa Hügel, the house of Herr and Frau Krupp von Bohlen, in the Ruhr valley near Essen. Bertha Krupp, the "Cannon Queen" and richest German heiress in Germany, if not the world, had been married to the South German diplomat, Gustav von Bohlen und Halbach, less than four years. She was only about twenty-four, but the coming of children had aged her as it does all German women apparently, and she had already ceased to look girlish. Her husband, who is sixteen or seventeen years senior to his wife, might have been no more than ten years older, to judge by their appearance when together. He put the name of Krupp in front of his own immediately after his marriage with the heiress, and few people add the "und Halbach" now, except officially. . . .

While I was in the "Spatzenhaus" with the boys, Herr Krupp von Bohlen brought in these four gentlemen and another, to see the celebrated visitors' book kept there since Bertha and Barbara were children. General von Bernhardi had arrived the night previous, and this was my first sight of him, as well, of course, of Herr Eccius and Doctor Linden.

I was more interested in the last of the three, because I had listened while Frau Krupp von Bohlen repeated to the children a wonderful story about the intelligence of some fish in the Naples Aquarium; and all I knew then of General von Bernhardi was that he was considered a great soldier, and had been the first officer to ride into Paris in 1871, or some tale of that sort. However, the minute I saw him I felt that here was a tremendous personality, and an intensely repellent one, a man to be reckoned with. I determined to ask a great many questions concerning him of the Countess, who knew everything about everybody, and did not object to telling what she knew with embellishments.

My name was politely mentioned by the host, and the visiting gentlemen all bowed to me. The only one who did so stiffly, as if he grudged bending his thick, short neck for my benefit, was General von Bernhardi. He gave me one sharp look from under his rather beetling eyebrows, and I wondered if he despised all women, or had merely taken a distaste to me.

"You are English?" he asked shortly, in German, his tone being that of a man accustomed to throw out commands as you might throw a battle-ax.

"She was born in Washington," said Herr Krupp von Bohlen, in his pleasant, cultivated voice. "Washington is the most interesting city of the United States, and holds pleasant memories for me. Miss ——'s grandfather was a distinguished American naval officer."

As he said this, he gave me a faint, rather humorous smile, which I interpreted as a warning or request not to try explaining my antecedents.

"Ach! That is better!" grunted the General. And I knew that, whatever might be his attitude toward women in general, Englishwomen were anyhow beyond the pale.

(Later I heard from the Countess that women were not much higher than the "four-footed animal kingdom" for Bernhardi; that he loudly contradicted his wife, even at hotel tables, when they traveled together;

that he always walked ahead of her in the street, and pushed past her or even other ladies, if strangers to him, in order to go first through a doorway.)

The General condescended to glance at me, and I thought again that he was the most ruthless, brutal-looking man I had ever met, the very type of militarism in flesh and blood—especially blood.

"You are a friend of the English?" he inquired.

I dared to stand up for England by answering that I thought her the greatest country in the world.

"That is nonsense," was his comment. I shall never forget it, or the cutting way in which it was spoken.

The Prince, though knowing me to be English (which Bernhardi, to do him justice, did not), backed the General up, explaining for my benefit as well as the children's that England might once have been nominally the most powerful nation, owing to her talent for grabbing possessions all over the world, and the cleverness of her diplomacy. But, he said, that was different now, under the Liberal Government. England was going down exactly as Rome had gone down, and the knell of her greatness was sounding already. Not one of her colonies would stand by her when her day of trouble should come, and most of them would go against her.

"You have only to read their own newspapers," said General Bernhardi, "to see that the English know they are degenerating fast. But the hand of Fate is on them. They are asleep, and they will wake up with a rude shock only when it is too late."

III—STORY OF THE CROWN PRINCE AND THE CROWN PRINCESS

Some quite innocent tales were told by the tattlers, of the Crown Princess. One was, that she had determined from the moment of her engagement to his Imperial Highness, to be the most beautiful and best dressed royal lady in Europe, as he strongly desired her to be, and that it almost broke her heart when she began to realize that being the mother of one baby after another was enlarging her slender waist. She was supposed to have had a wax model of herself made, soon after the birth of her first boy: face, hair, and figure all resembling her own as faithfully as possible. According to the story, she had every new fashion of hairdressing tried on this model, before deciding to use it herself, and would have milliners fit it with hats, rather than choose one to suit her own style merely from seeing it in the mirror. Gowns were shown to her in the same way when they arrived from Paris or Vienna, said the gossip who told me the tale, and the first time the measurements which fitted the figurine proved too small for the Princess's waist, there were tears.*

I did not fall in love with noisy Berlin, though Unter den Linden is so fine and imposing, with all its beautiful shops and trees. The city was so neat and square, so stolid and self-respecting that the capital of Prussia made me think of the Prussian character as I soon began to judge it. Potsdam I found more in-

---

* The Governess here tells of an interesting little flirtation between the Crown Princess and an Englishman because the Crown Prince "had flirted furiously with several athletic but beautiful ladies at a Winter Sports place in the Engadine."

teresting because it is old and historic. We spent a good deal of time in both places, and I used often to see the Emperor motoring in a yellow car with a very small Prussian royal standard on it to show who was the owner. The Crown Prince was always dashing about, too, generally driving himself, very recklessly, with a cigarette in his mouth, and looking about here and there, everywhere except where he was going. He had a black imp for a "mascot" on his automobile, a thing that waved its arms in a way to frighten horses, though it never seemed to do so. And sometimes the car would be full of ladies and children and several quite large dogs that walked over their owners and tried to jump out. The crowds seemed to like him, and the Crown Princess, whom they called "the sunshine of Berlin," even more. She was always very gracious, bowing and smiling, while the Crown Prince looked extremely bored. Still, if he had not been hailed with enthusiasm, I am sure he would have been vexed. Sometimes he would appear at a window of the palace, perhaps with one of the royal children in his arms, pretending not to notice the people outside gazing at him. But I thought he looked self-conscious, as if he were doing it all for effect. . . .

What I had heard from the Countess about the Crown Prince going to India and Egypt in the character of a "glorified spy" (even though I doubted the assertion) and the intimate talk of our Prince's "influence" in the Secret Service department, made me think more about spies and spying in a few months, than I had ever thought in my whole life. I began to look about for spies, and wonder if any of the much traveled, cultured people I met were engaged in spying with some of the highest in the land virtually at their head. The last person I should have connected with the profession of spying, however, was Herr Steinhauer. Even now I cannot be sure that he and the famous "master spy" of whom I have heard so much since I came back to England, are one and the same; but everything goes to prove that they are. . . .

IV—STORY OF A VISIT FROM COUNT ZEPPELIN

Once in Berlin, Count Zeppelin came, after having taken the Crown Prince, and my little Princes' father as well as one or two of their army friends, for a flight in his newest airship. Our Prince came back very enthusiastic after his trip, and wanted his elder son to go, but the Princess would not hear of this, and Count Zeppelin backed her up. He said that he did not know enough about children's nerves to risk an experiment, though he believed such boys as ours would stand it well. He told them, when they both begged to go, that they must content themselves with the "game" for a few years, and asked a good many questions of Lieutenant von X—— (who was present by request) as to how the little players got on with it. When he was talking of ordinary things, his face looked good-natured, even benevolent, with his rather scanty white hair and comfortable baldness. I thought, with a false beard, he would have exactly the right figure and face for Santa Claus; but as he listened to Lieutenant von X——'s account of how he taught the Princes to "play the game," and examined some of the toy buildings (so often powdered white with "bombs" that they could no longer be brushed completely clean), his face hardened, looking very stern and very old, his bright eyes almost hiding between wrinkled lids.

The Count took the elder boy between his knees, and catechised him as to some of the rules. The little boy was shy at first, but soon plucked up courage, and answered in a brisk and warlike way.

"This is a born soldier," said the airship inventor, laying his hand on the child's hair. "By the time he is ready for sky battles, we shall have something colossal to give him; but in the meantime, please Heaven, we shall make very good use of what we have got." ...

V—STORY OF GENERAL VON KLUCK—"THE OLD DARE-DEVIL"

Among other distinguished men who came to see my Princes and their plays, was General von Kluck —another one of those "great dome heads!" To me, it seemed the best part of his personality, and certainly the development was far superior to what I had named the "German officer head," a crude, unfinished type of head, which gives the impression that the skull has hardened before the brain had time to finish growing. General von Kluck did not talk at all to me, or appear to take any interest in the toy soldiers' battle. He had the air of being absent-minded and thinking deeply of something far away, in space. I heard him say that "they" wanted him to go to France to look at it. Who "they" were, I do not know, or what "it" was that they wished General von Kluck to see. But I knew that nearly a year after that visit the children had a present of a fancy red velvet box of chocolate. The Princess herself brought it into the schoolroom (we seldom had a lesson that was not interrupted in some way or other), and as the covering had already been removed, I do not know if the box had been sent from a distance or had come by hand. The Princess showed the boys General von Kluck's visiting card, and the writing on it, which said, "French chocolate from France, for two brave young German soldiers."

Later that day the Prince came and asked to see the box "from old von Kluck," which by that time was half empty. He looked at the card, and laughed. "The old dare-devil!" he chuckled. Then he said that, as we had eaten so much in such a short time it showed that French chocolate was good.

I seldom or never had any real conversation with the Prince, and it was not my place to ask questions; but I wondered why General von Kluck was an "old dare-devil" to go to France, and why the Prince seemed so pleased and amused about it. Also I remembered what I had heard the General say some months before, about France. I thought that there must be a mystery about it, either official, or something to do with a lady, perhaps a Frenchwoman. I know no more now than I knew then; but I have heard it said since I came back to England, by a Frenchman, that General von Kluck is supposed to have visited France incognito, to look at some quarries near Soissons, which Germans bought and secretly made ready to use as trenches, beginning their work a year before the war broke out.

VI—STORY OF THE CONFESSION OF LIEUTENANT VON X——

I often asked Lieutenant von X—— what the German army thought about the future of Germany, and I do not think he suspected in the least that I had any motive except "intelligent interest." He had come to look upon me as a family institution, and without telling lies in so many words, I allowed him to believe that I felt Germany's vast superiority over the rest of the world. It is a simple thing for any woman to make any German man believe this. The only difficult thing for him to understand is that a creature can be benighted enough to have a contrary opinion.

Lieutenant von X—— admitted that the German army as well as navy prayed for "The Day." He thought that Germany could "walk through France," and she, being far superior to Russia in every way, could not help but win in a war against that power, even without the help of Austria. He seemed to feel contempt for Austria and everything Austrian compared with what was German, but he said "she can be useful to us." As for England, she might be a tougher job, but it would "have to come," and with the improved Zeppelins (which England had been a "stupid-head" not to copy as well as she could) and the Krupp secrets, there was no doubt who would come out on top: Germany, the one power on earth who deserved by her gloriousness to be over all others. America, too, eventually must become Germanized, as Lieutenant von X—— believed she was already well on the way to be, with her growing German population, immense German financial interests, and influential newspapers. The plans for American conquest were already mapped out by the German War Office, who never left anything to chance. He said that this was no secret, or he would not mention it. There was once a hope that Germany and England might make a combination against the United States; but that had been abandoned, he said. Once I should have taken this for a joke, and also the expectation that when France was conquered (with Belgium thrown in as a matter of course) Antwerp and Dunkirk and Calais would all be German, becoming the

In the House of a German Prince

strongest military ports in the world; but I had learned better now. I knew that Lieutenant von X——, who seldom originated any ideas of his own, was simply repeating to me the sort of talk he heard among his brother officers. . . .

(The English-American Governess from this point relates a most remarkable story, every word of which is vouched for as the truth. She tells how Von Hindenburg, the Crown Prince, and other notables met in secret sessions at the palace where she was residing; about their relations with Prince Mohammed Ali and Enver Bey, the Envoy from Turkey; the intrigues in the days before the outbreak of the war; the scenes in the royal households when war was declared; and how she escaped at midnight, September 15, 1914. It is a revelation that gives one a clearer insight into the causes of the Great War and how the Hohenzollerns had planned for many years to enter upon a conquest of Europe and America.—EDITOR.)

"FROM CONVENT TO CONFLICT"—A VISION OF INFERNO

Or, A Nun's Account of the Invasion of Belgium

By Sister Antonia, Convent des Filles de Marie, Willebroeck, Province of Antwerp, Belgium

This is the appeal of a nun, who in the fullness of her heart tells the American people of the noble efforts of her Sisters to bring solace and comfort to agonized Belgium. Sisters Mary Antonia and Mary Cecilia were sent to the United States with the approval of Cardinal Mercier, Archbishop of Malines, with the following credentials: "The Superior of the Convent of the Daughters of Mary, Willebroeck, Provence of Antwerp, Belgium, state by this present (letter) that the Sisters Mary Antonia and Mary Cecilia are sent to the United States in order to examine if there are means of establishing a colony (mission) of the Daughters of Mary there; she gives to Sister M. Antonia the power to act in her name as to taking the measures necessary to this effect." Sister Antonia tells her noble story in a little volume (published by *John Murphy Company,* Baltimore. Copyright, 1916) with this introduction: "The hope is indulged that the harrowing scenes witnessed by the author in Belgium, after the German invasion in 1914, may induce her own countrymen and women to more fully appreciate the blessings of peace. The events narrated are set forth as actually occurring, and—'with malice to none, with charity for all.' Any profits derived from its favorable reception by the reading public or the charitably inclined are to be devoted to the reconstruction and repair of our school and convent, damaged during the engagement at the Fortress of Willebroeck, or for the establishment of a sewing school, with a lace making department, for young women in America or England, as our Reverend Superiors may decide." The editors take pleasure in commending this book and in extending their appreciation to the publishers for their courtesy in allowing these selections.

I—STORY OF THE FATEFUL DAY IN THE CONVENT

A merry group of Convent girls, in charge of Sister guardian, was seated in the shade of a huge old pear tree, discussing the joys and expectations of the approaching summer vacation. High are the walls enclosing this ancient cloister, and many are the gay young hearts protected and developed within its shady precincts.

Bright are the faces and happy the hearts of more than one hundred young girls on this midsummer day in the memorable year 1914. . . .

July's sun sank gently away on the western horizon, and its last rays lit up the ripening fruit, the plants and flowers in the garden. It seemed to linger for a last farewell to the groups of merry children who, unconscious of their fast-approaching woe, were cheerfully singing Belgium's well-known national song, "The Proud Flemish Lion."

In a few moments the "Golden Gate" closed on a field of purple haze, shutting out that blessed glimpse of heaven, while the black shroud of the most dismal night in history darkened the sky of that hapless nation.

The Sisters were together in the evening recreation of that fateful day, when word was received that King Albert of Belgium, in order to fulfill his obligations of neutrality, had refused the Kaiser's army access to his territory to attack the French. Had a thunderbolt fallen from a clear sky, or an earthquake shaken the ground under foot, it would scarcely have surprised or terrorized the people more than did the Kaiser's declaration of war against this free and happy little kingdom. . . .

One Sunday morning, about the middle of August, an unusual tumult was heard on the street. The door bell was loudly rung, and a messenger admitted with news that the officers of the Belgian War Department had commanded everything within firing range of the fortress to be cleared away at once. For some time previous the soldiers had been busy cutting down the groves and all the trees in the immediate vicinity of the fortress. The poor people were given just three hours to get away with bag and baggage.

This was a terrible misfortune for about six hundred families, whose dwellings, being located within the limits prescribed, had to be leveled to the ground. Even the tombstones in the cemetery, together with all the crops, trees, haystacks, barns and everything within range of the gaping mouths of the cannon, had to be laid flat or taken away.

No wonder that the people raced to and fro that hot Sunday morning, carrying bundles, dragging wagons with household furniture and fixtures; wheeling trunks, clothing, stoves, pictures, bedding and every article that could be taken up and carried away. Tears and perspiration rolled over the cheeks of men and women, whose faces glowed from the heat and intense excitement. . . .

II—STORY OF THE SOLDIERS AT LIEGE

In the meantime a most terrible battle was taking place at the fortification of Liege. Was ever attack so strong or resistance more determined? Belgian officers said, "The enemy were twenty to one against us; but, being obliged to face the terrible fires of the fortress, their ranks were cut down in about the same manner as wheat is cut off by the reaper." "So great was the number of the Germans that they seemed to spring up out of the ground." "They crawled ahead on hands and feet, and at a given signal sprang erect and fired, and then again prostrated themselves. Thus they advanced, avoiding as much as possible the heavy fires in front." Another Belgian officer at the fortress during the battle said: "It resembled a storm of fiery hailstones from a cloud of smoke, in an atmosphere suffocating with heat and the smell of powder."

Eyewitnesses relate that heaps of slain, yards high, were found on the battlefield, while columns of lifeless bodies were observed in a standing position, there being no place for the dead to fall.

A story was told by one of the Belgian officers of a German soldier who, when wounded by a Belgian in a hand-to-hand combat, took out a coin and presented it. The Belgian, surprised, exclaimed "Zijt gij zot?" (Are you crazy?) "Do you not know that I've broken your arm?" "Yes," said the German, "This is to show my gratitude for the favor you've rendered me, since it gives me the opportunity of leaving the battlefield."

Much was said about the valor of the soldiers on both sides during the siege of Liege. The Germans were obliged to advance in the face of destructive fires. If one should retreat, he would be pierced by the bayonet of the soldier behind him. . . .

While facing death in this first great battle at the fortress of Liege, one of the soldiers began to sing the well-known national hymn, "The Proud Flemish Lion." Immediately the strains were taken up by the whole regiment, and thus singing, they advanced until hundreds of them fell in that awful conflict.

In the heaviest of the fray we were told that King Albert had placed himself in the lines with his soldiers. He did not desire to be called king, but comrade. His military dress was distinguished from the others by only a small mark on one of the sleeves. He attended to the correspondence for his soldiers and was regarded by them as a friend and father, under whose guidance they were ready to fight and die.

When the siege was over he visited the wounded in many of the hospitals and addressed each soldier in person. . . .

After the fall of Liege and Namur, the destruction of Louvain and a number of noted cities, towns and villages, our minds were concerned with that awe-inspiring event—the advance of the enemy to Brussels.

Well do we remember that beautiful summer evening, when our prayers and evening meditation in the chapel were disturbed for about an hour by the continuous whirl of automobiles passing the Convent. We were told that evening that it was the departure of the legislative body from Brussels to Antwerp, with the archives and treasures of the Government.

Our hearts seemed to grow cold and leaden within us as we sat there hoping, praying, fearing, yet instinctively feeling the doom so rapidly approaching.

One gloomy, rainy day, word came that over two thousand soldiers of the Civil Guard had lowered their weapons at the approach of the enemy and quietly surrendered the City of Brussels, Belgium's beautiful capital. To have fought without fortifications against such superior forces as the Germans possessed would have been a useless sacrifice of life.

III—STORY OF THE PRIESTS, DOCTORS AND RED CROSS NURSES

One afternoon in the middle of August a large, heavy wagon was drawn into the yard. It bore the flag of the Red Cross on top, and on the side in great white letters the words "Military Hospital."

In a few minutes a fleshy little gentleman, who at once distinguished himself as the "Chef" (chief), and a number of other gentlemen, about thirty-five in all, wearing white bands with red crosses on their arms, and long white linen coats over their uniforms, such as bakers sometimes wear, were seen hurrying to and fro, unpacking and carrying their various instruments and utensils to the operating room.

A military chaplain and four or more doctors accompanied the group. All except the chaplain were dressed in uniform. Several young ladies of Willebroeck, former members of our Boarding-school, dressed in white and wearing the head-dress and armband of the Red Cross, came next day and graciously presented themselves to aid in taking care of the wounded.

Coffins were provided by our village for the soldiers who died in our hospital. . . .

The condition of the poor maimed soldiers (as they were brought into the convent) was sad to behold. One man, we were told by the Red Cross nurses, had twenty bullets in his body; another was pierced through the lung by a bayonet; one, aged twenty, lost an arm to the shoulder; one had only one or two fingers left on the hand; one was crazed by a bullet which touched the brain; another was shot through the mouth, the bullet lodging in the back of the throat. His case was especially distressing, his the most intense suffering of all. He lived for a week without eating, drinking or speaking.

Three wounded Germans were brought in, being picked up on the battlefield by members of our division of the Red Cross. They seemed greatly distressed and afraid, positively refusing to touch food or drink of which the Sisters or nurses did not first partake.

One day we were called upon to witness a most sorrowful sight. A small farmer's wagon drove up to the gate, bearing the lifeless bodies of two children, a girl aged eight and her brother, aged fourteen. The mother and a smaller child were also in the wagon. The mother related that they were taking flight as refugees. Seeing the enemy, they hastened to retreat, and were fired at by the soldiers. The children, who were in the back part of the wagon, were struck and wounded in a most frightful manner. The little girl's face was nearly all torn off, and the back of the boy's head had been shattered.

At the approach of Belgian soldiers, who fired at the enemy, the mother was enabled to pick up the lifeless bodies of her children, put them into the wagon and drive with them to our hospital, which was the nearest post.

A little after four o'clock one afternoon, shortly before the departure of the first division of the Red Cross, our attention was attracted by the heavy and continuous tread of cavalry and soldiers passing along the street. It was the Belgian army returning from a long and tiresome march.

Here was found a different kind of suffering from that which was ministered to in the hospital. Hunger and fatigue were stamped upon the countenance of each of these men, who, about a month before were industrious citizens at their daily occupations.

There were in the ranks priests, in their long black cassocks, wearing the arm-band of the Red Cross, who, as volunteer chaplains, had joined the army and were ever at the service of the soldiers on the march, and even on the battlefield. We were informed that priests, and those preparing for the priesthood, were not obliged to serve in the army in time of peace; but, in case of war, they may be called upon to serve as military chaplains. When the present war broke out, hundreds of them joined as volunteers, marching in the ranks with the soldiers and undergoing their sufferings and hardships.

Many doctors rode along in motor cars. They were distinguished by a special dark-colored uniform, with a red collar and gilded trimmings. They also wore the arm-band of the Red Cross. Officers on horse-back led each division of the army. The faces of all were disfigured with sweat and dust, while dust in abundance covered shoes and clothing. Some were staggering along, unable to walk straight, owing to the hard shoes and blistered feet. Hollow-cheeked, and with eyes which seemed to protrude from their sockets, they passed along, piteously imploring a morsel of bread.

Fortunately, the abundant supply of bread in the Convent had just been increased by the addition of forty of those immense loaves found only in Belgium. All of this was hastily cut, buttered and, with baskets full of pears, dealt out, piece by piece, to the passing soldiers, until, finally, only a small portion remained over for the supper of the wounded remaining in the hospital. . . .

Before the command was given to enter the schools, we saw soldiers, among whom were also priests, lying on the ground on the opposite side of the street, even as horses which, having run a great distance, fall down from sheer exhaustion. Some of these, we learned afterwards, did not have their shoes off in nearly three weeks. The socks, hard and worn out, were in some cases stamped into the blistered feet in such a manner as to cause excruciating pain. In some cases the feet were so painful and swollen that the patients had to be carried in on stretchers. In the meantime, several ambulance wagons had stopped at the school gate, and numerous wounded were carried in.

We retired at a late hour one night amid the incessant booming of cannon. Scarcely were our eyes closed when some one passed in the dormitory and knocked at each door. "Ave Maria," was the quiet greeting. "Deo Gratias," the response. "What is it?" was asked. "The Germans have entered and are crossing the bridge," was the reply.

With beating heart and trembling limbs, each sprang up and was dressed in a few minutes. In a state of great excitement, all stood in the hall ready to receive orders from the Superior, who had gone downstairs to make inquiries about the situation. . . .

The crackling of shells, the heavy cannonade from the fortress and field cannon, and the occasional proximity of those hostile aeroplanes, together with the reports of atrocities and destruction taking place around us, were fearsome in the extreme.

In striking contrast to the noise and commotion on all sides, was the calm tranquility which reigned in the chapel. The Sacred Heart stretched forth that same Fatherly hand which assisted the apostle sinking on the Sea of Galilee. The altar was still and solitary, but the little red light flickered in the sanctuary lamp and told of Him whose word alone stilled the winds and calmed the angry waves. . . .

IV—STORY OF THE HEROIC REFUGEES

Sorrowful scenes were witnessed along the streets. Our attention and sympathies were particularly attracted to the flight of the refugees.

For hours and days and weeks the doleful procession passed along the streets; a living stream made up of all ranks and classes of society. Here were seen the poor old farmer's household, whose sons had gone to the front; and young married women, with small children in their arms or by their sides, whose husbands had to don the soldier's uniform and go to the war. The sick, the old and the feeble were taken from their beds of suffering and, with shawls or blankets thrown over their shoulders, placed in carts or wagons and carried away, perhaps, to perish by the roadside. We have seen cripples and small children hurriedly driven along the street in wheelbarrows.

Packages carried on their arms, on their backs, or in little carts were about all that the poor people could take. . . .

It was most pitiful to see these poor people, whose only object was to get away as far as possible from the scenes of conflict. Some carried small loaves of bread; others had a little hay or straw in their wagons; some led a cow or two; others two or three pigs. In some of the carts we recognized faces of our former pupils, who only one short month before were longing for the pleasant vacation days. Their fathers or brothers were in the army, and their homes forsaken. Some children had lost their parents and were crying piteously.

When the Sisters left the parish church, where they daily took part in the public devotions for peace, they were besieged by hundreds of these poor, half-frantic refugees, beseeching shelter over night in the church or schools, which were already full to overflowing. The days were warm and pleasant, but the nights were very chilly and sometimes rainy. Where would those poor people go and what could they do without food or shelter for all those little children? The friendly stars looked down from the realms above upon thousands who lay along the roadside, while others crowded the barns and country schools, or made rude tent-like shelters in the bed of the new canal.

The Sisters, wholly absorbed in their work for the wounded, and relying on the word of the Belgian officers, that timely warning would be given as to the necessity of departure, had as yet no idea of joining the throngs of refugees who continuously filed through the main streets.

The shocks of the cannonade from the fortress caused the buildings to tremble on their foundations, while the ground under foot seemed agitated as by an earthquake. A large number of wounded soldiers had been brought in the night before, and three or four lay dead in the mortuary.

Our Sisters and servant maids, as also the generous women refugees of Willebroeck, continued their sickening task in the laundry. In wooden shoes they stood at those large cement tubs while suds and blood-dyed water streamed over the stone floor.

Night closed in again, but brought neither rest nor consolation. Fearing to retire, some of the Sisters remained in the chapel, while others spent the tedious hours of that dreary night in the refectory or adjoining rooms, and kept busy making surgical dressings for the wounded, of whom a larger number than usual had been brought into the hospital.

At intervals during the night the cannonade was heard, while the searchlights of the fortress penetrated the clouds on the look-out for the murderous Zeppelins. Morning came at last, with an increase of work and anguish. The enemy, with their usual determination, were trying to force their way through to Antwerp, while the Belgians were equally determined to prevent them, or to at least check their progress.

An officer called for the Reverend Superior and said in an excited manner, "Weg van hier, aanstonds! Geen tijd te verliezen." (Away from here at once! No time to be lost.) This message flew from one to another, even to the terror-stricken hearts of the numerous wounded.

Impossible to describe the scenes which followed. In a few minutes a long line of motor cars came whirling up to the gate to take away the wounded who, some of them in an almost dying condition, were being dragged out of their beds, dressed and hurriedly carried away to Antwerp, or to another place of refuge. One can never forget the look of anguish on some of their faces, while others seemed totally indifferent to all that was taking place around them. . . .

(Sister Antonia here tells about the flight of the nuns with the refugees to Antwerp and the sea; the exodus to England and Holland; and finally her own voyage to America.—EDITOR.)

"WAR LETTERS OF AN AMERICAN WOMAN"—IN BLEEDING FRANCE

Experiences in the Siege of Paris

By Marie Van Vorst, Distinguished American Novelist Residing in Paris

These letters present a singularly vivid chronicle of an American woman's experiences during the Great War. She was living in Paris, but brought her mother to London for safety. Here she went through a course of Red Cross lectures and returned to become a nurse at the American Ambulance in the Pasteur Institute in Neuilly, then under the control of Mrs. W. K. Vanderbilt. Her brilliant intellect and sympathizing heart are brought out in her letters to friends in America. Her whole soul is in the cause of the Allies and in her letters she tells many beautiful stories of her experiences in Paris, London, Nice and Rome. To read her impressions as she wrote them down for her friends is to recapture the thrill and the uplift, the sorrows and the hopes, the high resolves and unshakable purpose of those that will live forever in history. Several letters are reprinted here by permission of her publisher, *John Lane Company,* London and New York.

I—STORY OF ROBERT LE ROUX

To Miss Anna Lusk, New York.

Paris, Nov. 7th, 1914.

DEAREST ANNA:

In the contemplation of the great griefs of those who have lost their own, of those who have given their all; in the contemplation of the bravest country in the world—Belgium—ravaged from frontier to frontier, laid barren and waste, smoked, ruined, devastated and scarred by wholesale massacre of civilian women and children, our hearts have been crushed. Our souls have been appalled by the burdens of others, and by the future problems of Belguim, not to speak of one quarter of France. Much of the north has been wiped out, and the stories of individual suffering and insults too terrible to dwell upon, you will say.

One of my old clerks in the Bon Marché has had his little nephew come back to him from Germany—a peaceful young middle-class man pursuing his studies in a German town—with both his hands cut off!

The other day in the Gare du Nord, waiting for a train, there was a stunning Belgian officer—not a private —he was a captain in one of the crack regiments. His excitement was terrible, he was almost beside himself with anguish and with anger. In a little village he had seen one woman violated by seven Germans in the presence of her husband; then the husband shot, the woman shot and her little baby cut in four pieces on a butcher's block. You can hardly call this the common course of war. He was a Belgian gentleman, and I should consider this a document of truth.

But there are so many that I cannot prolong, and will not—what is the use? Every now and then a people needs to be wiped off the face of the earth, or a contingent blotted out that a newer and finer civilization shall prevail. Certainly this is the case with Germany. They say here that the Emperor and Crown Prince will be tried by law and sentenced to death as common criminals, the Emperor as a murderer and the Crown Prince as a robber, for his goods trains were stacked with booty and loot. Think of it, a Prince! Everywhere the Germans pass they leave their filthy insults behind them, in the beautiful châteaux and in the delicate rooms of the French women—the indications of their passing, not deeds of noble heroism that can be told of foes as well as of friends, but filthy souvenirs of the passing of creatures for whom the word "barbarism" is too mild!

Here is a more spiritual picture.

Robert Le Roux, jun., was buried yesterday. You will have read in the previous pages here the story of his exploits on the battlefield—the closing of his young life in bravely leading his troops up the hill to certain death. And yesterday I went to St. Germain to his funeral.

The last time I had seen young Robert he was a little boy, in short breeches and socks. His mother brought him to Versailles and he played with us in the garden there—a strong, splendid-looking young French boy. Now I was going to his funeral, and he was engaged to be married, with all his hopes before him, and on this same train was his little fiancée, in her long crêpe veil, broken-hearted; and his little sister, and the father, who had followed his son's campaign with such ardor and such tenderness; and his uncle, Dr. D., of whom I spoke previously—the splendid sergeant-major whose only son had just been killed by the enemy. A train of sorrow!—and only one of so many, so many.

The church at St. Germain is simple and very old. The doors were all hung with heavy snow-white cloth, and before the door stood the funeral car drawn by white horses, all in white, and instead of melancholy hearse plumes there were bunches of flags, and over all hung the November mist enveloping, softening, and there was a big company of Cuirassiers guarding the road.

We went in, and the church was crowded from the nave to the doors, and all the nave and the little chapels were blazing with the lily lights of the candles. It was all so white and so pure, so effulgent, so starry. There was an uplift about it, an élan; tragic as it all was, there was ever that feeling of beyond, beyond!

Before the altar lay the young man's coffin—that leaden coffin that had stood by his father in the fortress of Toul for three weeks, waiting for the dead. It was completely covered by the French flag, and the candles burnt around it.

Beside me was a woman with her husband. She wept so bitterly through the whole service that my heart was just wrung for her, and her husband's face, as his red-lidded eyes stared out in the misty church, was one of the most tragic things I ever saw. I wept, of course, and I have not cried very much since the war broke out, but her grief was too much for me. Finally she turned to me and said: "Madame, I only had one son, he was so charming, so good; he has fallen before the enemy, and I don't know where he is buried!" Just think of it! There she was, at the funeral of another man's son because he was a soldier! Link upon link of sorrow and suffering—such broken hearts. . . .

The whole service was musical, nothing else but violins and harps. It was the most beautiful thing I ever heard, so quiet and so sweet; and that little group touched me profoundly—Le Roux with his daughter and the little fiancée—and that was all. In that coffin lying under the flag Bessie had placed at Toul her little silk pillow for the young soldier's head, and his love-letters in a little packet lay by his side. Around his arm he had worn a little ribbon taken from the hair of his sweetheart, and at the very last when he was dying and the hospital nurse was about to unknot it—I don't know why—the boy put up his feeble hand to prevent her; of course they buried it with him, and, as you think of it, you can hear that unknown voice on the battlefield, that, as the stretcher-bearers came to look for the wounded, called out: "Take him, he is engaged to be married; and leave me."

Oh, if out of it all arise a better civilization, purer motives, less greed for money, more humanitarian and unselfish aims, we can bear it.

I think of America with an ever-increasing love; I am proud to belong to that young and far-off country, but if our voice is raised now in encouragement for Belgium, encouragement for the Allies, and in reprobation of these acts of dishonorable warfare and cruel barbarism, I shall love my country more.

How superb the figure of the Belgian king is, standing there among the remnant of his army, and surrounded by his destroyed and ruined empire, and the cries of the people in his ears—a sublime figure. . . .

II—STORY OF A SCHOOL TEACHER—AND A GARDENER

To Mr. F. B. Van Vorst, N. Y.

Nov. 20th, 1914.

MY DEAR BROTHER,

I wonder, as I sit here, in one of those rare, quiet moments that fall in a nurse's day, whilst I am preparing my charts, what they are thinking of in this silent room.

This group is singularly silent. They do not talk from bed to bed, as some of the more loquacious do. Directly opposite is one of those fragile bits of humanity that the violent wind of war has blown, like an unresisting leaf, into the vortex. Monsieur Gilet is a humble little school teacher from some humble little village school in a once peaceful commune, where in another little village school his humble little wife teaches school as he does. He is so light and so frail that I can lift him myself with ease. He has a shrapnel wound in his side and they have not found the ball. His thin cheeks are scarlet. He is gentleness and sweetness itself. What has he ever done to be crucified like this? Monsieur Gilet is not thinking of his burning wound. He is thinking of the little woman in the province of Cher. How can she come to see him? She has no congé. When will she come to see him? For his life is all there in that war-shattered country. She has a baby twelve weeks old, born since he went to battle. That's what he is thinking of. When will she come?

On his right is a superb Arab, with an arm and hand so broken and so mutilated that it is hard to hold it without shuddering when the doctors drain it. On his head I have carefully adjusted a bright yellow flannel fez. His mild, docile eyes follow the nurse as she does for him the few little things she can to make him more at ease. For every service done, he thanks her in a sweet, soft voice. Just now, when I left him to come over here and sit down before my table, his eyes filled with tears. He can say a few words of French. He kisses my hand with Oriental grace. "Merci, ma mére."

On Monsieur Gilet's left lies a man whose language is as hard to understand, very nearly, as the Arab's—almost unintelligible—a *patois* of the Midi. He is a gardener, used only to the care of plants and flowers. He is a big, rugged giant, and so strong, and so silent a sufferer that since his entrance to the hospital he has not made one murmur or one complaint, or asked one service, and excepting when spoken to, he never says a word. Then he gives you a radiant smile and some token of gratitude. They operated on him to-day. There is shrapnel in his eye. He will never fully see his gardens again, and he is so strong and so patient and so able to bear pain, that they operated on him without anæsthetics, and he walked to and from the operating room—a brave, silent, docile giant, singularly appealing. . . . He is thinking of his gardens, trodden out of all semblance of beauty, for he had been working in the north before the heel of the barbarian crushed out his flowers for ever and blotted out his sight.

III—STORY OF THE BOYS WHO SING "TIPPERARY"

To Mr. F. B. Van Vorst, Hackensack, N. J.

Paris, Dec. 4th, 1914.

MY DEAR FREDERICK,

To-morrow will be my last day at the hospital, as I start in the evening for Nice, on my way to Rome. I have lately found myself sole nurse in a ward with nine men. . . .

It is full of English Tommies, and unless you nurse them and help those English boys, you don't know what they are. They are too lovely and too fine for words. One perfectly fine young fellow has had his leg amputated at the thigh—his life ruined for ever. Another is blind, staring into the visions of his past—he will never have anything else to look at again. The chief amusement of these fellows seems to be watching the funerals, and they call me to run to the window to see the hearses covered with the Union Jack or the French flag, and they find nothing mournful in the processions. One Sunday afternoon, as I sat there, leaning against a table in the middle of the room, a few country flowers in a vase near by—for Miss Hickman asks for country flowers for country lads—I asked them if they wouldn't sing me a song that I had heard a good deal about but had never heard sung. "What's that, nurse?" asked the boy without a leg. "Tipperary"—for I had never heard it. "Why, of course we will, won't we, lads?" and he said to his companion, only nineteen, from some English shire: "You hit the tune." And the boy "hit it," and they sang me "Tipperary." Before they had finished I had turned away and walked out into the corridor to hide the way it made me feel, and I heard it softly through the door as they finished: "It's a long way to Tipperary." I shall never hear it again without seeing the picture of that ward, the country flowers and the country lads, and hearing the measure of that marching tune. . . .

I have seen Mrs. Vanderbilt constantly. She seems to be ubiquitous. Wherever there's need, she is to be found—whether in the operating-room, the bandaging-room, or in one of the great wards where she has charge. I have found her everywhere, just at the right moment: calm, poised, dignified, capable and sweet. But none of this expresses the strength that she has been to the American Ambulance since its foundation—the heart and soul of its organization; and her personal gifts to it have been generous beyond words. I don't know what we shall do when she finally returns to America. She animates the whole place with her spirit and her soul. . . .

IV—STORY OF THE "MIRACLES" OF THE BATTLES

Madame Le Roux, New York.

Paris, June 15th, 1915.

DEAR BESSIE,

Lady K. told such a beautiful thing, out at Bridget's, that I forgot to tell you before. She said that it was bruited in England that there had been a miracle wrought when von Kluck's army so unexpectedly turned back from Paris, which without doubt they could have taken. She said that it was rumored—and not only in the ranks, but among higher men—that there appeared in the sky a singular phenomenon, and that the German prisoners bore witness that a cavalcade like heavenly archers suddenly filled the heavens and shot down upon the Germans a rain of deadly darts. As you know, this was long before the use of any asphyxiating gas or turpinite; but on the field were found hundreds of Germans, stone dead, immovable, who had fallen without any apparent cause. You remember the armies of the old Scriptures that "the breath of the Lord withered away."

Lady K. said that the rumor that the woods of Compiègne were full of troops when the Germans made that famous retreat was absolutely untrue. There were no troops in the forest, and what they saw were, again, celestial soldiers.

No doubt these tales come always in the history of war. But, my dear, how beautiful they are—how much more heavenly and inspired than the beatings on the slavish backs of the German Uhlans, of the half-drunken, brutish hordes! Everywhere is the same uplifting spirit. When I speak of Paris being sad, it *is;* but it is not depressing. There is a difference. If it were not for the absence of those I love, I would rather be here than anywhere. In church on Sunday, the Bishop said that at one of the services near the firing line, when he asked the question: "How many of the men here have felt, since they came out, a stirring in their hearts, an awakening of the spirit?" as far as he could see, every hand was raised. And men have gone home to England, without arms and without legs, maimed for life, and have been heard to say that in spite of their material anguish they regretted nothing, for they had found their souls. . . .

I ought to tell you that all credulous and believing France thinks that the country is being saved by Jeanne d'Arc. You hear them say it everywhere. Just think of it, in the twentieth century, my dear, when the war is being fought in the air and under the sea, by machines so modern that only the latest invention can triumph! Think of it, and then consider that there remains enough of spiritual faith to believe that the salvation of a country comes through prayer.

V—STORY OF COMPTE HENRY DADVISARD

To Mrs. Louis Stoddard, N. Y.

June 25th, 1915.

MY DEAR MOLLY,

* Mme. de S. told me last night that once during the last year she had a little spray of blossoms that had been blessed by the Pope, and in writing to Henry on the field, she sent him a little bit of green—a tiny leaf pinned on a loving letter. When she looked through the uniform sent back to her, a few days ago, in his pocket was this little card, all stained with his blood. This card, with her few loving words, was all he carried on him into that sacred field. I must not forget the belt he wore around him, which she had made with her own hands, and it contained some money and in one of the folds of the chamois was a prayer that she had written out for him. The paper was so worn with reading and unfolding and folding that it was like something used by the years.

All the night before he went to that great battle, he spent in prayer. His aide told Mme. de S. that he had not closed his eyes. They say that if he could have been taken immediately from the field, he would have been saved, for he bled to death.

---

* In speaking of the death of Comte Henry Dadvisard.

I only suppose that you will be interested in these details because they mark the going out of such a brilliant life, and it is the intimate story of one soldier who has laid down his life, after months and months of fighting and self-abnegation and loneliness, on that distant field.

From the time he left her in August until his death, he had never seen any of his family—not a soul. I want to tell you the way she said good-bye to him, for I never knew it until last night. She had expected him to lunch —imagine!—and received the news by telephone that he was leaving his "quartier" in an hour. She rushed there to see the Cuirassiers, mounted, in their service uniform, the helmets all covered with khaki, clattering out of the yard. She sat in the motor and he came out to her, all ready to go; and they said good-bye, there in the motor, he sitting by her side, holding her hands. She said he looked then like the dead—so grave. You know he was a soldier, passionately devoted to his career. He had made all the African campaign and had an illustrious record. She says he asked her for her blessing and she lightly touched the helmet covered with khaki and gave it him. And neither shed a tear. And he kissed her good-bye. She never saw him again. . . .

She said that his General told her as follows: "The night before the engagement, Henry Dadvisard came into my miserable little shack on the field. He said to me: 'Mon général, just show me on the map where the Germans are.' A map was hanging on the wall and I indicated with my finger: '*Les Allemands sont là, mon enfant.*' And Dadvisard said: 'Why, is that all there is to do—just to go out and attack them there? Why, we'll be coming back as gaily as if it were from the races!' He turned to go, saying: '*Au revoir,* mon général.' But at the door he paused, and I looked up and saw him and he said: '*Adieu,* mon général.' And then I saw in his eyes a singular look, something like an appeal from one human soul to another, for a word, a touch, before going out to that sacrifice. I did not dare to say anything but what I did say: *'Bon courage, mon enfant; bonne chance!'* And he went. . . ."

After telling me this, Mme. de S. took out his watch, which she carries with her now—a gold watch, with his crest upon it—the one he had carried through all his campaigns, with the soldier's rough chain hanging from it. It had stopped at half-past ten; as he had wound it the night before, the watch had gone on after his heart had ceased to beat. . . .

The day before Henry left his own company of Cuirassiers to go into the dangerous and terrible experiences of the trenches, to take up that duty which ended in his laying down his life, he gathered his men together and bade them good-bye. Last night dear Mme. de S. showed me his soldier's note-book, in which he had written the few words that he meant to say to his men. I begged her to let me have them: I give them to you. This address stands to me as one of the most beautiful things I have ever read.

General Foch paid him a fine tribute when he mentioned him in despatches, and this mention of him was accompanied by the bestowal of the Croix de Guerre.

"Henry Dadvisard, warm-hearted and vibrant; a remarkable leader of men. He asked to be transferred to the infantry, in order to offer more fully to his country his admirable military talents. He fell gloriously on the 27th of April, leading an attack at the head of his company."

VI—STORY OF THE MORGAN-MARBURY HOSPITAL

To Mrs. Morawetz, New York.

Paris, June 22nd, 1915.

DEAREST VIOLET,

I went out the other day with Madame Marie to Versailles, *en auto*. I wanted to see the little hospital that Anne Morgan and Bessie Marbury have given out there. One of their pretty little houses is in the charge of some gentle-faced sisters of charity, and out in the garden, with the roses blooming and the sweet-scented hay being raked in great piles, were sitting a lieutenant, convalescing, and his *commandant,* who had come to see him, also wounded. Both men wore the Legion of Honor on their breasts. They were talking about the campaign. The lieutenant wore his *képi* well down over his face; he was totally blind for ever, at thirty! His interest in talking to his superior officer was so great that you can fancy I only stopped a second to speak to him. There were great scars on his hands and his face and neck were scarred too. I heard him say, as I turned to walk away: "*J'aime aussi causer des jours quand nous étions collégiens à Saint-Cyr. Ces souvenirs sont plus doux.*" It was terribly touching.

VII—STORY OF THE GAY FRENCH OFFICER

To Miss B. S. Andrews, New York.

Paris, July 12th, 1915.

DEAREST BELLE,

Mme. de S. is going next week on the cruel and dreadful mission of disinterring her belovèd dead. She is going down into the tomb in Belgium—if she can get through—to take her boy out of the charnel house, where he is buried under six other coffins. "God has his soul," she says; "I only ask his body" ... if she can find it. She has told no one of her griefs, but to me; and she bears herself like a woman of twenty-five, gallantly. ...

There is one gay officer of twenty-nine, and six feet two. I don't think you'd speak of "little insignificant Frenchmen" if you could see him! He's superb. One finger off on the left hand, and the right hand utterly useless. So we work at that for fifteen minutes, and all the little group of soldiers linger, because they love him so—he's so killing, so witty, so gay. He screams in mock agony, and laughs and makes the most outrageous jokes; and when he has gone, one of them says to me: *"Il est adoré par ses hommes, madame; il est si courageux."* The spirit between men and officers is so beautiful in the French army. They are all brothers. None of that lordly, arrogant oppression of the Germans. One of the soldiers said to me: *"Il n'y a pas de grade, maintenant, madame. Nous sommes tous des hommes qui aiment le pays."*

And Lieutenant ———, of whom I have just been speaking. I said to him: "Tell me something about the campaign, monsieur." And he answered: "Oh, madame, I would like to tell you about the *men*. They're superb. I have never seen anything like it. I had to lead a charge with 156 men into what we all believed was certain death. Why," he said, "they went like schoolboys—shouting, laughing, pushing each other up the parapet. ... We came back nine strong," he said.

Dr. Blake has been magnificent. His operations are something beyond words. Men came in to me for treatment and told me that he worked actual miracles with faces that were blown off, building new jaws, and oh, Heavens! I don't know what not.

VIII—STORY OF A FRENCH MOTHER AT MASS

Paris, July 20th, 1915.

DEAREST VIOLET,

I saw a very touching thing the other day in the Madeleine, where I went to Mass. A woman no longer young, in the heaviest of crape, came in and sat down and buried her face in her hands. She shook with suppressed sobs and terrible weeping. Presently there came in another worshipper, a stranger to her, and sat down by her side. He was a splendid-looking officer in full-dress uniform—a young man, with a wedding-ring upon his hand—one of those permissionnaires home, evidently, for the short eight days that all the officers are given now—a hiatus between the old war and the new. He bent too, praying; but the weeping of the woman at his side evidently tore his heart. Presently she lifted her face and wiped her eyes, and the officer put his hand on hers. And as I was sitting near, I heard what he said:

"*Pauvre madame, pauvre madame! . . . Ma mère pleure comme vous.*"

She glanced at him, then bent again in prayer. But when she had finished, before she left her seat, I heard her say to him:

"*Monsieur, j'ai beaucoup prié pour vous. Sachez que vous avez les prières d'une vielle mère à laquelle ne reste rien au monde.*"

He touched her hand again and said:

"Merci, madame. Adieu!"

It was just one of those intensely touching pictures in that dimly lighted church, full of worshippers, that one can never forget. . . .

IX—STORY OF A LITTLE SOLDIER FROM AFRICA

To Mrs. William K. Vanderbilt, Newport.

4, Place du Palais Bourbon,
Paris, Aug., 1915.

DEAREST ANNE,

Wandering about alone, as I have been doing a great deal lately, I have gone into many of the churches and prayed at the different shrines, and it is impressive to see the character of those who come in to pray. Men who can never kneel again; men who sit with bandaged eyes before the lighted altars, for whom all the visions of the world have been blotted out for ever; the poor women in their little shawls; women in their crape veils; the man going to the Front; the man who has come back from it, never to take an active part in life again; and the women who ask the Mother of Sorrows to remember theirs. . . .

A very agreeable Abbé dined with me last night. He told me that he was giving absolution to one dying German boy—only sixteen—on the field, and he put his hand under the boy's head and lifted it, and the boy, who was delirious, simply said: "Mama, mama, mama!" And the Abbé said to me: "It is a very curious thing, but in all the dying appeals I have ever heard, it is always for the *mother.*" That return, perhaps, to the lost childhood—the call just before going to sleep. . . .

One day when I was giving electricity lately at the Ambulance, a poor little Zouave hobbled in—he had only one leg left—and held up a maimed hand for me to treat. He was not a very interesting-looking specimen—rather sullen and discouraged, I thought—but as I looked at his frail little body and his disfigured hand, I looked at his breast too. Three medals were on it—the Legion of Honor, the Croix de Guerre, and the Médaille Militaire —all a man can get! And he was just a little soldier of Africa—a nondescript man whose name would only be heard at other times to be forgotten.

Jacquemin.

"Qu'est-ce que vous avez fait pour mériter tout cela, mon ami?"

Pour mériter tout cela, parbleu! He has one leg only, one hand only, and he has back of him eight months of hospital and eight months of horror, for his sufferings have been beyond words.

Jacquemin!

Oh, his name is pretty well known now in a certain Sector!

"Qu'est-ce que vous avez fait pour mériter tout cela?"

Three medals across that narrow chest!

Well, alone, on a bad night, in storm and rain, he was a volunteer patrol. Alone, he brought in four German prisoners. He was a volunteer for six *patrouilles* of the gravest danger—not always alone, but always fetching in prisoners and more prisoners. Bad for the Germans. He carried his superior officer, wounded, out under fire and saved his life. Then there was a line of trenches where a hundred and fifty-six men—they know his name: Jacquemin! Jacquemin with the little mongrel dog always at his heels—a hundred and fifty-six men had eaten nothing for four days but the sodden bread left in their haversacks. Jacquemin filled several wagons full of bread and seating himself on the driver's seat of the first, he drove in that life-giving line under the fire of shot and shell, right into the very jaws of death. He brought sufficient supplies to save the line of trenches, for otherwise they would have had to evacuate them through starvation, as indeed was the case with others where this gay little Zouave could not reach. Just the giving of food to the faint and hungry men whose stern faces were set against death. That act brought him one of those medals across his breast—I forget which. Finally, the shot and shell which he had braved so many times was bound to get him, and with his leg and arm almost shot away he lay for dead amongst the other slain, and they buried him. They buried Jacquemin. Fortunately or unfortunately—it depends upon how he regards a life which he will live through henceforth with only one leg and only one arm—a little bit of his soldier's coat sprouted out of the ground. (They don't always bury deep on those fields.) And his dog saw it and smelled and dug and dug, and whined and cried, until they came and unburied Jacquemin and brought him back.

He is sitting up there at the Ambulance now, and his little dog is sometimes in the kitchen and sometimes comes up to the wards.

Jacquemin!

"Qu'est-ce que vous avez fait pour mériter tout cela, mon ami?"

What countless thousands of them have done, all along those lines—Englishmen and Frenchmen, Scotchmen and Irishmen, Indians, Australians, Canadians—hearts and souls and bodies offered up magnificently and valiantly sacrificed for the greatest Cause for which humanity has ever fought! Jacquemin brought them bread to the fighting line; and that great fighting line, by its efforts, is giving bread for ever to the world. . . .

(Hundreds of these wonderful letters, revealing the great soul of this American woman, have been gathered into her book which forms one of the most beautiful insights into the "soul of the war."—EDITOR.)

"A GERMAN DESERTER'S WAR EXPERIENCE"—HIS ESCAPE

"The Inside Story of the German Army"

Told by—(His Name Must Be Witheld To Save the Lives of His Relatives and Himself)

This narrative is without doubt the greatest story yet told by a German soldier. It is a startling confession of the inward feelings of a young German miner in the Kaiser's ranks. Escaping to America after serving fourteen months, he first told his story to the *New Yorker Volkszeitung,* the principal organ of the German socialists in the United States. Believing that all the American people should know the truth, his experiences have been translated by J. Koettgen and published in book form by *B. W. Huebsch,* of New York. His stories are of historical value because he tells how he marched into Belgium with the first German army of invasion; the crossing of the Meuse; the Battle of the Marne. He also tells the first German story of the rout and flight of the Teutonic forces from the Marne—and his desertion from the "hell" within the German army. In these pages we can give but ten selected glimpses of the several hundred stories and scenes which he so graphically describes.

*I—STORY OF THE MARCH INTO BELGIUM

At the end of July, 1914, our garrison at Koblenz was feverishly agitated. Part of our men were seized by an indescribable enthusiasm, others became subject to a feeling of great depression. The declaration of war was in the air. I belonged to those who were depressed. For I was doing my second year of military service and was

---

* All numbers relate to the stories herein told—not to the chapters in the book.

to leave the barracks in six weeks' time. Instead of the long wished-for return home war was facing me. . . .

Our sapper battalion, No. 30, had been in feverish activity five days before the mobilization; work was being pushed on day and night. . . . Moreover, there was the suspicious amiability of the officers and sergeants, which excluded any doubt that any one might still have had. Officers who had never before replied to the salute of a private soldier now did so with the utmost attention. Cigars and beer were distributed in those days by the officers with great, uncommon liberality, so that it was not surprising that many soldiers were scarcely ever sober and did not realize the seriousness of the situation. But there were also others. There were soldiers who also in those times of good-humour and the grinning comradeship of officer and soldier could not forget that in military service they had often been degraded to the level of brutes, and who now thought with bitter feelings that an opportunity might perhaps be offered in order to settle accounts.

The order of mobilization became known on the 1st of August, and the following day was decided upon as the real day of mobilization. But without awaiting the arrival of the reserves we left our garrison town on August 1st. Who was to be our "enemy" we did not know; Russia was for the present the only country against which war had been declared.

We marched through the streets of the town to the station between crowds of people numbering many thousands. Flowers were thrown at us from every window; everybody wanted to shake hands with the departing soldiers. All the people, even soldiers, were weeping. Many marched arm in arm with their wife or sweetheart. The music played songs of leave-taking. People cried and sang at the same time. Entire strangers, men and women, embraced and kissed each other; men embraced men and kissed each other. It was a real witches' sabbath of emotion; like a wild torrent, that emotion carried away the whole assembled humanity. Nobody, not even the strongest and most determined spirit, could resist that ebullition of feeling.

But all that was surpassed by the taking leave at the station, which we reached after a short march. Here final adieus had to be said, here the separation had to take place. I shall never forget that leave-taking, however old I may grow to be. Desperately many women clung to their men; some had to be removed by force. Just as if they had suddenly had a vision of the fate of their beloved ones, as if they were beholding the silent graves in foreign lands in which those poor nameless ones were to be buried, they sought to cling fast to their possession, to retain what already no longer belonged to them.

Finally that, too, was over. We had entered a train that had been kept ready, and had made ourselves comfortable in our cattle-trucks. Darkness had come, and we had no light in our comfortable sixth-class carriages.

The train moved slowly down the Rhine, it went along without any great shaking, and some of us were seized by a worn-out feeling after those days of great excitement. Most of the soldiers lay with their heads on their knapsacks and slept. Others again tried to pierce the darkness as if attempting to look into the future; still others drew stealthily a photo out of their breast-pocket, and only a very small number of us spent the time by debating our point of destination. Where are we going to? Well, where? Nobody knew it. At last, after long, infinitely long hours the train came to a stop. After a night of quiet, slow riding we were at—Aix-la-Chapelle! At Aix-la-Chapelle! What were we doing at Aix-la-

Chapelle? We did not know, and the officers only shrugged their shoulders when we asked them.

After a short interval the journey proceeded, and on the evening of the 2nd of August we reached a farm in the neighbourhood of the German and Belgian frontier, near Herbesthal. Here our company was quartered in a barn. Nobody knew what our business was at the Belgian frontier. In the afternoon of the 3rd of August reservists arrived, and our company was brought to its war strength. We had still no idea concerning the purpose of our being sent to the Belgian frontier, and that evening we lay down on our bed of straw with a forced tranquillity of mind. Something was sure to happen soon, to deliver us from that oppressive uncertainty. How few of us thought that for many it would be the last night to spend on German soil! . . .

II—STORY OF THE FIRST ALARM TO BATTLE

At 1 o'clock in the morning an alarm aroused us again, and the captain honoured us with an address. He told us we were at war with Belgium, that we should acquit ourselves as brave soldiers, earn iron crosses, and do honour to our German name. . . .

The soldier is told, "The Belgian is your enemy," and he has to believe it. The soldier, the workman in uniform, had not known till then who was his enemy. If they had told us, "The Hollander is your enemy," we would have believed that, too; we would have been compelled to believe it, and would have shot him by order. We, the "German citizens in uniform," must not have an opinion of our own, must have no thoughts of our own, for they give us our enemy and our friend according to requirements, according to the requirements of their own interests. The Frenchman, the Belgian, the

Italian, is your enemy. Never mind, shoot as we order, and do not bother your head about it. . . .

About ten minutes we might have lain in the grass when we suddenly heard rifle shots in front of us. Electrified, all of us jumped up and hastened to our rifles. Then the firing of rifles that was going on at a distance of about a mile or a mile and a half began steadily to increase in volume. We set in motion immediately. . . .

Though I was aware that we should be in the firing line within half an hour, I endeavoured to convince myself that our participation in the fight would no longer be necessary. I clung obstinately, nay, almost convulsively to every idea that could strengthen that hope or give me consolation. That not every bullet finds its billet; that, as we had been told, most wounds in modern wars were afflicted by grazing shots which caused slight flesh-wounds; those were some of the reiterated self-deceptions indulged in against my better knowledge. And they proved effective. It was not only that they made me in fact feel more easy; deeply engaged in those thoughts I had scarcely observed that we were already quite near the firing line. . . .

We were lying flat on the ground, and fired in the direction indicated to us as fast as our rifles would allow. So far we had not seen our opponents. That, it seemed, was too little interesting to some of our soldiers; so they rose partly, and fired in a kneeling position. Two men of my company had to pay for their curiosity with their lives. Almost at one and the same time they were shot through the head. The first victim of our group fell down forward without uttering a sound; the second threw up his arms and fell on his back. Both of them were dead instantly.

Who could describe the feelings that overcome a man in the first hail of bullets he is in? When we were leaping forward to reach the firing line I felt no longer any fear and seemed only to try to reach the line as quickly as possible. But when looking at the first dead man I was seized by a terrible horror. For minutes I was perfectly stupefied, had completely lost command over myself and was absolutely incapable to think or act. I pressed my face and hands firmly against the ground, and then suddenly I was seized by an irrepressible excitement, took hold of my gun, and began to fire away blindly. Little after little I quieted down again somewhat, nay, I became almost quite confident as if everything was normal. Suddenly I found myself content with myself and my surroundings, and when a little later the whole line was commanded, "Leap forward! March, march!" I ran forward demented like the others, as if things could not be other than what they were. . . .

It was a hand to hand fight; every kind of weapon had to be employed; the opponent was attacked with the butt-end of the rifle, the knife, the fist, and the teeth. One of my best friends fought with a gigantic Belgian; both had lost their rifles. They were pummeling each other with their fists. I had just finished with a Belgian who was about twenty-two years of age, and was going to assist my friend, as the Herculean Belgian was so much stronger than he. Suddenly my friend succeeded with a lightning motion in biting the Belgian in the chin. He bit so deeply that he tore away a piece of flesh with his teeth. The pain the Belgian felt must have been immense, for he let go his hold and ran off screaming with terrible pain.

All that happened in seconds. The blood of the Belgian ran out of my friend's mouth; he was seized by a horrible nausea, an indescribable terror, the taste of the warm blood nearly drove him insane. That young, gay, lively fellow of twenty-four had been cheated out of his youth in that night. He used to be the jolliest among us; after that we could never induce him even to smile.

Whilst fighting during the night I came for the first time in touch with the butt-end of a Belgian rifle. I had a hand to hand fight with a Belgian when another one from behind hit me with his rifle on the head with such force that it drove my head into the helmet up to my ears. I experienced a terrific pain all over my head, doubled up, and lost consciousness. When I revived I found myself with a bandaged head in a barn among other wounded.

I had not been severely wounded, but I felt as if my head was double its normal size, and there was a noise in my ears as of the wheels of an express engine. . . .

We were quite hungry and ate the tinned soup with the heartiest of appetites. Many of our soldiers were sitting with their dinner-pails on the dead horses that were lying about, and were eating with such pleasure and heartiness as if they were home at mother's. Nor did some corpses in the neighbourhood of our improvised camp disturb us. There was only a lack of water and after having eaten thirst began to torment us.

We continued our march in the scorching midday sun; dust was covering our uniforms and skin to the depth of almost an inch. We tried in vain to be jolly, but thirst tormented us more and more, and we became weaker and weaker from one quarter of an hour to another. Many in our ranks fell down exhausted. . . .

III—STORY OF THE POISONED WELLS

Finally, towards four o'clock, we saw a village in front of us; we began at once to march at a much brisker pace. Among other things we saw a farm-cart on which were several civilian prisoners, apparently snipers.

There was also a Catholic priest among them who had, like the others, his hands tied behind his back with a rope. Curiosity prompted us to enquire what he had been up to, and we heard that he had incited the farmers of the village to poison the water.

We soon reached the village and the first well at which we hoped to quench our thirst thoroughly. But that was no easy matter, for a military guard had been placed before it who scared us off with the warning, "Poisoned"! Disappointed and terribly embittered the soldiers, half dead with thirst, gnashed their teeth; they hurried to the next well, but everywhere the same devilish thing occurred—the guard preventing them from drinking. In a square, in the middle of the village, there was a large village well which sent, through two tubes, water as clear as crystal into a large trough. Five soldiers were guarding it and had to watch that nobody drank of the poisoned water. I was just going to march past it with my pal when suddenly the second, larger portion of our company rushed like madmen to the well. The guards were carried away by the rush, and every one now began to drink the water with the avidity of an animal. All quenched their thirst, and not one of us became ill or died. We heard later on that the priest had to pay for it with his death. . . .

In every army one finds men with the disposition of barbarians. The many millions of inhabitants in Germany or France are not all civilized people, much as we like to convince ourselves of the contrary. Compulsory military service in those countries forces all without distinction into the army, men and monsters. I have often bitterly resented the wrong one did to our army in calling us all barbarians only because among us—as, naturally also among the French and English—there were to be found elements that really ought to be in the penitentiary.

I will only cite one example of how we soldiers ourselves punished a wretch whom we caught committing a crime.

One evening—it was dark already—we reached a small village to the east of the town of Bertrix, and there, too, found "poisoned" water. We halted in the middle of the village. I was standing before a house with a low window, through which one could see the interior. In the miserable poverty-stricken working man's dwelling we observed a woman who clung to her children as if afraid they would be torn from her. Though we felt very bitter on account of the want of water, every one of us would have liked to help the poor woman. Some of us were just going to sacrifice our little store of victuals and to say a few comforting words to the woman, when all at once a stone as big as a fist was thrown through the window-pane into the room and hurt a little girl in the right hand. There were sincere cries of indignation, but at the same moment twenty hands at least laid hold of the wretch, a reservist of our company, and gave him such a hiding as to make him almost unconscious. If officers and other men had not interfered the fellow would have been lynched there and then. He was to be placed before a court-martial later on, but it never came to that. He was drowned in the river at the battle of the Meuse. Many soldiers believed he drowned himself, because he was not only shunned by his fellow soldiers, but was also openly despised by them. . . .

IV—STORY OF THE BELGIAN SNIPERS

We had to proceed, and soon reached the town of Bertrix. Some few houses to the left and right of the road were burning fiercely; we soon got to know that they had been set alight because soldiers marching past were said to have been shot at from those houses. Before one of these houses a man and his wife and their son, a boy of 15 or 16, lay half burnt to cinders; all had been covered with straw. Three more civilians lay dead in the same street.

We had marched past some more houses when all at once shots rang out; they had been shooting from some house, and four of our soldiers had been wounded. For a short while there was confusion. The house from which the shots must have come was soon surrounded, and hand grenades were thrown through all the windows into the interior. In an instant all the rooms were in flames. The exploding hand grenades caused such an enormous air pressure that all the doors were blown from their hinges and the inner walls torn to shreds. Almost at the same time, five men in civilian clothes rushed into the street and asked for quarter with uplifted hands. They were seized immediately and taken to the officers, who formed themselves into a tribunal within a few minutes. Ten minutes later sentence had already been executed; five strong men lay on the ground, blindfolded and their bodies riddled by bullets.

Six of us had in each of the five cases to execute the sentence, and unfortunately I, too, belonged to those thirty men. The condemned man whom my party of six had to shoot was a tall, lean man, about forty years of age. He did not wince for a moment when they blindfolded him. In a garden of a house nearby he was placed with his back against the house, and after our captain had told us that it was our duty to aim well so as to end the tragedy quickly, we took up our position six paces from the condemned one. The sergeant commanding us had told us before to shoot the condemned man through the chest. We then formed two lines, one behind the other. The command was given to load and secure, and we pushed five cartridges into the rifle. Then the command rang out, "Get ready!" The first line knelt, the second stood up. We held our rifles in such a position that the barrel pointed in front of us whilst the butt-end rested somewhere near the hip. At the command, "Aim!" we slowly brought our rifles into shooting position, grasped them firmly, pressed the plate of the butt-end against the shoulder and, with our cheek on the butt-end, we clung convulsively to the neck of the rifle. Our right forefinger was on the trigger, the sergeant gave us about half a minute for aiming before commanding, "Fire!"

Even to-day I cannot say whether our victim fell dead on the spot or how many of the six bullets hit him. . . .

V—STORY OF MURDEROUS FIGHTS IN THE NIGHT

After a short march we engaged the French to the northeast of Donchéry. On this side of the Meuse the enemy had only his rear-guard, whose task was to cover the crossing of the main French armies, a movement which was almost exclusively effected at Sédan and Donchéry. We stuck close to the heels of our opponents, who did not retreat completely till darkness began to fall. The few bridges left did not allow him to withdraw his forces altogether as quickly as his interest demanded. Thus it came about that an uncommonly murderous nocturnal street fight took place in Donchéry which was burning at every corner. The French fought with immense energy; an awful slaughter was the result. Man against man! That "man against man!" is the most terrible thing I have experienced in war. Nobody can tell afterwards how many he has killed. You have gripped your opponent, who is sometimes weaker, sometimes stronger than yourself. In the light of the burning houses you observe that the white of his eyes has turned red; his mouth is covered with a thick froth. With head uncovered, with disheveled hair, the uniform unbuttoned and mostly ragged, you stab, hew, scratch, bite and strike about you like a wild animal. It means life or death. You fight for your life. No quarter is given. You only hear the gasping, groaning, jerky breathing. You only think of your own life, of death, of home. In feverish haste, as in a whirlwind, old memories are rushing through your mind. Yet you get more excited from minute to minute, for exhaustion tries to master you; but that must not be—not now! And again the fight is renewed; again there is hewing, stabbing, biting. Without rifle, without any weapon in a life and death struggle. You or I. I? I?—Never! you! The exertion becomes superhuman. Now a thrust, a vicious bite, and you are the victor. Victor for the moment, for already the next man, who has just finished off one of your mates, is upon you— You suddenly remember that you have a dagger about you. After a hasty fumbling you find it in the prescribed place. A swift movement and the dagger buries itself deeply in the body of the other man.

Onward! onward! new enemies are coming up, real enemies. How clearly the thought suddenly flashes on you that that man is your enemy, that he is seeking to take your life, that he bites, strikes, and scratches, tries to force you down and plant his dagger in your heart. Again you use your dagger. Thank heavens! He is down. Saved!— Still, you must have that dagger back! You pull it out of his chest. A jet of warm blood rushes out of the gaping wound and strikes your face. Human blood, warm human blood! You shake yourself, horror strikes you for only a few seconds. The next one approaches; again you have to defend your skin. Again and again the mad murdering is repeated, all night long— . . .

VI—STORY OF THE MEN WHO DIE

Many of my mates envied the dead soldiers and wished to be in their place in order to be at least through with all their misery. Yet all of us were afraid of dying—afraid of dying, be it noted, not of death. All of us often longed for death, but we were horrified at the slow dying lasting hours which is the rule on the battle-field, that process which makes the wounded, abandoned soldier die piecemeal. I have witnessed the death of hundreds of young men in their prime, but I know of none among them who died willingly. A young sapper of the name of Kellner, whose home was at Cologne, had his whole abdomen ripped open by a shell splinter. Maddened by pain he begged me to assure him that he would not have to die. Of course, I assured him that his wounds were by no means severe and that the doctor would be there immediately to help him. My words comforted him. He died ten minutes later. . . .

We common soldiers were here handling the dead and wounded as if we had never done anything else, and yet in our civilian lives most of us had an abhorrence and fear of the dead and the horribly mangled. War is a hard school-master who bends and reshapes his pupils.

One section was busy with digging a common grave for the dead. We took away the papers and valuables of the dead, took possession of the eatable and drinkable stores to be found in the saddle bags attached to the horses and, when the grave was ready, we began to place the dead bodies in it. They were laid close together in order to utilize fully the available space. I, too, had been ordered to "bring in" the dead. The bottom of the grave was large enough for twenty-three bodies if the space was well utilized. When two layers of twenty-three had already been buried a sergeant of the artillery, who was standing near, observed that one of the "dead" was still alive. He had seen the "corpse" move the fingers of his right hand. On closer examination it turned out that we came near burying a living man, for after an attempt lasting two hours we succeeded in restoring him to consciousness. The officer of the infantry who supervised the work now turned to the two soldiers charged with getting the corpses ready and asked them whether they were sure that all the men buried were really dead.

"Yes," the two replied, "we suppose they are all dead." That seemed to be quite sufficient for that humane officer, for he ordered the interments to proceed. Nobody doubted that there were several more among the 138 men whom we alone buried in one grave (two other, still bigger, graves had been dug by different burial parties) from whose bodies life had not entirely flown. . . .

We were as merry as boys and as noisy as street urchins. "Oh, what a joy to be a soldier lad!"—that song rang out, subdued at first, then louder and louder. It died away quickly enough as one after the other laid down his tired head. We slept like the dead.

A soldier in war never knows the date or day of the week. One day is like another. Whether it is Saturday, Thursday or Sunday, it means always the same routine of murdering. "Remember the Sabbath day to keep it holy!" "Six days shalt thou labor and do all thy work. But the seventh day—thou shalt not do any work." These, to our Christian rulers, are empty phrases. "Six days shalt thou murder and on the seventh day, too."

VII—STORY OF THE "MISSING" OFFICERS

However, not all the soldiers approved of that senseless, that criminal murdering. Some of the "gentlemen" who had ordered us to massacre our French comrades were killed "by mistake" in the darkness of the night, by their own people, of course. Such "mistakes" repeat themselves almost daily, and if I keep silence with regard to many such mistakes which I could relate, giving the exact name and place, the reader will know why.

During that night it was a captain and first lieutenant who met this fate. An infantryman who was serving his second year stabbed the captain through the stomach with his bayonet, and almost at the same time the first lieutenant got a stab in the back. Both men were dead in a few minutes. Those that did the deeds showed not the slightest signs of repentance, and not one of us felt inclined to reproach them; on the contrary, every one knew that despicable, brutal murderers had met their doom.

In this connection I must mention a certain incident which necessitates my jumping a little ahead of events. When on the following day I conversed with a mate from my company and asked him for the loan of his pocket knife he drew from his pocket three cartridges besides his knife. I was surprised to find him carrying cartridges in his trousers' pockets and asked him whether he had no room for them in his cartridge case. "There's room enough," he replied, "but those three are meant for a particular purpose; there's a name inscribed on each of them." Some time after—we had meanwhile become fast friends—I inquired again after the three bullets. He had one of them left. I reflected and remembered two sergeants who had treated us like brutes in times of peace, whom we had hated as one could only hate slave-drivers. They had found their grave in French soil. . . .

A company of the Hessian landwehr, all of them old soldiers, were marching past with sore feet and drooping heads. They had probably marched for a long while. Officers were attempting to liven them up. They were to sing a song, but the Hessians, fond of singing and good-natured as they certainly are known to be, were by no means in a mood to sing. "I tell you to sing, you swine!" the officer cried, and the pitifully helpless-looking "swine" endeavored to obey the command. Here and there a thin voice from the ranks of the overtired men could be heard to sing, *"Deutschland, Deutschland über alles, über alles in der Welt."* With sore feet and broken energy, full of disgust with their "glorious" trade of warriors, they sang that symphony of supergermanism that sounded then like blasphemy, nay, like a travesty— *"Deutschland, Deutschland über alles, über alles in der Welt."* . . .

VIII—STORY OF THE SACKING OF SUIPPES

I have never in war witnessed a greater general pillaging than here in Suippes. It was plain that we had to live and had to have food. The inhabitants and storekeepers having fled, it was often impossible to pay for the things one needed. Men simply went into some store, put on socks and underwear, and left their old things; they then went to some other store, took the food they fancied, and hied themselves to a wine-cellar to provide themselves to their hearts' content.

The finest and largest stores—Suippes supplied a large tract of country and had comparatively extensive stores of all descriptions—were empty shells in a few hours.

One of our sappers had for weeks carried about with

him a pair of handsome boots for his fiancée and then had them sent to her in two parcels. However, the field-post did not guarantee delivery; and thus the war bride got the left boot, and not the right one. . . .

The occupant of one house was evidently a young bride, for the various pieces of the trousseau, trimmed with dainty blue ribbons, could be seen in the wardrobes in a painfully spick and span condition. All the wardrobes were unlocked. We did not touch a thing. We were again reminded of the cruelty of war. Millions it turned into beggars in one night; the fondest hopes and desires were destroyed. When, the next morning, we entered the house again, driven by a presentiment of misfortune, we found everything completely destroyed. Real barbarians had been raging here, who had lost that thin varnish with which civilization covers the brute in man. The whole trousseau of the young bride had been dragged from the shelves and was still partly covering the floor. Portraits, photographs, looking-glasses, all lay broken on the floor. Three of us had entered the room, and all three of us clenched our fists in helpless rage. . . .

When a man is accustomed to step over corpses with a cold smile on his lips, when he has to face death every minute day and night, he gradually loses that finer feeling for human things and humanity. Thus it must not surprise one that soldiers could laugh and joke in the midst of awful devastation, that they brought wine to a concert room in which there was a piano and an electric organ, and had a joyful time with music and wine. They drank till they were unconscious; they drank with sergeants and corporals, pledging "brotherhood"; and they rolled arm in arm through the streets with their new "comrades." . . .

IX—STORY OF THE TRAGEDY OF THE MARNE

At the Marne—in the maw of death. It was dark, and rained. From all directions one heard in the darkness the wounded calling, crying, and moaning. The wounded we had with us were likewise moaning and crying. All wanted to have their wounds dressed, but we had no more bandages. We tore off pieces of our dirty shirts and placed the rags on those sickening wounds. Men were dying one after the other. There were no doctors, no bandages; we had nothing whatever. You had to help the wounded and keep the French off at the same time. It was an unbearable, impossible state of things. It rained harder and harder. We were wet to our skins. We fired blindly into the darkness. The rolling fire of rifles increased, then died away, then increased again. We sappers were placed among the infantry. My neighbor gave me a dig in the ribs. "I say," he called out.

"What do you want?" I asked.

"Who are you?"

"A sapper."

"Come here," he hissed. "It gives you an uncanny feeling to be alone in this hell of a night. Why are you here too?—They'll soon come again, those over there; then there'll be fine fun again. Do you hear the others cry?"

He laughed. Suddenly he began again: "I always shoot at those until they leave off crying—that's great fun."

Again he laughed, that time more shrilly than before.

I knew what was the matter. He had become insane. A man passed with ammunition. I begged him to go at once and fetch the section leader. The leader, a lieutenant of the infantry, came up. I went to meet him and told him that my neighbor was continually firing at the wounded, was talking nonsense, and was probably insane. The lieuenant placed himself between us. "Can you see anything?" he asked the other man. "What? See? No; but I hear them moaning and crying, and as soon as I hit one—well, he is quiet, he goes to sleep—" The lieutenant nodded at me. He took the gun away from the man. But the latter snatched it quickly away again and jumped out of the trench. From there he fired into the crowd of wounded men until, a few seconds after, he dropped down riddled by several bullets.

(Here the soldier gives a wonderful description of the rout and flight from the Battle of the Marne which is too long to be included in this collection, but which the reader will find complete, in his book: "A Deserter's War Experiences."—EDITOR.)

X—STORY OF A FURLOUGH—AND ESCAPE

It was not until September that I managed to obtain furlough at the request of my relations, and I left for home with a resolve that at times seemed to me impossible to execute. All went well until I got to Diedenhofen.

As far as that station the railroads are operated by the army authorities. At Diedenhofen they are taken over by the Imperial Railroads of Alsace-Lorraine and the Prusso-Hessian State Railroads. So I had to change, and got on a train that went to Saarbruecken. I had scarcely taken a seat in a compartment in my dirty and ragged uniform when a conductor came along to inspect the tickets. Of course, I had no ticket; I had only a furlough certificate and a pass which had been handed to me at the field railroad depot of Chatel. The conductor looked at the papers and asked me again for my ticket. I drew his attention to my pass. "That is only good for the territory of the war operations," he said; "you are now traveling on a state railroad and have to buy a ticket."

I told him that I should not buy a ticket, and asked him to inform the station manager. "You," I told him, "only act according to instructions. I am not angry with you for asking of me what I shall do under no circumstances." He went off and came back with the manager. The latter also inspected my papers and told me I had to pay for the journey.

"I have no means for that purpose," I told him. "For these last three years I have been in these clothes" (I pointed to my uniform), "and for three years I have therefore been without any income. Whence am I to get the money to pay for this journey?"

"If you have no money for traveling you can't take furlough." I thought to myself that if they took me deep into France they were in conscience bound to take me back to where they had fetched me. Was I to be a soldier for three years and fight for the Fatherland for more than a year only to find that now they refused the free use of their railroads to a ragged soldier? I explained that I was not going to pay, that I could not save the fare from the few pfennigs' pay. I refused explicitly to pay a soldier's journey with my private money, even if—as was the case here—that soldier was myself. Finally I told him, "I must request you to inform the military railroad commander; the depot command attends to soldiers, not you." He sent me a furious look through his horn spectacles and disappeared. Two civilians were sitting in the same compartment with me; they thought it an unheard-of thing that a soldier coming from the front should be asked for his fare. Presently the depot commander came up with a sergeant. He demanded to see my furlough certificate, pay books, and all my other papers.

"Have you any money?"

"No."

"Where do you come from?"

"From Chatel in the Argonnes."

"How long were you at the front?"

"In the fourteenth month."

"Been wounded?"

"No."

"Have you no money at all?"

"No; you don't want money at the front."

"The fare must be paid. If you can't, the company must pay. Please sign this paper."

I signed it without looking at it. It was all one to me what I signed, as long as they left me alone. Then the sergeant came back.

"You can not travel in that compartment; you must also not converse with travelers. You have to take the first carriage marked 'Only for the military.' Get into that."

"I see," I observed; "in the dogs' compartment."

He turned round again and said, "Cut out those remarks."

The train started, and I arrived safely home. After the first hours of meeting all at home again had passed I found myself provided with faultless underwear and had taken the urgently needed bath. Once more I could put on the civilian dress I had missed for so long a time. All of it appeared strange to me. I began to think. Under no conditions was I going to return to the front. But I did not know how I should succeed in getting across the frontier. I could choose between two countries only —Switzerland and Holland. It was no use going to Switzerland, for that country was surrounded by belligerent states, and it needed only a little spark to bring Switzerland into the war, and then there would be no loophole for me. There was only the nearest country left for me to choose—Holland. But how was I to get there? There was the rub. I concocted a thousand plans and discarded them again. Nobody, not even my relatives, must know about it.

(How this German soldier fled from the war and escaped to America is told in his book: "A German Deserter's War Experiences;"—Copyright, 1917, B. W. Huebsch.)

"THE SOUL OF THE WAR"—TALES OF THE HEROIC FRENCH

Revelations of a War Correspondent

Told by Philip Gibbs, Special Correspondent for the "London Daily Chronicle"

The eye-witness stories of this gifted English author lay bare the soul of the Great War. He tells of the human and psychological side of warfare as he has seen it on the battle field under heavy shell fire, in bombarded towns, in field hospitals and amid great movements of troops. He reveals the throbbing heart of the ghastly brute force that mangles the body and tortures the mind of heroic men. The author says in his conclusion: "More passionate than any other emotion that has stirred man through life is my conviction that any man that has seen these things, if he has . . . any human pity, should dedicate his head and heart to the sacred duty of preventing another war like this." The stories herein given are by permission of his publishers, *Robert M. McBride and Company* (Copyright 1915), and are taken from but one chapter of this notable book, in which he relates nearly a thousand anecdotes.

*I—STORY OF THE SOLDIERS OF FRANCE

The Germans, however great their army, could never have captured the soul of Paris. . . .

When in the first days of the war I saw the soldiers of France on their way to the front, I had even then a conviction that the fighting qualities of the nation had not degenerated in forty-four years of peace. . . . Afterwards, during many months as a wanderer in this war, I

---

* All numerals relate to stories told herein, not to chapters in the book.

came to know the French soldier with the intimacy of long conversations to the sound of guns, in the first line of trenches facing the enemy, in hospitals, where he spoke quietly while comrades snored themselves to death, in villages smashed to pieces by shell-fire, in troop trains overcrowded with wounded, in woods and fields pockmarked by the holes of "marmites," and in the restaurants of Paris and provincial towns where, with an empty sleeve or one trouser-leg dangling beneath the tablecloth, he told me his experiences of war with a candor in which there was no concealment of truth; and out of all these friendships and revelations of soul the character of the soldiers of France stands before my mind in heroic colors. . . .

He does not like death—he dreads the thought of it—but without questioning his soul he springs forward to save this mother-country of his and dies upon her bosom with a cry of "Vive la France!"

The French soldier . . . needs feminine consolation, and all his ideals and his yearnings and his self-pity are intimately associated with the love of women, and especially of one woman—his mother. When Napoleon, in the island of St. Helena, used to talk about the glories of his victorious years, and then brooded over the tragedy of his overthrow so that all his soul was clouded with despair, he used to rouse himself after the silence which followed those hours of self-analysis and say, "Let us talk about women—and love." Always it is the feminine spirit in which a Frenchman bathes his wounds. One small incident I saw a year or two ago gave me the clue to this quality in the French character. It was when Védrines, the famous airman, was beaten by only a few minutes in the flight round England. Capitaine Conneau—"Beaumont," as he called himself—had outraced his rival and waited, with French gallantry, to shake the hand of the adversary he had defeated on untiring wings. A great crowd of smart men and women waited also at Brooklands to cheer the second in the race, who in England is always more popular than the prize-winner. But when Védrines came to earth out of a blue sky he was savage and bitter. The loss of the prize-money was a great tragedy to this mechanic who had staked all his ambition on the flight. He shouted out harsh words to those who came to cheer him, and shook them off violently when they tried to clap him on the back. He was savagely angry. Then suddenly something seemed to break in his spirit, and his face quivered.

"Is there any woman to embrace me?" he asked. Out of the crowd came a pretty Frenchwoman and, understanding the man, though she had not met him before, she held out her arms to him and raised her face.

"Allons-donc, mon vieux!" she said.

The man put his arms about her and kissed her, while tears streamed down his face, covered in sweat and dust. He was comforted, like a boy who had hurt himself, in his mother's arms. It was a queer little episode—utterly impossible in the imagination of an Englishman—but a natural thing in France.

So when a Frenchman lies dying, almost unconscious before the last breath, it is always a woman's name that he cries out, or whispers, though not always the name of his wife or mistress. One word is heard again and again in the hospital wards, where the *poilus* lie, those bearded fellows, so strong when they went out to the war, but now so weak and helpless before death.

"Maman! Maman!"

It is to the bosom of motherhood that the spirit of the Frenchman goes in that last hour.

"Oh, my dear little mamma," writes a young lieutenant of artillery, "it would be nice to be in my own room again, where your picture hangs over my bed looking down on the white pillows upon which you used to make the sign of the Cross before I went to sleep. I often try to dream myself into that bedroom again, but the cold is too intense for dreams, and another shell comes shrieking overhead. War is nothing but misery, after all."

Yet if the English reader imagines that because this thread of sentiment runs through the character of France there is a softness in the qualities of French soldiers, he does not know the truth. Those men whom I saw at the front and behind the fighting lines were as hard in moral and spiritual strength as in physical endurance. . . .

II—STORY OF THE FIGHTERS FROM ARGONNE AND LORRAINE

The slopes of Hartmansweilerkopf were already washed by waves of blood which surged round it for nine months and more, until its final capture by the French. St. Mihiel and Les Eparges and the triangle which the Germans had wedged between the French lines were a shambles before the leaves had fallen from the autumn trees in the first year of war. In the country of the Argonne men fought like wolves and began a guerrilla warfare with smaller bodies of men, fighting from wood to wood, from village to village, the forces on each side being scattered over a wide area in advance of their main lines. Then they dug themselves into trenches from which they came out at night, creeping up to each other's lines, flinging themselves upon each other with bayonets and butt-ends, killing each other as beasts kill, without pity and in the mad rage of terror which is the fiercest kind of courage.

In Lorraine the tide of war ebbed and flowed over

the same tracts of ground, and neither side picked up its dead or its wounded. Men lay there alive for days and nights, bleeding slowly to death. The hot sun glared down upon them and made them mad with thirst. Some of them lay there for as long as three weeks, still alive, with gangrened limbs in which lice crawled, so that they stank abominably.

"I cannot tell you all the things I saw," said one of the young soldiers who talked to me on his way back from Lorraine. He had a queer look in his eyes when he spoke those words which he tried to hide from me by turning his head away. But he told me how the fields were littered with dead, decomposing and swarmed with flies, lying there in huddled postures, yet some of them so placed that their fixed eyes seemed to be staring at the corpses near them. And he told me how on the night he had his own wound French and German soldiers not yet dead talked together by the light of the moon, which shed its pale light upon all those prostrate men, making their faces look very white. He heard the murmurs of voices about him, and the groans of the dying, rising to hideous anguish as men were tortured by ghastly wounds and broken limbs. In that night enmity was forgotten by those who had fought like beasts and now lay together. A French soldier gave his water-bottle to a German officer who was crying out with thirst. The German sipped a little and then kissed the hand of the man who had been his enemy. "There will be no war on the other side," he said.

Another Frenchman—who came from Montmartre—found lying within a yard of him a Luxembourgeois whom he had known as his *chasseur* in a big hotel in Paris. The young German wept to see his old acquaintance. "It is stupid," he said, "this war. You and I were happy when we were good friends in Paris. Why should we have been made to fight each other?" He died with his arms round the neck of the soldier who told me the story, unashamed of his own tears.

Round this man's neck also were clasped the arms of a German officer when a week previously the French *piou-piou* went across the field of a battle—one of the innumerable skirmishes—which had been fought and won four days before another French retirement. The young German had had both legs broken by a shell, and was wounded in other places. He had strength enough to groan piteously, but when my friend lifted him up death was near to him.

"He was all rotten,' said the soldier, "and there came such a terrible stench from him that I nearly dropped him, and vomited as I carried him along."

I learned something of the psychology of the French soldier from this young infantryman with whom I traveled in a train full of wounded soon after that night in Lorraine, when the moon had looked down on the field of the dead and dying in which he lay with a broken leg. He had passed through a great ordeal, so that his nerves were still torn and quivering, and I think he was afraid of going mad at the memory of the things he had seen and suffered, because he tried to compel himself to talk of trivial things, such as the beauty of the flowers growing on the railway banks and the different badges on English uniforms. But suddenly he would go back to the tale of his fighting in Lorraine and resume a long and rapid monologue in which little pictures of horror flashed after each other as though his brain were a cinematograph recording some melodrama. Queer bits of philosophy jerked out between this narrative. "This war is only endurable because it is for a final peace in Europe." "Men will refuse to suffer these things again. It is the end of militarism." "If I thought that a child of mine would have to go through all that I have suffered during these last weeks, I would strangle him in his cradle to save him from it."

Sometimes he spoke of France with a kind of religion in his eyes.

"Of course, I am ready to die for France. She can demand my life as a right. I belong to her and she can do with me what she likes. It's my duty to fight in her defense, and although I tell you all the worst of war, Monsieur, I do not mean that I am not glad to have done my part. In a few weeks this wound of mine will be healed and I shall go back, for the sake of France, to that Hell again. It is Hell, *quand même!*"

III—STORIES OF THE FRENCH ZOUAVES

Some of the letters from French soldiers, scrawled in the squalor of the trenches by men caked in filth and mud, are human documents in which they reveal themselves with extraordinary intimacy, and in which they put the whole truth, not disguising their terror or their blood-lust in the savage madness of a bayonet charge, or the heartache which comes to them when they think of the woman they love, or the queer little emotions and sentiments which come to them in the grim business of war. . . .

"I send this letter," writes a young Zouave, "as I sit huddled under an earth-heap at twenty yards from a German trench, less to be envied than a rabbit in its burrow, because when the hunter is far away it can come out and feed at pleasure. You who live through the same agonies, old friend, must learn and rejoice that I have been promoted adjutant on the night of November 13 on the banks of the Yser. There were seventy men out of 250—the rest of the company sleep forever round that ferryman's house which the papers have made famous. . . . What moral sufferings I have endured! We have now been brought to the south of Ypres and continue this depressing life in advanced trenches. Not a quarter of an hour's respite; shells, shrapnels, bombs and bullets fall around us continuously. How courage has changed with this modern war! The hero of olden times was of a special type, who put on a fine poise and played up to the gallery because he fought before admiring spectators. Now, apart from our night attacks, always murderous, in which courage is not to be seen, because one can hardly discern one's neighbour in the darkness, our valour consists in a perfect stoicism. Just now I had a fellow killed before a loophole. His comrades dragged him away, and with perfect quietude replaced the man who is eternally out of action. Isn't that strange? Isn't it courage to get the brains of one's comrade full in the face, and then to stand on guard in the same place while suffering the extremes of cold and dampness? . . . On the night of the 13th I commanded a section of corps which a mitrailleuse had raked. I had the luck to escape, and I shouted to these poor devils to make a last assault. Then I saw what had happened and found myself with a broken rifle and a uniform in rags and tatters. My commandant spoke to me that night, and said: 'You had better change those clothes. You can put on an adjutant's stripes.'" . . .

"The greater number of the bodies," writes a soldier, "still lie between the trenches, and we have been unable to withdraw them. We can see them always, in frightful quantity, some of them intact, others torn to bits by the shells which continue to fall upon them. The stench of this corruption floats down upon us with foul odours. Bits of their rotting carcasses are flung into our faces and over our heads as new shells burst and scatter them.

It is like living in a charnel house where devils are at play flinging dead men's flesh at living men, with fiendish mockery. The smell of this corruption taints our food, and taints our very souls, so that we are spiritually and physically sick. That is war!"

"This horrible game of war," writes another man, "goes on passionately in our corner. In seventy-four days we have 'progressed' about 1200 yards. That tells you everything. Ground is gained, so to speak, by the inch, and we all know now how much it costs to get back a bit of free France."

Along the French lines Death did not rest from his harvesting whatever the weather, and although for months there was no general advance on either side, not a day passed without new work for the surgeons, the stretcher-bearers, and the grave-diggers. One incident is typical of a hospital scene near the front. It was told in a letter from a hospital nurse to a friend in Paris.

"About midday we received a wounded general, whom we made as comfortable as possible in a little room. Although he suffered terribly, he would submit to no special care, and only thought of the comfort of two of his officers. By an extraordinary chance a soldier of his own regiment was brought in a few moments later. Joy of the general, who wanted to learn at once what had happened to his children. He asked to see the soldier immediately:

" 'Tell me—the commandant?'

" 'Dead, mon général.'

" 'And the captain?'

" 'Dead, mon général.'

"Four times questions were asked, and four times the soldier, whose voice became lower, made his answer of death. Then the general lowered his head and asked no more. We saw the tears running down his scarred old face, and we crept out of the room on tiptoe."

IV—STORY OF THE GHASTLY SCENES IN FRANCE

In spite of all this tragedy, the French soldier into whose soul it sank, and who will never forget, wrote home with a gaiety which gleamed through the sadness of his memories. There was a new series of "Lettres de mon moulin" from a young officer of artillery keeping guard in an old mill-house in an important position at the front. They were addressed to his "dearest mamma," and, thoughtful of all the pretty hands which had been knitting garments for him, he described his endeavours to keep warm in them:

"To-night I have piled on to my respectable body a flannel waistcoat, a flannel shirt, and a flannel belt going round three times, a jacket with sleeves sent by mamma herself, a leather waistcoat from Aunt Charlotte, a woolen vest which came to me from the unknown mother of a young dragoon, a warm undercoat recently received from my tailor, and a woolen jacket and wrap knitted by Madame P. J. So I prepare to sleep in peace, if the 'Boches' will kindly allow me."

The enemy did not often allow the young gentleman to sleep and about the windmill the shells were bursting.

They reached one Sunday morning almost as far as the little twelfth-century church to which the young officer had stepped down from his windmill to hear Mass in the middle of a crowd of soldiers chanting the office, recited by a soldier, accompanied by a harmonium played by another soldier. The windows were shattered, and a beautiful old house next to the church lay in ruins.

The officer spent lonely hours in the windmill in charge

of the telephone exchange, from which the batteries were worked. The men in the trenches and the gun-pits pitied his loneliness, and invented a scheme to cheer him up. So after dark, when the cannonade slackened, he put the receiver to his ears and listened to a Tyrolese ballad sung by an orderly, and to the admirable imitation of a barking dog performed by a sapper, and to a Parisian *chanson* delightfully rendered by the aviator.

"Bonne nuit, maman," wrote the officer of artillery at the end of each letter from his windmill. . . .

There was a little farm near Steinbach round which a battle raged for many days. Leading to it was a sunken road, defended by the enemy, until one day they put up a number of non-combatants from captured villages to prevent a French attack.

"Among them we could distinguish a woman, with her hair falling to her shoulders and her hands tied behind her back. This new infamy inflamed the courage of our soldiers. A company rushed forward with fixed bayonets. The road to the farm was swept by the enemy's fire, but nothing stopped our men. In spite of our losses we carried the position and are masters of the farm. There was no mercy in those moments of triumph. The ghastly business of war was done to the uttermost."

There were ghastly things in some of the enemy's trenches. One of the worst of them was seen in the forest of Apremont, in the district of Woevre, where the enemy was strongly intrenched in some quarries quite close to the French trenches, which sapped their way forward to those pits. When the guns ceased firing the French soldiers often heard the sound of singing. But above the voices of the Germans there came sometimes a series of piercing cries like the screeching of an owl in a terrible plaint, followed by strange and blood-curdling laughter. It was the voice of a mad woman who was one of those captured from neighbouring villages and brought into the trenches by the Germans. One day the German soldiers carried her the length of their own trenches. Only her head was visible above the ground. She wore a German helmet above the wild hair which blew in wisps about her death-white face, and it seemed like a vision of hell as she passed shrieking with the laughter of insanity.

V—STORY OF THE PRIEST-SOLDIERS

One turns from such horrors to the heroism of the French soldier, his devotion to his officers, his letters to that *chère maman* before whom his heart is always that of a little child, to the faith which saves men from at least the grosser brutalities of war. . . .

The priest-soldier in France has been a spiritual influence among his comrades, so that some of them fought with nobler motives than that of blood-lust, and went to death or victory, influenced not by hatred of fellow men, but by a conviction that out of all that death there would come a new life to nations, and that in killing their enemy they were killing a brutal tyranny with its grip upon the world, and a barbarism which would make human life a slavery. . . .

Not a week passed without some priest being cited in the Order of the Day. . . .

The Abbé Bertrand, vicar of St. Germain de Coulamer, was mobilized on the outbreak of war, and for his gallantry in the field promoted successively to the ranks of sergeant, sergeant-major, sub-lieutenant, and lieutenant. He fell on November 4 at the battle of Audrechy, leading his men to the assault. A few days before his death he wrote: "I always look upon this war as an expiation, and I am proud to be a victim." And again: "Oh, how cold the rain is, and how severe the weather! For our faith in France I have offered God to let me be wet and soaked to the very bones."

The story of the Abbé Armand, in the 14th battalion of the Chasseurs Alpins, is that of a hero. A simple man, he used to open his heart to his rough comrades, and often in the trenches, under shell-fire, he would recite the Psalms in a clear voice so that they could hear him. On November 17, to the south of Ypres, his company was selected to hold a dangerous position, swept by the heavy guns of the Germans and near the enemy's trenches. All day until the evening the priest and his comrades stayed there, raked by a hideous shell-fire. At last nearly all the men were killed, and on his side of the emplacement the Abbé Armand was left with two men alive. He signaled the fact to those below by raising three fingers, but shortly afterwards a bullet struck him so that he fell and another hit him in the stomach. It was impossible to send help to him at the time, and he died half an hour later on the tumulus surrounded by the dead bodies of his comrades. They buried him up there, and that night his loss was mourned, not without tears, by many rough soldiers who had loved the man for his cheeriness, and honoured him for the simple faith, which seemed to put a glamour about the mudstained uniform of a soldier of France.

There were scores of stories like that, and the army lists contained the names of hundreds of these priest-soldiers decorated with the Legion of Honour or mentioned in despatches for gallant acts.

Not all French soldiers are like these priests who were valiant with the spirit of Christian faith. Side by side with the priest was the apache, or the slum-dweller, or the peasant from the fields, who in conversation was habitually and unconsciously foul. Not even the mild protest of one of these priests could check the flow of richly imagined blasphemies which are learned in the barracks during the three years' service, and in the *bistros* of the back streets of France from Cherbourg to Marseilles. But, as a rule, the priest did not protest, except by the example of keeping his own tongue clean. "What is the use?" said one of them. "That kind of thing is second nature to the men and, after all, it is part of my sacrifice."

VI—STORY OF GAIETY ON THE ROADS OF FRANCE

Along the roads of France, swinging along to dig a new line of trenches, or on a march from a divisional headquarters to the front, the soldiers would begin one of their Rabelaisian songs which have no ending, but in verse after verse roam further into the purlieus of indecent mirth, so that, as one French officer told me, "these ballads used to make the heather blush." After the song would come the great game of French soldiers on the march. The humourist of the company would remark upon the fatigued appearance of a *sous-officier* near enough to hear.

"He is not in good form to-day, our little corporal. Perhaps it has something to do with his week-end in Paris!"

Another humourist would take up the cue.

"He has a great thirst, our corporal. His first bottle of wine just whets his whistle. At the sixth bottle he begins to think of drinking seriously!"

"He is a great amorist, too, they tell me, and very passionate in his love-making!"

So the ball is started and goes rolling from one man to another in the ranks, growing in audacity and wallowing along filthy ways of thought, until the *sous-officier,* who had been grinning under his *képi,* suddenly turns red with anger and growls out a protest. . . .

VII—STORY OF THE EVENING OF LIQUID FLAMES

The soldiers of France have learned the full range of human suffering, so that one cannot grudge them their hours of laughter, however coarse their mirth. There were many armies of men from Ypres to St. Mihiel who were put to greater tasks of courage than were demanded of the human soul in medieval torture chambers, and they passed through the ordeal with a heroism which belongs to the splendid things of history. As yet the history has been written only in brief bulletins stating facts baldly, as when on a Saturday in March of 1915 it was stated that "In Malancourt Wood, between the Argonne and the Meuse, the enemy sprayed one of our trenches with burning liquid so that it had to be abandoned. The occupants were badly burned." That official account does not convey in any way the horror which overwhelmed the witnesses of the new German method of attacking trenches by drenching them with inflammatory liquid. A more detailed narrative of this first attack by liquid fire was given by one of the soldiers:

"It was yesterday evening, just as night fell, that it happened. The day had been fairly calm, with the usual quantity of bursting shells overhead, and nothing forewarned us of a German attack. Suddenly one of my comrades shouted, 'Hallo! what is this coming down on us? Any one would think it was petroleum.' At that time we could not believe the truth, but the liquid which began to spray on us was certainly some kind of petroleum. The Germans were pumping it from hoses. Our sub-lieutenant made us put out our pipes. But it was a useless precaution. A few seconds later incendiary bombs began to rain down on us and the whole trench burst into flame. It was like being in hell. Some of the men began to scream terribly, tearing off their clothes, trying to beat out the flames. Others were cursing and choking in the hot vapour which stifled us. 'Oh, my Christ!' cried a comrade of mine. 'They've blinded me!' In order to complete their work those German bandits took advantage of our disturbance by advancing on the trench and throwing burning torches into it. None of us escaped that torrent of fire. We had our eyebrows and eyelashes burned off, and clothes were burned in great patches and our flesh was sizzling like roasting meat. But some of us shot through the greasy vapour which made a cloud about us and some of those devils had to pay for their game."

Although some of them had become harmless torches and others lay charred to death, the trench was not abandoned until the second line was ready to make a counter-attack, which they did with fixed bayonets, frenzied by the shrieks which still came from the burning pit where those comrades lay, and flinging themselves with the ferocity of wild beasts upon the enemy, who fled after leaving three hundred dead and wounded on the ground.

Along five hundred miles of front such scenes took place week after week, month after month, from Artois to the Argonne, not always with inflammatory liquid, but with hand grenades, bombs, stink-shells, fire balls, smoke balls, and a storm of shrapnel.

VIII—STORY OF THE HAND GRENADIERS

Out of the monotonous narratives of trench-warfare, stories more horrible than the nightmare phantasies of

Edgar Allan Poe, stories of men buried alive by sapping and mining, and of men torn to bits by a subterranean explosion which leaves one man alive amidst the litter of his comrades' limbs so that he goes mad and laughs at the frightful humour of death, come now and then to reveal the meaning of this modern warfare which is hidden by censors behind decent veils. It is a French lieutenant who tells this story, which is heroic as well as horrid:

"We were about to tidy up a captured trench. At the barrier of sand bags which closed up one end of it, two sentinels kept a sharp lookout so that we could work in peace of mind. Suddenly from a tunnel, hidden by a fold in the ground, an avalanche of bombs was hurled over our heads, and before we could collect our wits ten of our men had fallen dead and wounded, all hugger-mugger. I opened my mouth to shout a word of command when a pebble, knocked by a piece of shell, struck me on the head, and I fell, quite dazed. But my unconsciousness only lasted a second or two. A bursting shell tore off my left hand and I was awakened by the pain of it. When I opened my eyes and groaned, I saw the Germans jump across the sand-bags and invade the trench. There were twenty of them. They had no rifles, but each man carried a sort of wicker basket filled with bombs. I looked round to the left. All our men had fled except those who were lying in their blood. And the Germans were coming on. Another slip or two and they would have been on the top of me. At that moment one of my men, wounded in the forehead, wounded in the chin, and with his face all in a pulp of blood, sat up, snatched at a bag of hand grenades, and shouted out:

"'Arise, ye dead!'

"He got on his knees, and began to fling his bombs into the crowd of Germans. At his call, the other wounded men struggled up. Two with broken legs grasped their rifles and opened fire. The hero with his left arm hanging limp, grabbed a bayonet. When I stood up, with all my senses about me now, some of the Germans were wounded and others were scrambling out of the trench in a panic. But with his back to the sandbags stayed a German *Unter-offizier*, enormous, sweating, apoplectic with rage, who fired two revolver shots in our direction. The man who had first organized the defense of the trench—the hero of that 'Arise, ye dead!'—received a shot full in the throat and fell. But the man who held the bayonet and who had dragged himself from corpse to corpse, staggered up at four feet from the sand-bags, missed death from two shots, and plunged his weapon into the German's throat. The position was saved, and it was as though the dead had really risen."

IX—STORY OF THE FRENCH DRAGOONS

A young Russian officer in the French dragoons told me that he had been fighting since the beginning of the war with never more than three hours' sleep a night and often no sleep at all. On many nights those brief hours of rest were in beetroot fields in which the German shrapnel had been searching for victims, and he awakened now and then to listen to the well-known sound of that singing death before dosing off again.

It was "Boot and saddle" at four o'clock in the morning, before the dawn. It was cold then—a cold which made men tremble as with an ague. A cup of black coffee was served, and a piece of bread.

The Russian officer of French dragoons, who has lived in British colonies, saw a vision then—a false mirage—of a British breakfast. It was the thought of grilled bloaters, followed by ham and eggs, which unmanned him for a moment. Ten minutes later the cavalry was moving away. A detachment was sent forward on a mission of peril, to guard a bridge. There was a bridge near Béthune one night guarded by a little patrol. It was only when the last man had been killed that the Germans made their way across.

Through the darkness these mounted men leaned forward over their saddles, peering for the enemy, listening for any jangle of stirrup or clink of bit. On that night there came a whisper from the cavalry leader.

"They are coming! . . . Quiet there!"

A file of dark shadows moved forward. The dragoons swung their carbines forward. There was a volley of shots before the cry rang out.

"Cessez feu! Cessez feu!"

The cry had been heard before from German officers speaking excellent French, but this time there was no treachery in it. The shadows who moved forward through the night were Frenchmen changing from one trench to another.

The risk of death is taken lightly by all these men. It is curious, indeed, that almost every French soldier has a conviction that he will die in battle sooner or later. In moments of imagination he sees his own corpse lying out in the field, and is full of pity for his wife and children. But it does not destroy his courage or his gift of gaiety or his desire to fight for France or his sublime endurance of pain.

X—STORY OF THE SINGING ARMY AT AMIENS

It is curious how long the song of La Marseillaise has held its power. It has been like a leit-motif through all the drama of this war in France, through the spirit of the French people waiting patiently for victory, hiding their tears for the dead, consoling their wounded and their cripples, and giving their youngest and their manhood to the God of War. What is the magic in this tune so that if one hear it even on a cheap piano in an auxiliary hospital, or scraped thinly on a violin in a courtyard of Paris, it thrills one horribly? On the night of August 2, when I traveled from Paris to Nancy, it seemed to me that France sang La Marseillaise—the strains of it rose from every wayside station—and that out of its graveyards across those dark hills and fields, with a thin luminous line on the far horizon the ghosts of slain soldiers rose to sing it to those men who were going to fight again for liberty.

Since then it has always been in my ears. I heard it that night in Amiens when the French army was in retreat, and when all the young men of the city, not yet called to the colours because of their youth, escaped hurriedly on truck trains before a bridge was blown up, so that if they stayed they would be prisoners in German hands. It was these boys who sang it, with fresh, clear voices, joining in a fine chorus, though not far away the soldiers of France were limping through the night from abandoned positions:

> *Entendez-vous, dans les campagnes,*
> *Mugir ces féroces soldats?*
> *Ils viennent jusque dans nos bras*
> *Egorger nos fils, nos compagnes!*
> *Aux armes, citoyens!*
> *Aux armes, citoyens!*
> *Formez vos bataillons!*
> *Marchons! . . .*

I listened to those boys' voices, and something of the history of the song put its spell upon me then. There was the passion of old heroism in it, of old and bloody deeds. . . .

Poor devils! Hundreds of them have told me their stories and at the end of a tale of misery have said: "I do not complain, you know. It's war, and I am glad to do my duty for the sake of France." And yet sometimes, when they thought back, to the homes they had left, and their old ways of civil life, they had moments of weakness in which all the strength of their souls seemed to ebb away.

"It's fatal to think of one's life before the war," said a young Frenchman who sat with me at the table of a little café not far from the front. He was a rich young man, with a great business in Paris which had been suspended on the first day of mobilization, and with a pretty young wife who had just had her first baby. Now he was a simple soldier, and for nine months he had not seen Paris or his home or his pretty wife. The baby's eyes were gray-blue, it seemed, but he had not been able to test the truth of that description.

"As a rule," he said, "one doesn't think back to one's old life. A great gulf lies between us and the past and it is as though one had been born again just to be a soldier in this war. The roots of our former existence have been torn up. All one's old interests have been buried. My wife? I hardly ever think of her. My home? Is there such a place? . . . It is only at night, or suddenly, sometimes, as one goes marching with one's company that one's thoughts begin to roam back over old grounds for a moment or two. The other fellows know what one's silence means, and one's deafness, so that one doesn't hear a neighbour's joke or answer his question. It gives one a horrible heartache and one is overwhelmed with depression. . . . Great God, how long is this war going to last?"

(This brilliant young English author continues to relate the scenes his eyes have witnessed with the skill of the master. His description of Paris during the siege is a literary masterpiece.—EDITOR.)

"TRENCHING AT GALLIPOLI"—IN THE LAND OF THE TURKS

Adventures of a Newfoundlander

Told by John Gallishaw, Member of the First Newfoundland Regiment

This is the personal narrative of a loyal Newfoundlander soldiering in the disastrous Dardanelles campaign. This is an adventurous story stranger than fiction; as well as a reliable account by an unusually keen participant of the gigantic failure at Gallipoli. Mr. Gallishaw was a student at Harvard when the War began and he gives an extraordinarily vivid impression of trench fighting and trench living. He tells how seven weeks after the outbreak of the War, the Newfoundlanders joined the flotilla containing the first contingent of Canadians. He was on garrison duty for a time at Edinburg Castle in Scotland and then sent to Egypt. His book: "Trenching in Gallipoli" is published by the *Century Company*, Copyright 1916, with whose permission the following stories are taken.

*I—STORY OF A HARVARD STUDENT IN TURKEY

THE afternoon sun poured down steadily on little groups of men preparing dugouts for habitation (at Gallipoli). I had a good many details to attend to before I could look about for a suitable place for a dugout. Men had to be told off for different fatigues. Men for pick and shovel work that night were placed in sections so that each group would get as much sleep as possible. All the available dugouts had been taken up by the first comers. . . .

---

* All numerals relate to stories herein told—not to chapters in the book.

After much hunting, I found a likely looking place. It was about seven feet square, and where I planned to put the head of my dugout a large boulder squatted. It was so eminently suitable that I wondered that no one else had preëmpted it. I took off my equipment, threw my coat on the ground, and began digging. It was soft ground and gave easily.

A short distance away, I could see Art Pratt, digging. He was finding it hard work to make any impression. He saw me, stopped to mop his brow, and grinned cheerfully.

"You should take soft ground like this, Art," I yelled.

"I've gone so far now," said Art, "that it's too late to change," and we resumed our work.

After a few more minutes' digging, my pick struck something that felt like the root of a tree, but I knew there was no tree on that God-forsaken spot large enough to send out big roots. I disentangled the pick and dug a little more, only to find the same obstruction. I took my small intrenching tool, scraped away the dirt I had dug, and began cleaning away near the base of a big boulder. There were no roots there, and gradually I worked away from it. I took my pick again, and at the first blow it stuck. Without trying to disengage it I began straining at it. In a few seconds it began to give, and I withdrew it. Clinging to it was a part of a Turkish uniform, from which dangled and rattled the dried-up bones of a skeleton. Nauseated, I hurriedly filled in the place, and threw myself on the ground, physically sick. While I was lying there one of our men came along, searching for a place to bestow himself. He gazed inquiringly at the ground I had just filled in.

"Is there anybody here?" he asked me, indicating the place with a pick-ax.

"Yes," I said, with feeling, "there is."

"It looks to me," he said, "as if some one began digging and then found a better place. If he don't come back soon I'll take it."

For about fifteen minutes he stood there, and I lay regarding him silently. At last he spoke again.

"I think I'll go ahead," he said. "Possession is nine points of the law, and the fellow hasn't been here to claim it."

"I wouldn't if I were you," I said. "That fellow's been there a hell of a long while."

I left him there digging, and crawled away to a safe distance. In a few minutes he passed me.

"Why didn't you tell me?" he demanded, reproachfully.

"Because half of the company saw me digging there and didn't tell me," I said.

I was prospecting around for another place when Art Pratt hailed me. "Why don't you come with me," he said, "instead of digging another place?"

I went to where he was and looked at the dugout. It wasn't very wide, and I said so. Together we began widening and deepening the dugout, until it was big enough for the two of us. It was grueling work, but by supper time it was done. The night before, a fatigue party had gone down to the beach and hauled up a big field kitchen. Our cooks had made some tea, and we had been issued some loaves of bread. Art unrolled a large piece of cloth with all the pomp and ceremony of a man unveiling a monument. He did it slowly and carefully. There was a glitter in his eyes that one associates with an artist exhibiting his masterpiece. He gave a triumphant switch to the last fold and held toward me a large piece of fresh juicy steak.

"Beefsteak!" I gasped. "Sacred beefsteak! Where did you get it?"

Art leaned toward me mysteriously. "Officers' mess," he whispered.

"I've got salt and pepper," I said, "but how are you going to cook it?"

"I don't know," said Art, "but I'm going up to the field kitchen; there's some condensed milk that I may be able to get hold of to spread on our bread."

II—STORY OF THE ROYAL ENGINEERS

While Art was gone, I strolled down the ravine a little way to where some of the Royal Engineers were quartered. The Royal Engineers are the men who are looked on in training as a noncombatant force, with safe jobs. In wartime they do no fighting, but their safe jobs consist of such harmless work as fixing up barbed wire in front of the parapet and setting mines under the enemy's trenches. For a rest they are allowed to conduct parties to listening posts and to give the lines for advance saps. Sometimes they make loopholes in the parapet, or bolster up some redoubt that is being shelled to pieces.

The Turks were sending over their compliments just as I came abreast of the Engineers' lines. One of the engineers was sifting some gravel when the first shell landed. He dropped the sieve, and turned a back somersault into some gorse-bushes just behind him. The sieve rolled down, swayed from side to side, and settled close to my head, in the depression where I was conscientiously emulating an ostrich. I gathered it to my bosom tenderly and began crawling away. From behind a boulder I heard the engineer bemoaning to an officer the loss of his sieve, and he described in detail how a huge shell had blown it out of his hands. Joyfully I returned to Art with my prize.

"What's that for?" said Art.

"Turn it upside down," I said, "and it's a steak broiler."

"Where did you get it?" said Art.

I told him, and related how the engineer had explained it to his officer.

Up at the field kitchen a group was standing around.

"What's the excitement?" I asked Art.

"Those fellows are a crowd of thieves," answered Art, virtuously. "They're looking about to see what they can steal. I was up there a few minutes ago and saw a can of condensed milk lying on the shaft of the field kitchen. They were watching me too closely to give me a chance, but you might be able to get away with it."

The two of us strolled up slowly to where Hebe Wheeler, the creative artist who did our cooking, was holding forth to a critical audience.

"It's all very well to talk about giving you things to eat, but I can't cook pancakes without baking powder. You can't get blood out of a turnip. I'd give you the stuff if I got it to cook, but I don't get it, do I, Corporal?" said Hebe, appealing to me.

I moved over and stood with my back to the shaft on which rested the tin of condensed milk.

"No, Hebe," I said, "you don't get the things; and when you do get them, this crowd steals them on you."

"By God," said Hebe, "that's got to be put a stop to. I'll report the next man I find stealing anything from the cookhouse."

I put my hand cautiously behind my back, until I felt my fingers close on the tin of milk. "You let me know, Hebe," I said, as I slipped the tin into the roomy pocket of my riding breeches, "and I'll make out a crime sheet against the first man whose name you give." I stayed about ten minutes longer talking to Hebe, and then returned to my dugout. Art had finished broiling the piece of steak, and we began our supper. I put my hand in my breeches' pocket to get the milk. Instead of grasping the tin, my fingers closed on a sticky, gluey mass. The tin had been opened when I took it and I had it in my pocket upside down. About half of it had oozed over my pocket. Art was just pouring the remainder on some bread when some one lifted the rubber sheet and stuck his head into our dugout. It was the enraged Hebe Wheeler. As soon as he had missed his precious milk he had made a thorough investigation of all the dugouts. He looked at Art accusingly.

"Come in, Hebe," I said pleasantly. "We don't see you very often."

Hebe paid no attention to my invitation, but glared at Art.

"I've caught you with the goods on," he said. "Give me back that milk, or I'll report you to the platoon officer."

"You can report me to Lord Kitchener if you like," said Art, calmly, as he drained the can; "but this milk stays right here."

Hebe disappeared, breathing vengeance.

III—STORY OF A NIGHT IN THE DUG-OUTS

After supper that night a crowd sat around the dying embers of the fires. This was one of the first positions we had been in where there was cover sufficient to warrant fires being lighted. A mail had been distributed that day, and the men exchanged items of news and swapped gossip. There were men there from all parts of Newfoundland. They spoke in at least thirty different accents. . . .

Sometimes a friend of the absent "Half" would tell of Half's exploit of stealing a trolley from the Reid Newfoundland Company and going twenty miles to see a girl. Sometimes the hero was a married man. Then it was opined that his conjugal relations were not happy, and the reason he enlisted was that "he had heard something." . . . The lumbermen of Notre Dame Bay and Green Bay told fearsome and wondrous tales of driving and swamping, of teaming and landing, until one almost heard the blows of ax, the "gee" and "haw" of the teamsters, and smelt the pungent odor of new-cut pine. The Reid Newfoundland Railway, the single narrow gauge road that twists a picturesque trail across the Island, had given largely of its personnel toward the making of the regiment. Firemen and engineers, brakemen and conductors, talked reminiscently of forced runs to catch expresses with freight and accommodation trains. There is an interesting tale of two drivers who blew their whistles in the Morse code, and kept up communication with each other, until a girl learned the code and broke up the friendship. A steamship fireman contributed his quota with a story of laboring through mountainous seas against furious tides when the stokers' utmost efforts served only to keep steamers from losing way. By comparison with the homeland, Turkey suffered much; and the things they said about Gallipoli were lamentable. From the gloom on the other side of the fire a voice chanted softly, "It's a long, long way to Tipperary, It's a long way to go." Gradually all joined in. After Tipperary, came many marching songs. "Are we downhearted? NO," with every one booming out the "No." "Boys in Khaki, Boys in Blue," and at last their own song; to the tune of "There is a tavern in the town."

And when those Newfoundlanders start to yell, start to yell,
Oh, Kaiser Bill, you'll wish you were in hell, were in hell;
For they'll hang you high to your Potsdam palace wall,
You're a damn poor Kaiser, after all.

The singing died down slowly. The talk turned to the trenches and the chances of victory, and by degrees to personal impressions.

"I'd like to know," said one chap, "why we all enlisted."

"When I enlisted," said a man with an accent reminiscent of the Placentia Bay, "I thought there'd be lots of fun, but with weather like this, and nothing fit to eat, there's not much poetry or romance in war any more."

"Right for you, my son," said another; "your King and Country need you, but the trouble is to make your King and Country feed you."

"Don't you wish you were in London now, Gal?" said one chap, turning to me. "You'd have a nice bed to sleep in, and could eat anywhere you liked."

"Well," I said, "enough people tried to persuade me to stop. One fellow told me that the more brains a man had, the farther away he was from the firing-line. He'd been to the front too. I think," I added, "that General Sherman had the right idea."

"I wish you fellows would shut up and go to sleep," said a querulous voice from a nearby dugout.

"You don't know what you're talking about, Gal; General Sherman was an optimist."

"It doesn't do any good to talk about it now," said Art Pratt, in a matter of fact voice. "Some of you enlisted so full of love of country that there was patriotism running down your chin, and some of you enlisted because you were disappointed in love, but the most of you enlisted for love of adventure, and you're getting it."

Again the querulous subterranean voice interrupted: "Go to sleep, you fellows—there's none of you knows what you're talking about. There's only one reason any of us enlisted, and that's pure, low down, unmitigated ignorance." Amid general laughter the class in applied psychology broke up, and distributed themselves in their various dugouts.

Halfway down to my dugout, I was arrested by the sound of scuffling, much blowing and puffing, and finally the satisfied grunt that I knew proceeded from Hebe Wheeler.

"I've got a spy," he yelled. "Here's a bloody Turk."

"Turk nothing," said a disgusted voice. "Don't you know a man from your own company?"

Hebe relinquished his hold on his captive and subsided, grumbling. The other arose, shook himself, and went his way, voicing his opinion of people who built their dugouts flush with the ground.

"What do you think of the news from the Western front?" said Art, when I located him.

"What is it?" I asked.

"The enemy are on the run at the Western front. The British have taken four lines of German trenches for a distance of over five miles in the vicinity of Loos. The bulletin board at Brigade headquarters says that they have captured several large guns, a number of machine guns, and seventeen thousand unwounded prisoners. If they can keep this up long enough for the Turks to realize that it is hopeless to expect any help from that quarter, Abdul Pasha will soon give in."

IV—STORY OF THE BOMB-THROWING AUSTRALIANS

We were talking about Abdul Pasha's surrendering when we dropped off to sleep. We must have been asleep about two hours when the insistent, crackling sound of rapid fire, momentarily increasing in volume, brought us to our feet. Away up on the right, where the Australians were, the sky was a red glare from the flashing of many rifles. Against this, we oculd see the occasional flare of different coloured rockets that gave the warships their signals for shelling. Very soon one of our officers appeared.

"Stand to arms for the Newfoundlanders," he said.

"What is it?" I asked.

"The Australians are advancing," he answered. "We'll go up as reinforcements if we're needed. Tell your men to put on their ammunition belts, and have their rifles ready. They needn't put on their packs; but keep them near them so that they can slip them on if we get the order to move away."

I went about among the men of my section, passing along the word. Everybody was tingling with excitement. Nobody knew just what was about to happen; but every one thought that whatever it was it would prove interesting. For about half an hour the rapid fire kept up, then by degrees died down.

"Did you see that last rocket?" said a man near me; "that means they've done it. A red rocket means that the navy is to fire, a green to continue firing, and a white one means that we've won."

In a few minutes Mr. Nunns walked toward us. "You can put your equipments off, and turn in again," he said, "nothing doing to-night."

"What is all the excitement?" I asked.

"Oh, it's the Anzacs again," he said; "when they heard of the advance at Loos, they went over across, and surprised the Turks. They've taken two lines of trenches. They did it without any orders—just wanted to celebrate the good news."

I was awakened the next morning by the sound of a whizz-bang flying over our dugout. Johnny Turk was sending us his best respects. I shook Art, who was sleeping heavily.

"Get up, Art," I said. I might as well have spoken to a stone wall. I tried again. Putting my mouth to his ear, I shouted, "Stand to, Art. Stand to."

Art turned over, sleeping. "I'll stand three if you like, but don't disturb me," he muttered, and relapsed into coma.

In a few minutes, two or three more shells came along. They were well over the ridge behind us, but were landing almost in the midst of another line of dugouts. I stood gazing at them for a little while. A man passed me running badly. "Come on," he gasped, "and yell for the stretcher." I followed him without further question. "It's all right," he said, slowing up just before we came to the line of dugouts that had just been shelled. "They've got him all right." We continued toward a group that was crowded about a stretcher. A man was lying on it, with his head raised on a haversack. He rolled his eyes slowly and surveyed the group. "What the hell is the matter?" he said dazedly; then felt himself over gingerly for wounds. Apparently he could find none. "What hit me?" he asked, appealing to a grinning Red Cross man.

"Nothing," said the other, "except about a ton of earth. It's a lucky thing some one saw you. That last shell buried you alive."

The whistle of a coming shell dispersed the grinning spectators. I went back to my dugout, and found Art busily toasting some bread over the sieve that I had commandeered the day before.

"What was the excitement?" he asked.

"Charlie Renouf," I said, "was buried alive."

"Heavens," said Art, "he's the postman; we can't afford to lose him. That reminds me that I've got to write some letters."

While we were writing, the orderly sergeant, that

dread of loafers, who appoints all details for fatigue work, bore down upon our dugout. "Two men from you, Corporal Gallishaw," he said, "for bomb throwers. Give me their names as soon as you can. They're for practice this afternoon."

"One here, right away," said Art, "and put Lew O'Dea down for the other."

Lew O'Dea was a character. He was in the next dugout to me. The first day on the Peninsula, his rifle had stuck full of sand, and some one had stolen his tin canteen for cooking food. He immediately formed himself into an anti-poverty society of one thereafter, and went around like a walking arsenal. I never saw him with fewer than three rifles, usually he carried half a dozen. He always kept two or three of them spotlessly clean; so that no matter when rifle inspection came, he always had at least one to show. He had been a little late in getting his rifle clean once and was determined not to be caught any more. His equipment always contained a varied assortment of canteens, seven or eight gas masks, and his dugout was luxurious with rubber sheets and blankets. "I inherited them," he always answered, whenever anybody questioned him about them. With ammunition for his several rifles, when he started for the trenches in full marching order, he carried a load that a mule need by no means have been ashamed of.

"Do you want to go on bomb throwing detail this afternoon?" I called to O'Dea across the top of the dugout.

"Sure," he answered; "does a swim want to duck?"

"Fine," I said; "report here at two o'clock."

At two o'clock, accompanied by an officer and a sergeant, we went down the road a little way to where some Australians were conducting a class in bomb throwing. A brown-faced chap from Sydney showed me the difference between bombs that you explode by lighting a match, and bombs that are started by pulling out a plug, and the dinky little three-second "cricket balls" that explode by pressing a spring. I asked him about the attack the night before. He told me that they had been for some time waiting for a chance to make a local advance and that would capture an important redoubt in the Turkish line. Every night at exactly nine o'clock, the Navy had thrown a searchlight on the part of the line the Anzacs wanted to capture. For ten minutes they kept up heavy firing. Then, after a ten minutes' interval of darkness and suspended firing, they began a second illumination and bombardment, commencing always at twenty minutes past nine, and ending precisely at half past. After a little while, the enemy, knowing just the exact minute the bombardment was to begin, took the first beam of the searchlight as a hint to clear out. But the night before, a crowd of eager Australians had crept softly along in the shadow made doubly dark by the glare of the searchlight, the noise of their advance covered by the sound of the bombardment. As soon as the bombardment ceased and the searchlight's beam was succeeded by darkness, they poured into the Turkish position. They had taken the astonished Turks completely by surprise.

"We didn't expect to make the attack for another week," said the Australian; "but as soon as our boys heard that we were winning in France, they thought they'd better start something. There hasn't been any excitement over our way now for a long time," he said. "I'm about fed up on this waiting around the trenches." He fingered one of the little cricket-ball bombs caressingly. "Think of it," he said; "all you do is press that little spring, and three seconds after you're a casualty."

"Pressing the little spring," said I, "is my idea of

nothing to do, unless you're a particularly fast sprinter."

"By the Lord Harry, Newfoundland," said the Australian, with a peculiar, excited glint in his eye, "that's an inspiration."

"What's an inspiration?" I asked, in bewilderment.

The Australian stretched himself on the ground beside me, resting his chin in his cupped hands. "When I was in Sydney," he said slowly and thoughtfully, "I did a hundred yards in ten seconds easily. Now if I can get in a traverse that's only eight or nine yards long, and press the spring of one of those little cricket balls, I ought to be able to get out on the other side of the traverse before it explodes."

Art and Lew O'Dea passed along just then and I jumped up to go with them. "Don't forget to look for me if you're over around the Fifteenth Australians," said the Australian. "Ask for White George."

"I won't forget," I said, as I hurried away to join the others.

We were about half way to our dugouts when we passed a string of our men carrying about twenty mail bags. It was the second instalment of a lot of mail that had been landed the day before. We followed the sweating carriers up the road to the quarter-master sergeant's dugout, and waited around humbly while that autocrat leisurely sorted out the mail, making remarks about each letter and waiting after each remark for the applause he felt it deserved. With maddening deliberation he scanned each address. "Corporal W. P. Costello." "He's at the base," some one answered. Corporal Costello's letter was put aside. "Private George Butler." Private Butler, on the edge of the crowd, pushed and elbowed his way toward the quarter-master sergeant. "Here you are; letter for Butler."

I received one letter, and was sitting on the edge of

my dugout reading it when one of our men passing along, yelled to me. "Hey," he said, "you come from the United States, don't you?"

"Yes," I said; "what do you want to know that for?"

"I've got something here," he said, stopping, "that comes from there too." He dived into his pocket, and produced a medley of articles. From these he selected a small paper-wrapped parcel.

"What's that?" I said.

"It's chewing gum," he answered; "real American chewing gum like the girls chew in the subway in New York." He unwrapped it, selected a piece, placed it in his mouth, and began chewing it with elaborated enjoyment. After a few minutes, he came nearer. "By golly," he said, with an exaggerated nasal drawl, "it's good gum, I'll soon begin to feel like a blooming Yank. I'm talking like a Yank already. Don't you wish you had some of this?"

"I'll make you a sporting offer," I answered. "I'll fight you for the rest of what you've got."

"No, you won't," he answered nasally; "it's made me feel exactly like a Yank; I'm too proud to fight."

(This Newfoundland soldier-boy here tells about his experiences in "No Man's Land"; his fights with the Turks; how he was wounded and sent his last message "home"; how he finally recovered and returned to America.—EDITOR.)

SCENES "IN A FRENCH HOSPITAL"

Stories of a Nurse

By M. Eydoux-Demians—Translated by Betty Yeomans

This is a wonderful revelation of the soul of France. It gives "impressions of things actually seen and heard, revealing the wonderful courage and emotion that exists today in a French provincial hospital." These notes have been collected in a volume dedicated: "To My Five Brothers Wounded in the Service of France." These touching and inspiring stories of the wounded and nurses in a French hospital and told with a dramatic and literary power which make them little masterpieces. They form a most realistic picture of the human side of the Great War. The selections herein given are from the hundreds of thrilling anecdotes in the book, by courtesy of the publishers, *Duffield and Company:* Copyrighted 1915.

*I—STORIES OF THE WOUNDED ON THEIR BEDS

On October sixth, (1914) last, I received a message from the directress of the Hospital of Saint Dominic, reading as follows:

"A large number of wounded have just arrived. We can't take care of any more ourselves, and the moment has come to call for volunteers. I shall expect your help."

One hour later, as you can easily imagine, I was at

---

* All numerals relate to stories herein told, not to chapters in the original books.

Saint Dominic. This specially privileged hospital is under the gentle management of the Sisters of St. Vincent de Paul. Several years ago some of its devoted trustees made one effort after another on its behalf in Paris, and, after overcoming many difficulties, reëstablished the Sisters of Charity amongst us once again. They had not a doubt even then that they were working in the interests of France's soldiers, those same soldiers whose faces light up now with such a special joy when they lie on their painful stretchers, and catch sight, near the large entrance porch, of the good white cornettes of the Sisters waiting for them.

With my heart beating fast I entered the room to which I had been assigned. There they all were before me, these lads that had undergone that terrible and fierce adventuring into war. I remember how they went away in our wonderful mobilisation trains, those make-shift, flower-bedecked trains that sped all of them to the same destination, the same region of glory and bloodshed. One long war cry seemed to rise up from them over all our land. Our young soldiers who went away in them had acquired an entirely new way of shouting *"Vive la France."* It was no longer as if they were on parade, notwithstanding all the flowers that people tossed to them: it was already the cry of men who were to lead in war's assaults, and make the supreme sacrifice of their lives. I remember one little infantryman of twenty years, standing erect with folded arms in the back of his compartment, his eyes flashing, and all the muscles of his pale face taut. He kept repeating threateningly, *"Vive la France—vive la France,"* without a look toward any one; saying it just to himself and for his country. And I felt that it was as if he said: "We shall get them: we must get them, no matter what it costs. As for me, well, you see, to begin with, my life doesn't count any more." This very fellow is the one, perhaps, who has come back now and sleeps here in this first cot, where a face both energetic and infantile shows in the midst of the blood-stained linen.

Sister Gabrielle made a tour with me of all the patients. The memory of certain of them particularly is fixed in my mind. There is number 3, here, who got a bullet wound in the region of the liver, and has to lie absolutely still, lest an internal hemorrhage may occur at any moment. A warrior of twenty-three he is, with cheeks as rosy as a girl's, and clear blue eyes. He fought like a lion, they say, but here nothing could be gentler. His appreciation for the least thing that is done for him is touching. Number 8, little eight, as they call him, a volunteer, who seems about fifteen, and who has to live week after week propped on his right side, on a hard hospital bed, on account of an abscess following his wound. Number 12, an infantryman, who got a bullet in the left temple; it was extracted from his right maxillary, and in passing cut his tongue in two. "Everything has been put back," said the Sister, "but he can't talk yet, and he'll have to learn to talk all over again, like a little child. In taking care of him you must come every once in a while and see if you can guess what he wants." Number 17, a brave among the braves, who, under the enemy's fire, crawled ten kilometres on his hands and knees, dragging his twice-wounded foot behind him, to deliver an order that he had been charged with. His wounds cause him cruel suffering, and yet he seems illuminated as with some strange inward joy. Number 24, nicknamed the little sieve, because of his fifteen wounds. Number 32, who suffers like a real martyr. His leg was literally shattered by the fragments of a shell. It was a question whether it could be saved at all, but following the directions of the war surgeon, we are keeping up the attempt. Antiseptic injections are made twice a day as deep as the bone. Number 30, who has lost an eye and has two open fractures in his right arm. When I said to him: "You have given a good deal for France," he answered, "It's the least I could do." And he added, laughing, "I was so clumsy with my hands. This will teach me to be clever even with my left one." . . .

One cannot repeat too often or too admiringly, "Our wounded." Our wounded, that is to say, those men who have come back from that hell, "whose horrors," they say themselves, "are indescribable;" those who have marched beneath "that terrible, moving curtain of iron," to which an officer compared the mass of balls and shells in battle, a mass so compact that it obscured the very daylight on the firing line. Our wounded! Those, in a word, who have brought back in their very flesh the frightful scars of the enemy's iron, those who have cemented with their own blood the human wall that is now our frontier. They have come back, not with their courage drained, broken down, horror-stricken, stunned—not at all. They forget themselves to talk smilingly of the great hope in which we all share. They are touched, deeply touched, by the few hours of fatigue we undergo for them each day—for them who have given almost their lives.

My tasks were laid out for me, and I began work at once, thanked by the soldiers almost in advance for my trouble.

"It's a bit too much to see you work like this for us."

"All the same, no one has ever been served like this."

They are not a bit difficult, but pleased with everything, these men who suffer so much, who have such a right to every care. Alas, there are too many of them (this hospital alone has as many as a thousand) to permit of all the little comforting things that we should like to do for them without stint. The Sister who cooks is sorely driven, and even the prescribed dishes that she sends up for the sickest ones are often far from appetizing. For instance, I have just taken Number 13, who is consumed by a lingering fever (a bullet passed through his lung), a milk soup that smelt badly burned, and in which pieces of half-cooked rice floated round. I sighed a little about it as I put the napkin on the bed. Did he understand what worried me? In any case, he shows no distaste, and a quarter of an hour later, when I pass by him, he motions to me, and says gently, "It was delicious, madame."

That's the way they all are—all of them.

II—STORY OF SISTER GABRIELLE— "ARCHANGEL"

I STUDY with emotion the admirable vision of the human soul which the Sister of Charity and the wounded soldier set before me. It is a vision which has intervened always, as with an element of the supernatural, in our war-time pictures, and, behold, now we find it again, almost miraculously, in the supreme struggle of 1914.

Sister Gabrielle, who has charge of my room, her identity quite hidden as it is by her archangel's name, is the daughter of a general, as I know. She has three brothers that have served beneath the colours. The oldest, a quite young captain, has just met his death on the field of honour. I happen to have learned the circumstances: how, covered with blood already flowing from three different wounds, Captain X nevertheless struggled on bravely at the head of his men, and after several hours of conflict was struck by a bullet full in the breast. He fell, crying: "Don't fall back! That's my last order!"

Sister Gabrielle was told only last week of the glorious grief that had been thrust upon her, but no one around her would have guessed her sorrow. Possibly her smile for the patients that day was a little more compassionate and tender than usual, when she thought of her brother enduring his moment of supreme agony alone down there in the forests of the Vosges. . . .

She is thin and frail—mortally ill herself, they say; she was quite ill one month ago. But if you speak to her of her health she interrupts you a little impatiently:

"We have given ourselves, body and soul, according to our vows. To last a little longer or a little less doesn't matter. The main thing is to fulfill our tasks. Besides," she adds, indicating her patients, "they have given their lives for France. It is quite right, if it must be so, that our lives be sacrificed to save them." . . .

In the lot of wounded that were sent in yesterday, forty came to Sister Gabrielle directly from the Aisne. They arrived toward the close of the day, and I shall never forget the spectacle of that room. One stretcher succeeded another, all borne slowly by the litter-men and set down near the hastily prepared beds. Here and there you caught a cry of pain that could not be kept in, though there were no complaints, no continued groanings. Yet now, when you lean over those glorious and lamentable blue bonnets, cut as they are by bullets and stained with the mud of the trenches, when you take off the caps that have grown stiff with the dampness of the long rains, you perceive their suffering by the glittering look in their fevered eyes, their poor, worn faces and ravaged features, sunken and hollow with suffering. Then, all at once, at the least word, the old gallantry that we know so well reasserts itself. For example, they ask the most touching and childish favours of us. Thus if a limb that hurts too much must be lifted, or a piece of clothing that binds a wound eased up, they all ask:

"Not the orderly, not the orderly, please! the Sister or the lady."

The first words that the newcomers exchange with their cot neighbours are not about their own hardships; they speak first, and before anything else, of France.

"How are things going down there?"

"All right. We'll get them."

Then the newcomers, worn out as they are, sink into feverish sleep, struggling sometimes for days between realities and the persistent nightmare of the visions that pursue them. That night in the room that was always so still, but that now seemed more feverish than usual, I heard a sound of smothered sobs. It was Number 25, a big, good-looking soldier, whom each day I had seen having his wound dressed, a real torture, without a word, and who was sobbing now with his head in his pillow, ashamed of his tears, but powerless to keep them back. I went to him and tried to question him, but the soldiers don't readily speak to you of the sorrows that touch their hearts the deepest and most nearly.

"Thank you, lady; don't bother yourself about me. I don't need anything."

"Is your pain worse, maybe?"

"I'm in pain, yes, terribly, but it isn't that."

"What is it, then? Won't you tell me?"

He denied me still, then, all at once, under the pressure of his grief, he said:

"Oh, yes, I do feel like confiding in you. I'll tell you what it is. The comrade who was waiting next to me till his bed was ready brought me news of the death of my best friend. He was in his regiment and was killed by his side. Oh, madame, he was such a fine fellow, so devoted and full of courage. We were brought up together. He was more than my chum; he was my friend."

He cried and cried. He had borne everything without giving way—the continual nearness of death, the so hard life in the trenches, the incessant physical suffering; but the death of his friend crushed him and brought him down to earth. And while I murmured words that, alas, were futile for any change they made in his sorrow, but which did some good, just the same, I heard him sobbing in his pillow:

"My friend was killed. My friend was killed."

His friend—when one knows what the word *comrade* means to them, one divines all that word friend may mean, too.

Sister Gabrielle, whose infallible instinct brings her alway to the cots where the sickest of her children are, passed near Number 25 and stopped a moment. She did not ask him anything. She just put her hand caressingly on his brown head, so young and virile, and said in her firm, sweet voice:

"All right, my boy, all right. Courage. Remember all this is for France."

Then turning to me, she said:

"Before night-time wouldn't you like to play a game of dominoes with this good boy? He'll represent the French forces, and in the morning he must be able to tell me that he has won."

In the midst of his tears the young soldier, his heart swelling in his distress, smiled at finding himself thus treated like a child. They have such need of it, the soldiers, after having done so valiantly the work of men!

III—STORIES OF THE SOLDIERS FROM THE AISNE

It is comforting to hear them talk about their superior officers, as a soldier of the 149th Infantry has just talked to me about his captain.

"Oh, I can tell you, my captain had plenty of good blood in his veins. There was nothing suspicious about him. I saw him standing straight up among the whistling bullets, giving his orders without flinching, without recoiling one inch, as if he were sitting at his desk and only flies were buzzing round his head. And so gentle, too. Good to the men and always jolly. We were in luck to have him over us."

I asked him questions about his campaign, and he talked freely, having only good things to tell. The taciturn ones are those who have sad memories to conceal.

"We were the ones told off to take the village of S———," he said, "where the enemy was. My captain, who acted as chief of battalion, got us all together, and said to us:

"'There seem to be two or three Boches down there. We must get them out, eh?'"

"Everybody knew very well what that meant, but we laughed and went to it in good part. What fights those were! Two days of bloody battles in the streets. Finally the village was ours. We had one night's rest in a farmhouse, three-quarters of which had been destroyed. When we got there we spied an unfortunate porker in a corner. He had taken refuge there, frightened by the firing. He came in very handy, I can tell you, for our stomachs were hollow.

"'Charge again on that Boche, there,' said the Captain. When he had eaten and slept and assembled again next day, he said:

"Well, well, my lads, we're in danger of getting too soft here. Suppose we go on a little further and see what's happening.'

"We marched on further, but the enemy, who were in force, began to shoot at us all at once from below. My Captain didn't expose us needlessly. He made us lie down in the deserted trenches. There were corpses there and dead horses, and water, water everywhere. It rained without stopping. We spent the night up to our waists in water. It was enough to make one laugh."

To laugh—this word turns up all the time in their recitals, and in the most unexpected manner. Oh, this French courage, which faces not only the bitter struggle with danger, but disdains and mocks it, too; that elegant courage of our fathers that has been born again amongst us.

My foot-soldier, Number 149, was seized with quite a touching emotion when I told him that I knew his Captain's lady.

"Tell her she may be proud," he said, "and that I'd willingly go back down there; for my country's sake, of course, but also and a good deal, on my Captain's account."

Then I let him know something that I'd kept till the end of our interview, that his Captain, young as he was, had just been promoted to the rank of battalion chief; that the Cross of the Legion of Honour had been given him, and that, thanks to him, no doubt, the entire regiment had been mentioned in the order of the day. I won't attempt to picture the little soldier's moving and disinterested joy.

Near Number 3's bed I caught sight of a peasant woman from the Cher, in a white headdress, and an old man, who wore a medallion of 1870 on his breast.

"They are his parents," Sister Gabrielle explained to

me. "I had word sent to them. The poor lad is in grave danger. Luckily I've got the management's permission to let the mother pass the nights here."

In this way I became acquainted with the Mèchins, French peasants of the old order, unalterably attached to the soil. They hope, nay, they are sure, that their son is going to get well. The sick man says nothing. They're all like that, our soldiers—no foolish tenderness, no pain given to their parents. Who knows, besides, how much their desire to live may have dwindled down after their tragic voyages to the frontier? The soul must possess new powers of detachment when it has risen to the heights of absolute self-sacrifice. The little soldier does not deceive himself, Sister Gabrielle has told me, and when I expressed my admiration for the strange moral force that he gave proof of, she answered me proudly:

"But they are all like that."

Just as I was going to leave the room the sick man summoned me with his eyes. I went up to him and bent over him.

"Do you want anything?" I asked.

He made a sign of No, and with a great effort raised his hand outside the bed and reached it toward me, murmuring: "Thanks."

I understood. It was his good-bye. He thought that he should perhaps not be there in the morning when I came back.

IV—STORIES OF THE HOSPITAL ORDERLIES

THE corps of orderlies is not always sympathetic. I must say, however, that in the room where I am employed, each one does his duty, thanks, no doubt, to the active supervision of the Sister, thanks also perhaps to three singularly moving personalities among the orderlies themselves.

To begin with, there is Nicolas Indjematoured, twenty-two, a Greek, and a subject of the Ottoman empire. He held a highly lucrative position, of which he was very proud, in a bank at Constantinople, but when the war broke out, he could not bear the thought of being drawn into service with the Germans against France, and did not hesitate to give up his job. He would not even see his old mother again, but made a will providing for her with all his small store of property, and sailed away as a stowaway on a steamer which landed him at Marseilles. He enlisted as a volunteer in the Legion and was ordered here, where, however, soon after his arrival, he received a serious finger wound, and was sent to St. Dominic to be cured. He explained his state of mind to me with simplicity and emotion:

"You can understand, madame, how ashamed I am, among all these brave men, not to have done anything yet for France. Luckily I can help Sister in serving them It's a great honour for me."

In the hospital room they all call him "the little Greek." Night and day he holds himself in readiness to do things for the invalids, whom he treats with touching consideration, refusing doggedly to accept the least remuneration from the management.

Boisset, a stubbly little orderly of some sixty years, is an old employee of the hospital. An ex-pastry cook with no family, he was operated on and cared for at the hospital ten years ago. His case is one of those mysterious stories of conversion that work themselves out in secret near this cross-shaped chapel, with its four great doors wide open on the wards of suffering.

Boisset, once cured, begged permission not to leave the hospital, "hoping," as he said, "to consecrate my life to God in the service of the poor wounded."

Do not his words recall those of the brothers of St.

Francis? Like them, Boisset has summed up his whole life in these two words: simplicity and heroism. He is at others' service night and day, just as he desired to be. The Sister calls him "her right arm," something at which he only half shows his pride. He is the one that's called upon, with never any fear of putting him out, if there's anything to be done in the way of lifting some fellow on whom a specially delicate operation has been performed, or doing some other difficult bit of duty. "Boisset, Boisset!" You get accustomed to hearing his name called out each moment. And Boisset, untiring, runs from one bed to the other, with his mincing, weary step, incessantly. In his moments of leisure he harks back to his old trade, begging from the kitchen some left-over bits of milk and whites of eggs, with which he cooks up some sweet dishes for his beloved patients, by whom they are much appreciated. What strikes me especially in Boisset is his *joyful spirit*. This man, who deliberately leads the hardest kind of life, has a smile always on his lips, and cheerfulness always in his heart. In the little recess where he does the patients' dishes you can hear him humming the canticles, especially the magnificat, of which he is very fond, as he confided to me, because it's the song of joy. When I find myself with Boisset I always want to talk to him about "Dame Poverty" and "Charity, her hand-maiden."

Our third orderly, the Marquess of X, belongs to one of the greatest Italian families. His mother was a French woman, and from the very beginning of hostilities, "he felt," as he put it, "the French blood boiling in his veins."

He found a simple and admirable way of doing something for his mother's country accordingly, by coming and putting himself at the service of the wounded. He wanted "to perform the humblest duties," he particularly specified. He did each day, from morning till night, very humble and sometimes repulsive duties, without apparently recoiling from them. He is but one in the nameless crowd of orderlies, yet the patients very easily distinguish him from the others, and the consolation and care that he gives them are specially sweet to them, because it includes the admiration of a noble soul and of a whole race for the French soldier.

The day he arrived, the Marquess of X, after making a tour of the wounded, came up to me with tears in his eyes.

"What extraordinary reserves of energy and heroism the French still have," he remarked to me, much moved. "To hear these young fellows tell of the dangers they've gone through, talking about sufferings, not only without complaining of them, but laughing about them, is *'the finest part of it all.'*"

V—STORIES FROM THE COTS OF THE DYING

SISTER GABRIELLE accosted me this morning with a luminous smile:

"We shall certainly save Number 32's leg. The work of disinfection is finished. The flesh begins to form again over the wound."

She is radiant. Such are her joys, the only ones she asks of life. Nothing else exists, or ever will exist for her, and yet her face is still young. Let us incline our heads before such lives as hers! In a flash I understand whence comes the deep-seated affinity of soul that rules between Sister Gabrielle and our soldiers; she has given as they have given, everything, even themselves. Only in her case, it is for always and under all circumstances. I ask her what she thinks of Number 3, who seems to me to be picking up a bit. She shakes her head sadly.

"His parents are full of illusions about him, but we can only prolong things for him, with all our care."

Sad, oh, how sad! A little later Mother Mèchin comes and talks to me in a low voice about her son.

"Such a good boy, madame! He never gave us one hour of trouble. He fought so well, they say, and at home he was as gentle as a girl. And he didn't drink or waste his money. Just imagine, he has saved up a thousand francs, in little pieces, since he was a child. We didn't want him to cut into this money to go to the wars. We preferred to go without things ourselves to fit him out, and let him keep his little savings. He will be very glad of it when he gets married." Married! Alas, poor boy! A terrible spouse is waiting for him, one who will not give him up. But already he has marched before her with as much courage as now perhaps he guesses at her coming near. He is very feeble, but he makes a sign that he would like to speak to me. I bend over his bed, and he whispers in my ear:

"I took communion this morning: I am very glad."

I had just brought him a medal of the Holy Virgin. He smiled with pleasure, and I am moved to the bottom of my soul, seeing him kiss the medal and then place it on his heart.

All this time we are making the acquaintance of newer patients, as they are always coming into this ward, which is reserved for those that have undergone the most serious operations. "One never has the consolation of seeing them completely cured," Sister Gabrielle warned me with a sigh. I stop a moment before a little Turco, who took part in the battle of the Aisne. Both his legs are broken. His face stiffens with pain, and now and then a groan escapes him, though it is at once suppressed. He scolds himself about it, and warns himself, or calls me to witness, I am not sure which, when I hear him murmuring:

"Just look! When you think of the ones who stayed down there, ought you ever to groan? We are happier here. It isn't right."

Those who stayed down there! The imagination recoils before the picture evoked by those simple words; those who stay behind down there in the cold and the night, under constant menace by the barbarian enemy, who stay to suffer agonies alone, to die; to see their blood, without the help even of a single bandage, flow from their broken flesh and fall to the last drop upon the soil of France. I remember the words of another wounded soldier:

"After the battle, that day, you couldn't hear yourselves talk any more in the trenches for the cries of the wounded. It was like one great uninterrupted wail. You could make out appeals, prayers, calls for help, women's names. Then, little by little, silence came again, as a good many of them died. What we heard sound longest on the battlefield, from one end to the other, was the word 'Mother!' It is always those who are dying who call like that; we know that well now."

Alas! What do we not know now of the many-sided anguish and horror of death! We must certainly begin, like the little Turco, to qualify as lucky the fellows whom destiny delivers up to the hospital. And yet how they suffer, even these. To physical torture is added too often the worst tortures of the spirit.

"In the two months I've been away, not one bit of news of my family has reached me," a soldier told me, "except a despatch announcing my father's death."

Another had lost a fifteen-year-old son, whom he adored, two hours before his departure.

"His body was still warm: my wife was as if mad with sorrow."

They tell you these things without complaint. France called them: it was quite natural to answer her, to go to her out of the midst of the greatest sorrows, the depest affections, the keenest happiness; sometimes, like that young engineer there of twenty, married eleven months ago to a girl of eighteen, to tear yourself away from a whole romance! He had been rejected for defective vision, but, and his wife agreed, he decided this did not matter any more, now that mobilization was under way, and that he must go. Two days after the birth of a fine boy—a future soldier, the mother said—he left his life of ease and tenderness and reported at the barracks as a simple soldier; and he had been encouraged to do so by that little Parisienne whom we should have thought absorbed in nothing but society and dress.

VI—STORY OF THE DEATH OF A MARTYR

The little soldier Mèchin had a serious hemorrhage in the night; he was in the operating room when I arrived at the hospital this morning. The Sister had sent his parents to pray in the chapel, they explained to me. The work of attending to the sick went on as usual; nothing must be allowed to stop the movement of the wheels. Toward ten o'clock I saw the litter coming back, borne slowly and with infinite precautions. Sister Gabrielle walked quite near it, and never stopped repeating: "Gently, more gently still."

The little soldier's face was as pale as a corpse; his eyes, which seemed to have sunk back in their orbits, were closed. When he was lifted up to put him on the bed, the shock, light as it was, brought on the supreme crisis. His breath, slow and scarcely perceptible, quickened strangely. His candid blue eyes opened, dilated, immense, as if looking for some one.

"He wants his parents," the Sister said to me in a low voice. "Go and find them quickly. It's the end."

In the quiet chapel that opened from the big wards, the poor Mèchins wept and prayed. I called them. The mother clasped her hands together, turning to me:

"The operation was successful, wasn't it, madame?"

Alas! I don't know, I fear not; but they must come quickly. Their tears blind them, she can't see her steps; she stumbles, and I have to give her my arm for support.

The moment she approaches her son she recognizes the shadow of death on his dear face, and would have given a cry of sorrow, but that Sister Gabrielle stops her, putting a finger on her lips. Soldiers who die must be surrounded by so great a peace.

"Here is your mother, here quite near to you," says the calm voice of the Sister in the ear of the dying man. "She embraces you. Your father is here, too. And here is the crucified One, Our Lord, here on your lips."

The little soldier kisses the cross and smiles at his mother; then his eyes, wide open, and as if drawn by some invincible attraction, turn and fix themselves on the open window opposite the bed, through which can be seen the infinite depths of the sky. Nothing again, till his last breath was drawn, could make his gaze turn elsewhere. Where have I already beheld a scene like this? I remember—it was in Greece, at Athens, last year. In the room of the tombs, a simple and admirable funeral monument represents death. A fine young man of twenty is standing ready to depart. His parents, their faces torn with sorrow, stretch out their arms to him, calling him, but he, so calm in the purity of the white marble, his eyes as if fascinated, looks fixedly, with all his thought, into the distance, one knows not where. As we passed this masterpiece, the young Greek who was with me whispered to me:

"Look at that boy there. He sees *something else.*"

Our little soldier, too, seemed to see something else. The chaplain gave him the last blessings. The mysterious shore drew nearer moment by moment. A deep silence, solemnly calm and very moving, fell suddenly on the great room into which the terrible visitor was so soon to penetrate; truly he must die well, surrounded thus by his comrades, upheld until the end by a Sister of Charity. The wings of her white cornette tremble above the young face in its last agony. The Sister's voice, already a supernatural one, is the last of this world's voices that Private Mèchin is to hear. She says, and he repeats slowly, the supreme invocation: "O God, receive me into Thy Paradise. Jesus, have mercy on me. Holy Mother of God, pray for us in the hour of our death."

It is over . . . the last breath exhales gently. The young soldier's gaze is fixed forever on the great light of God. Sister Gabrielle gently closes his eyelids and places the crucifix on the boy's heart. All is so calm, so evangelical, that the parents themselves dare not weep. Ah, how truly he spoke, the chaplain who wrote from the front: "The soldiers of France die without pain, like angels."

When the parents were led away for a while Sister Gabrielle piously replaced the sheet on the dead face, and said to me:

"This is the time for the patients' dinners. If you will, we'll go and serve them, and then we'll come back and lay out the body of this poor lad here."

I look at her wonderingly; she is very pale, and her eyes are full of unshed tears. She busies herself with the necessities of them all, with her usual clear-headedness.

Have they already broken with everything of earth, these Sisters, lifted themselves for good above the most pardonable frailty?

(Thus the author, M. Eydoux-Demians, continues to relate her experiences in the hospitals, telling of "The Funeral," "The First Communion," "Our Priests," "The Little Refugee," and a half hundred other little tragedies that bring tears to the eyes, a pain to the heart, and a sense of overwhelming joy that manhood and womanhood can rise to such noble heights in these days of terrible suffering.—EDITOR.)

"FLYING FOR FRANCE"—HERO TALES OF BATTLES IN THE AIR

With the American Escadrille at Verdun

Told by James R. McConnell, Sergeant-Pilot in the French Flying Corps

The story of how Jim McConnell, the young North Carolinian, went to France and gave his life to the cause of human liberty, is a noble tribute to young Americanism. His heroic deeds at the battle of Verdun when he fought with the American aviators in a sea of clouds is a classic that would do credit to the ancient Greeks. A comrade tells this story: "One day in January, 1915, I saw Jim McConnell in front of the Court House at Carthage, North Carolina. 'Well,' he said, 'I am all fixed up and I am leaving on Wednesday.' 'Where for?' I asked. 'I have got a job to drive an ambulance in France' was his answer. And then he went on to tell me, first, that as he saw it the greatest event of history was going on right at hand. 'These sand hills,' he said, 'will be here forever but the war won't— and so I am going.' So he went. He joined the American Ambulance Service in the Vosges, was mentioned many times in the Orders of the Day for conspicuous bravery in saving wounded under fire, and received the much-coveted Croix de Guerre." As a Sergeant-Pilot in the Lafayette Escadrille of American Aviators, McConnell was killed in March, 1917, in an encounter with two Boche-driven aeroplanes. It was his hope that he might lead a United States Army Aero Corps on the French front. He, indeed, had a part in great deeds and left the best description yet published of the most terrific battle in the war up to the time of his death. His book, titled "Flying for France," is published by *Doubleday, Page and Company*, Copyright 1916-17. Some of his experiences herein related are presented with their full authority in this collection of stories.

*I—STORY OF THE AMERICAN AIRMEN

Beneath the canvas of a huge hangar mechanicians are at work on the motor of an airplane. Outside, on the borders of an aviation field, others loiter awaiting their aërial charge's return from the sky. Near the hangar stands a hut-shaped tent. In front of it several short-winged biplanes are lined up; inside it three or four young men are lolling in wicker chairs.

They wear the uniform of French army aviators. These uniforms, and the grim-looking machine guns mounted on the upper planes of the little aircraft, are the only warlike note in a pleasantly peaceful scene. The war seems very remote. It is hard to believe that the greatest of all battles—Verdun—rages only twenty-five miles to the north, and that the field and hangars and mechanicians and aviators and airplanes are all playing a part therein.

Suddenly there is the distant hum of a motor. One of the pilots emerges from the tent and gazes fixedly up into the blue sky. He points, and one glimpses a black speck against the blue, high overhead. The sound of the motor ceases, and the speck grows larger. It moves earthward in steep dives and circles, and as it swoops closer, takes on the shape of an airplane. Now one can make out the red, white, and blue circles under the wings which mark a French war-plane, and the distinctive insignia of the pilot on its sides.

"Ton patron arrive!" one mechanician cries to another. "Your boss is coming!"

The machine dips sharply over the top of a hangar, straightens out again near the earth at a dizzy speed a

---

* All numerals relate to the stories herein, not to chapters of the book.

few feet above it and, losing momentum in a surprisingly short time, hits the ground with tail and wheels. It bumps along a score of yards and then, its motor whirring again, turns, rolls toward the hangar, and stops. A human form, enveloped in a species of garment for all the world like a diver's suit, and further adorned with goggles and a leather hood, rises unsteadily in the cockpit, clambers awkwardly overboard and slides down to terra firma.

A group of soldiers, enjoying a brief holiday from the trenches in a cantonment near the field, straggle forward and gather timidly about the airplane, listening open-mouthed for what its rider is about to say.

"Hell!" mumbles that gentleman, as he starts divesting himself of his flying garb.

"What's wrong now?" inquires one of the tenants of the tent.

"Everything, or else I've gone nutty," is the indignant reply, delivered while disengaging a leg from its Teddy Bear trousering. "Why, I emptied my whole roller on a Boche this morning, point blank at not fifteen metres off. His machine gun quit firing and his propeller wasn't turning and yet the darn fool just hung up there as if he were tied to a cloud. Say, I was so sure I had him it made me sore—felt like running into him and yelling, 'Now, you fall, you bum!'"

The eyes of the *poilus* register surprise. Not a word of this dialogue, delivered in purest American, is intelligible to them. Why is an aviator in a French uniform speaking a foreign tongue, they mutually ask themselves. Finally one of them, a little chap in a uniform long since bleached of its horizon-blue color by the mud of the firing line, whisperingly interrogates a mechanician as to the identity of these strange air folk.

"But they are the Americans, my old one," the latter explains with noticeable condescension.

Marvelling afresh, the infantrymen demand further details. They learn that they are witnessing the return of the American Escadrille—composed of Americans who have volunteered to fly for France for the duration of the war—to their station near Bar-le-Duc, twenty-five miles south of Verdun, from a flight over the battle front of the Meuse. They have barely had time to digest this knowledge when other dots appear in the sky, and one by one turn into airplanes as they wheel downward. Finally all six of the machines that have been aloft are back on the ground and the American Escadrille has one more sortie over the German lines to its credit.

II—STORY OF THE PERSONNEL OF THE ESCADRILLE

Like all worth-while institutions, the American Escadrille, of which I have the honour of being a member, was of gradual growth. When the war began, it is doubtful whether anybody anywhere envisaged the possibility of an American entering the French aviation service. Yet, by the fall of 1915, scarcely more than a year later, there were six Americans serving as full-fledged pilots, and now, in the summer of 1916, the list numbers fifteen or more, with twice that number training for their pilot's license in the military aviation schools.

The pioneer of them all was William Thaw, of Pittsburg, who is to-day the only American holding a commission in the French flying corps. Lieutenant Thaw, a flyer of considerable reputation in America before the war, had enlisted in the Foreign Legion in August, 1914. With considerable difficulty he had himself transferred, in the early part of 1915, into aviation, and the autumn of that year found him piloting a Caudron biplane, and doing excellent observation work. At the same time, Sergeants Norman Prince, of Boston, and Elliot Cowdin, of New York—who were the first to enter the aviation service coming directly from the United States—were at the front on Voisin planes with a cannon mounted in the bow.

Sergeant Bert Hall, who signs from the Lone Star State and had got himself shifted from the Foreign Legion to aviation soon after Thaw, was flying a Nieuport fighting machine, and, a little later, instructing less-advanced students of the air in the Avord Training School. His particular chum in the Foreign Legion, James Bach, who also had become an aviator, had the distressing distinction soon after he reached the front of becoming the first American to fall into the hands of the enemy. Going to the assistance of a companion who had broken down in landing a spy in the German lines, Bach smashed his machine against a tree. Both he and his French comrade were captured, and Bach was twice court-martialed by the Germans on suspicion of being an American *franc-tieur* —the penalty for which is death! He was acquitted but of course still languishes in a prison camp "somewhere in Germany." The sixth of the original sextet was Adjutant Didier Masson, who did exhibition flying in the States until—Carranza having grown ambitious in Mexico—he turned his talents to spotting *los Federales* for General Obregon. When the real war broke out, Masson answered the call of his French blood and was soon flying and fighting for the land of his ancestors.

Of the other members of the escadrille Sergeant Givas Lufbery, American citizen and soldier, but dweller in the world at large, was among the earliest to wear the French airman's wings. Exhibition work with a French pilot in the Far East prepared him efficiently for the task of patiently unloading explosives on to German military centres from a slow-moving Voisin which was his first mount. Upon the heels of Lufbery came two more graduates of the Foreign Legion—Kiffin Rockwell, of Asheville, N. C., who had been wounded at Carency; Victor Chapman, of New York, who after recovering from his wounds became an airplane bomb-dropper and so caught the craving to become a pilot. At about this time one Paul Pavelka, whose birthplace was Madison, Conn., and who from the age of fifteen had sailed the seven seas, managed to slip out of the Foreign Legion into aviation and joined the other Americans at Pau.

There seems to be a fascination to aviation, particularly when it is coupled with fighting. Perhaps it's because the game is new, but more probably because as a rule nobody knows anything about it. Whatever be the reason, adventurous young Americans were attracted by it in rapidly increasing numbers. Many of them, of course, never got fascinated beyond the stage of talking about joining. Among the chaps serving with the American ambulance field sections a good many imaginations were stirred, and a few actually did enlist, when, toward the end of the summer of 1915, the Ministry of War, finding that the original American pilots had made good, grew more liberal in considering applications.

Chouteau Johnson, of New York; Lawrence Rumsey, of Buffalo; Dudley Hill, of Peekskill, N. Y.; and Clyde Balsley, of El Paso; one after another doffed the ambulance driver's khaki for the horizon-blue of the French flying corps. All of them had seen plenty of action, collecting the wounded under fire, but they were all tired of being non-combatant spectators. More or less the same feeling actuated me, I suppose. I had come over from Carthage, N. C., in January, 1915, and worked with an American ambulance section in the Bois-le-Prêtre. All along I had been convinced that the United States ought to aid in the struggle against Germany. With that conviction, it was plainly up to me to do more than drive an ambulance. The more I saw the splendour of the fight the French were fighting, the more I felt like an *embusqué*—what the British call a "shirker." So I made up my mind to go into aviation.

A special channel had been created for the reception of applications from Americans, and my own was favourably replied to within a few days. It took four days more to pass through all the various departments, sign one's name to a few hundred papers, and undergo the physical examinations. Then I was sent to the aviation depot at Dijon and fitted out with a uniform and personal equipment. The next stop was the school at Pau, where I was to be taught to fly. My elation at arriving there was second only to my satisfaction at being a French soldier. It was a vast improvement, I thought, to the American Ambulance.

Talk about forming an all-American flying unit, or escadrille, was rife while I was at Pau. What with the pilots already breveted, and the élèves, or pupils in the training-schools, there were quite enough of our compatriots to man the dozen airplanes in one escadrille. Every day somebody "had it absolutely straight" that we were to become a unit at the front, and every other day the report turned out to be untrue. But at last, in the month of February, our dream came true. We learned that a captain had actually been assigned to command an American escadrille and that the Americans at the front had been recalled and placed under his orders. Soon afterward we élèves got another delightful thrill.

III—STORY OF THE FLIERS IN TRAINING

Thaw, Prince, Cowdin, and the other veterans were training on the Nieuport! That meant the American Escadrille was to fly the Nieuport—the best type of *avion de chasse*—and hence would be a fighting unit. It is necessary to explain parenthetically here that French military aviation, generally speaking, is divided into three groups—the *avions de chasse* or airplanes of pursuit, which are used to hunt down enemy aircraft or to fight them off; *avions de bombardement,* big, unwieldy monsters for use in bombarding raids; and *avions de rélage,* cumbersome creatures designed to regulate artillery fire, take photographs, and do scout duty. The Nieuport is the smallest, fastest-rising, fastest-moving biplane in the French service. It can travel 110 miles an hour, and is a one-man apparatus with a machine gun mounted on its roof and fired by the pilot with one hand while with the other and his feet he operates his controls. The French call their Nieuport pilots the "aces" of the air. No wonder we were tickled to be included in that august brotherhood!

Before the American Escadrille became an established fact, Thaw and Cowdin, who had mastered the Nieuport, managed to be sent to the Verdun front. While there Cowdin was credited with having brought down a German machine and was proposed for the *Médaille Militaire,* the highest decoration that can be awarded a non-commissioned officer or private.

After completing his training, receiving his military pilot's brevet, and being perfected on the type of plane he is to use at the front, an aviator is ordered to the reserve headquarters near Paris to await his call. Kiffin Rockwell and Victor Chapman had been there for months, and I had just arrived, when on the 16th of April orders came for the Americans to join their escadrille at Luxeuil, in the Vosges.

The rush was breathless! Never were flying clothes and fur coats drawn from the quartermaster, belongings packed, and red tape in the various administrative bureaux unfurled, with such headlong haste. In a few hours we were aboard the train, panting, but happy. Our party consisted of Sergeant Prince, and Rockwell, Chapman, and myself, who were only corporals at that time. We were joined at Luxeuil by Lieutenant Thaw and Sergeants Hall and Cowdin.

For the veterans our arrival at the front was devoid of excitement; for the three neophytes—Rockwell, Chapman, and myself—it was the beginning of a new existence, the entry into an unknown world. Of course Rockwell and Chapman had seen plenty of warfare on the ground, but warfare in the air was as novel to them as to me. For us all it contained unlimited possibilities for initiative and service to France, and for them it must have meant, too, the restoration of personality lost during those months in the trenches with the Foreign Legion. Rockwell summed it up characteristically.

"Well, we're off for the races," he remarked. . . .

On our arrival at Luxeuil we were met by Captain Thénault, the French commander of the American Escadrille—officially known as No. 124, by the way—and motored to the aviation field in one of the staff cars assigned to us. I enjoyed that ride. Lolling back against the soft leather cushions, I recalled how in my apprenticeship days at Pau I had had to walk six miles for my laundry. . . .

Rooms were assigned to us in a villa adjoining the famous hot baths of Luxeuil, where Cæsar's cohorts were wont to besport themselves. We messed with our officers, Captain Thénault and Lieutenant de Laage de Mux, at the best hotel in town. An automobile was always on hand to carry us to the field. I began to wonder whether I was a summer resorter instead of a soldier.

Among the pilots who had welcomed us with open arms, we discovered the famous Captain Happe, commander of the Luxeuil bombardment group. The doughty bomb-dispenser, upon whose head the Germans have set a price, was in his quarters. After we had been introduced, he pointed to eight little boxes arranged on a table.

"They contain *Croix de Guerre* for the families of the men I lost on my last trip," he explained, and he added: "It's a good thing you're here to go along with us for protection. There are lots of Boches in this sector."

I thought of the luxury we were enjoying: our comfortable beds, baths, and motor cars, and then I recalled the ancient custom of giving a man selected for the sacrifice a royal time of it before the appointed day. . . .

IV—STORY OF THE FIRST SORTIE IN THE CLOUDS

The memory of the first sortie we made as an escadrille will always remain fresh in my mnd because it was also my first trip over the lines. We were to leave at six in the morning. Captain Thénault pointed out on his aërial map the route we were to follow. Never having flown over this region before, I was afraid of losing myself. Therefore, as it is easier to keep other airplanes in sight when one is above them, I began climbing as rapidly as possible, meaning to trail along in the wake of my companions. Unless one has had practice in flying in formation, however, it is hard to keep in contact. The diminutive *avions de chasse* are the merest pinpoints against the great sweep of landscape below and the limitless heavens above. The air was misty and clouds were gathering. Ahead there seemed a barrier of them. Although as I looked down the ground showed plainly, in the distance everything was hazy. Forging up above the mist, at 7,000 feet, I lost the others altogether. Even when they are not closely joined, the clouds, seen from immediately above, appear as a solid bank of white. The spaces between are indistinguishable. It is like being in an Arctic ice field.

To the south I made out the Alps. Their glittering peaks projected up through the white sea about me like majestic icebergs. Not a single plane was visible anywhere, and I was growing very uncertain about my position. My splendid isolation had become oppressive, when, one by one, the others began bobbing up above the cloud level, and I had company again.

We were over Belfort and headed for the trench lines. The cloud banks dropped behind, and below us we saw the smiling plain of Alsace stretching eastward to the Rhine. It was distinctly pleasurable, flying over this conquered land. Following the course of the canal that runs to the Rhine, I sighted, from a height of 13,000 feet over Dannemarie, a series of brown, woodworm-like tracings on the ground—the trenches!

My attention was drawn elsewhere almost immediately, however. Two balls of black smoke had suddenly appeared close to one of the machines ahead of me, and with the same disconcerting abruptness similar balls began to dot the sky above, below, and on all sides of us. We were being shot at with shrapnel. It was interesting to watch the flash of the bursting shells, and the attendant smoke puffs—black, white, or yellow, depending on the kind of shrapnel used. The roar of the motor drowned the noise of the explosions. Strangely enough, my feelings about it were wholly impersonal.

We turned north after crossing the lines. Mulhouse seemed just below us, and I noted with a keen sense of satisfaction our invasion of real German territory. The Rhine, too, looked delightfully accessible. As we continued northward I distinguished the twin lakes of Gérardmer sparkling in their emerald setting. Where the lines crossed the Hartmannsweilerkopf there were little spurts of brown smoke as shells burst in the trenches. One could scarcely pick out the old city of Thann from among the numerous neighbouring villages, so tiny it seemed in the valley's mouth. I had never been higher than 7,000 feet and was unaccustomed to reading country from a great altitude. It was also bitterly cold, and even in my fur-lined combination I was shivering. I noticed, too, that I had to take long, deep breaths in the rarefied atmosphere. Looking downward at a certain angle, I saw what at first I took to be a round, shimmering pool of water. It was simply the effect of the sunlight on the congealing mist. We had been keeping an eye out for German machines since leaving our lines, but none had shown up. It wasn't surprising, for we were too many.

Only four days later, however, Rockwell brought down the escadrille's first plane in his initial aërial combat. He was flying alone when, over Thann, he came upon a German on reconnaissance. He dived and the German turned toward his own lines, opening fire from a long distance. Rockwell kept straight after him. Then, closing to within thirty yards, he pressed on the release of his machine gun, and saw the enemy gunner fall backward and the pilot crumple up sideways in his seat. The plane flopped downward and crashed to earth just behind the German trenches. Swooping close to the ground

Rockwell saw its débris burning away brightly. He had turned the trick with but four shots and only one German bullet had struck his Nieuport. An observation post telephoned the news before Rockwell's return, and he got a great welcome. All Luxeuil smiled upon him—particularly the girls. But he couldn't stay to enjoy his popularity. The escadrille was ordered to the sector of Verdun.

While in a way we were sorry to leave Luxeuil, we naturally didn't regret the chance to take part in the aërial activity of the world's greatest battle. The night before our departure some German aircraft destroyed four of our tractors and killed six men with bombs, but even that caused little excitement compared with going to Verdun. We would get square with the Boches over Verdun, we thought—it is impossible to chase airplanes at night, so the raiders made a safe getaway. . . .

The fast-flowing stream of troops, and the distressing number of ambulances brought realization of the near presence of a gigantic battle.

Within a twenty-mile radius of the Verdun front aviation camps abound. Our escadrille was listed on the schedule with the other fighting units, each of which has its specified flying hours, rotating so there is always an *escadrille de chasse* over the lines. A field wireless to enable us to keep track of the movements of enemy planes became part of our equipment.

Lufberry joined us a few days after our arrival. He was followed by Johnson and Balsley, who had been on the air guard over Paris. Hill and Rumsey came next, and after them Masson and Pavelka. Nieuports were supplied them from the nearest depot, and as soon as they had mounted their instruments and machine guns, they were on the job with the rest of us. Fifteen Americans are or have been members of the American Escadrille, but there have never been so many as that on duty at any one time.

V—STORY OF THE BATTLES IN THE SKIES

Before we were fairly settled at Bar-le-Duc, Hall brought down a German observation craft and Thaw a Fokker. Fights occurred on almost every sortie. The Germans seldom cross into our territory, unless on a bombarding jaunt, and thus practically all the fighting takes place on their side of the line. Thaw dropped his Fokker in the morning, and on the afternoon of the same day there was a big combat far behind the German trenches. Thaw was wounded in the arm, and an explosive bullet detonating on Rockwell's wind-shield tore several gashes in his face. Despite the blood which was blinding him Rockwell managed to reach an aviation field and land. Thaw, whose wound bled profusely, landed in a dazed condition just within our lines. He was too weak to walk, and French soldiers carried him to a field dressing-station, whence he was sent to Paris for further treatment. Rockwell's wounds were less serious and he insisted on flying again almost immediately.

A week or so later Chapman was wounded. Considering the number of fights he had been in and the courage with which he attacked it was a miracle he had not been hit before. He always fought against odds and far within the enemy's country. He flew more than any of us, never missing an opportunity to go up, and never coming down until his gasolene was giving out. His machine was a sieve of patched-up bullet holes. His nerve was almost superhuman and his devotion to the cause for which he fought sublime. The day he was wounded he attacked four machines. Swooping down from behind, one of them, a Fokker, riddled Chapman's plane. One bullet cut deep into his scalp, but Chapman, a master pilot, escaped from the trap, and fired several shots to show he was still safe. A stability control had been severed by a bullet. Chapman held the broken rod in one hand, managed his machine with the other, and succeeded in landing on a near-by aviation field. His wound was dressed, his machine repaired, and he immediately took the air in pursuit of some more enemies. He would take no rest, and with bandaged head continued to fly and fight.

The escadrille's next serious encounter with the foe took place a few days later. Rockwell, Balsley, Prince, and Captain Thénault were surrounded by a large number of Germans, who, circling about them, commenced firing at long range. Realizing their numerical inferiority, the Americans and their commander sought the safest way out by attacking the enemy machines nearest the French lines. Rockwell, Prince, and the captain broke through successfully, but Balsley found himself hemmed in. He attacked the German nearest him, only to receive an explosive bullet in his thigh. In trying to get away by a vertical dive his machine went into a corkscrew and swung over on its back. Extra cartridge rollers dislodged from their case hit his arms. He was tumbling straight toward the trenches, but by a supreme effort he regained control, righted the plane, and landed without disaster in a meadow just behind the firing line.

Soldiers carried him to the shelter of a near-by fort, and later he was taken to a field hospital, where he lingered for days between life and death. Ten fragments of the explosive bullet were removed from his stomach. He bore up bravely, and became the favourite of the wounded officers in whose ward he lay. When we flew over to see him they would say: *Il est un brave petit gars, l'aviateur américain.* [He's a brave little fellow, the

American aviator.] On a shelf by his bed, done up in a handkerchief, he kept the pieecs of bullet taken out of him, and under them some sheets of paper on which he was trying to write to his mother, back in El Paso.

Balsley was awarded the *Médaille Militaire* and the *Croix de Guerre,* but the honours scared him. He had seen them decorate officers in the ward before they died.

VI—STORY OF CHAPMAN'S LAST FIGHT

Then came Chapman's last fight. Before leaving, he had put two bags of oranges in his machine to take to Balsley, who liked to suck them to relieve his terrible thirst, after the day's flying was over. There was an aërial struggle against odds, far within the German lines, and Chapman, to divert their fire from his comrades, engaged several enemy airmen at once. He sent one tumbling to earth, and had forced the others off when two more swooped down upon him. Such a fight is a matter of seconds, and one cannot clearly see what passes. Lufberry and Prince, whom Chapman had defended so gallantly, regained the French lines. They told us of the combat, and we waited on the field for Chapman's return. He was always the last in, so we were not much worried. Then a pilot from another fighting escadrille telephoned us, that he had seen a Nieuport falling. A little later the observer of a reconnaissance airplane called up and told us how he had witnessed Chapman's fall. The wings of the plane had buckled, and it had dropped like a stone he said.

We talked in lowered voices after that; we would read the pain in one another's eyes. If only it could have been some one else, was what we all thought, I suppose. To lose Victor was not an irreparable loss to us merely, but to France, and to the world as well. I kept thinking of him lying over there, and of the oranges he was taking to Balsley. As I left the field I caught sight of Victor's mechanician leaning against the end of our hangar. He was looking northward into the sky where his *patron* had vanished, and his face was very sad.

By this time Prince and Hall had been made adjutants, and we corporals transformed into sergeants. I frankly confess to a feeling of marked satisfaction at receiving that grade in the world's finest army. I was a far more important person, in my own estimation, than I had been as a second lieutenant in the militia at home. The next impressive event was the awarding of decorations. We had assisted at that ceremony for Cowdin at Luxeuil, but this time three of our messmates were to be honoured for the Germans they had brought down. Rockwell and Hall received the *Médaille Militaire* and the *Croix de Guerre,* and Thaw, being a lieutenant, the *Légion d'honneur* and another "palm" for the ribbon of the *Croix de Guerre* he had won previously. Thaw, who came up from Paris specially for the presentation, still carried his arm in a sling.

There were also decorations for Chapman, but poor Victor, who so often had been cited in the Orders of the Day, was not on hand to receive them.

VII—STORY OF THE MORNING SORTIE OVER VERDUN

Our daily routine goes on with little change. Whenever the weather permits—that is, when it isn't raining, and the clouds aren't too low—we fly over the Verdun battlefield at the hours dictated by General Headquarters. As a rule the most successful sorties are those in the early morning.

We are called while it's still dark. Sleepily I try to reconcile the French orderly's muttered, *C'est l'heure, monsieur,* that rouses me from slumber, with the strictly

American words and music of "When That Midnight Choo Choo Leaves for Alabam'" warbled by a particularly wide-awake pilot in the next room. A few minutes later, having swallowed some coffee, we motor to the field. The east is turning gray as the hangar curtains are drawn apart and our machines trundled out by the mechanicians. All the pilots whose planes are in commission—save those remaining behind on guard—prepare to leave. We average from four to six on a sortie, unless too many flights have been ordered for that day, in which case only two or three go out at a time.

Now the east is pink, and overhead the sky has changed from gray to pale blue. It is light enough to fly. We don our fur-lined shoes and combinations, and adjust the leather flying hoods and goggles. A good deal of conversation occurs—perhaps because, once aloft, there's nobody to talk to.

"Eh, you," one pilot cries jokingly to another, "I hope some Boche just ruins you this morning, so I won't have to pay you the fifty francs you won from me last night!"

This financial reference concerns a poker game.

"You do, do you?" replies the other as he swings into his machine. "Well, I'd be glad to pass up the fifty to see you landed by the Boches. You'd make a fine sight walking down the street of some German town in those wooden shoes and pyjama pants. Why don't you dress yourself? Don't you know an aviator's supposed to look *chic?*"

A sartorial eccentricity on the part of one of our colleagues is here referred to.

The raillery is silenced by a deafening roar as the motors are tested. Quiet is briefly restored, only to be broken by a series of rapid explosions incidental to the trying out of machine guns. You loudly inquire at what altitude we are to meet above the field.

"Fifteen hundred metres—go ahead!" comes an answering yell.

"*Essence et gaz!* [Oil and gas!]" you call to your mechanician, adjusting your gasolene and air throttles while he grips the propeller.

"*Contact!*" he shrieks, and "*Contact!*" you reply. You snap on the switch, he spins the propeller, and the motor takes. Drawing forward out of line, you put on full power, race across the grass and take the air. The ground drops as the hood slants up before you and you seem to be going more and more slowly as you rise. At a great height you hardly realize you are moving. You glance at the clock to note the time of your departure, and at the oil gauge to see its throb. The altimeter registers 650 feet. You turn and look back at the field below and see others leaving.

In three minutes you are at about 4,000 feet. You have been making wide circles over the field and watching the other machines. At 4,500 feet you throttle down and wait on that level for your companions to catch up. Soon the escadrille is bunched and off for the lines. You begin climbing again, gulping to clear your ears in the changing pressure. Surveying the other machines, you recognize the pilot of each by the marks on its side— or by the way he flies. The distinguishing marks of the Nieuports are various and sometimes amusing. Bert Hall, for instance, has BERT painted on the left side of his plane and the same word reversed (as if spelled backward with the left hand) on the right—so an aviator passing him on that side at great speed will be able to read the name without difficulty, he says!

The country below has changed into a flat surface of varicoloured figures. Woods are irregular blocks of dark green, like daubs of ink spilled on a table; fields are geometrical designs of different shades of green and brown, forming in composite an ultra-cubist painting; roads are thin white lines, each with its distinctive windings and crossings—from which you determine your location. The higher you are the easier it is to read.

In about ten minutes you see the Meuse sparkling in the morning light, and on either side the long line of sausage-shaped observation balloons far below you. Red-roofed Verdun springs into view just beyond. There are spots in it where no red shows and you know what has happened there. In the green pasture land bordering the town, round flecks of brown indicate the shell holes. You cross the Meuse.

Immediately east and north of Verdun there lies a broad, brown band. From the Woevre plain it runs westward to the "S" bend in the Meuse, and on the left bank of that famous stream continues on into the Argonne Forest. Peaceful fields and farms and villages adorned that landscape a few months ago—when there was no Battle of Verdun. Now there is only that sinister brown belt, a strip of murdered Nature. It seems to belong to another world. Every sign of humanity has been swept away. The woods and roads have vanished like chalk wiped from a blackboard; of the villages nothing remains but gray smears where stone walls have tumbled together. The great forts of Douaumont and Vaux are outlined faintly, like the tracings of a finger in wet sand. One cannot distinguish any one shell crater, as one can on the pockmarked fields on either side. On the brown band the indentations are so closely interlocked that they blend into a confused mass of troubled earth. Of the trenches only broken, half-obliterated links are visible.

Columns of muddy smoke spurt up continually as high explosives tear deeper into this ulcered area. During heavy bombardment and attacks I have seen shells falling like rain. The countless towers of smoke remind one of Gustave Doré's picture of the fiery tombs of the arch-heretics in Dante's "Hell." A smoky pall covers the sector under fire, rising so high that at a height of 1,000 feet one is enveloped in its mist-like fumes. Now and then monster projectiles, hurtling through the air close by, leave one's plane rocking violently in their wake. Airplanes have been cut in two by them.

For us the battle passes in silence, the noise of one's motor deadening all other sounds. In the green patches behind the brown belt myriads of tiny flashes tell where the guns are hidden; and those flashes, and the smoke of bursting shells, are all we see of the fighting. It is a weird combination of stillness and havoc, the Verdun conflict viewed from the sky.

Far below us, the observation and range-finding planes circle over the trenches like gliding gulls. At a feeble altitude they follow the attacking infantrymen and flash back wireless reports of the engagement. Only through them can communication be maintained when, under the barrier fire, wires from the front lines are cut. Sometimes it falls to our lot to guard these machines from Germans eager to swoop down on their backs. Sailing about high above a busy flock of them makes one feel like an old mother hen protecting her chicks. . . .

Getting started is the hardest part of an attack. Once you have begun diving you're all right. The pilot just ahead turns tail up like a trout dropping back to water, and swoops down in irregular curves and circles. You follow at an angle so steep your feet seem to be holding you back in your seat. Now the black Maltese crosses on the German's wings stand out clearly. You think of him as some sort of big bug. Then you hear the rapid tut-tut-tut of his machine gun. The man that dived ahead of you becomes mixed up with the topmost

German. He is so close it looks as if he had hit the enemy machine. You hear the staccato barking of his mitrailleuse and see him pass from under the German's tail.

The rattle of the gun that is aimed at you leaves you undisturbed. Only when the bullets pierce the wings a few feet off do you become uncomfortable. You see the gunner crouched down behind his weapon, but you aim at where the pilot ought to be—there are two men aboard the German craft—and press on the release hard. Your mitrailleuse hammers out a stream of bullets as you pass over and dive, nose down, to get out of range. Then, hopefully, you re-dress and look back at the foe. He ought to be dropping earthward at several miles a minute. As a matter of fact, however, he is sailing serenely on. They have an annoying habit of doing that, these Boches.

VIII—STORY OF A FIGHT OVER FORT DOUAUMONT

Rockwell, who attacked so often that he has lost all count, and who shoves his machine gun fairly in the faces of the Germans, used to swear their planes were armoured. Lieutenant de Laage, whose list of combats is equally extensive, has brought down only one. Hall, with three machines to his credit, has had more luck. Lufbery, who evidently has evolved a secret formula, has dropped four, according to official statistics, since his arrival on the Verdun front. Four "palms"—the record for the escadrille, glitter upon the ribbon of the *Croix de Guerre* accompanying his *Médaile Militaire*.*

---

* This book was written in the fall of 1915. Since that time many additional machines have been credited to the American flyers.

A pilot seldom has the satisfaction of beholding the result of his bull's-eye bullet. Rarely—so difficult it is to follow the turnings and twistings of the dropping plane—does he see his fallen foe strike the ground. Lufbery's last direct hit was an exception, for he followed all that took place from a balcony seat. I myself was in the "nigger-heaven," so I know. We had set out on a sortie together just before noon, one August day, and for the first time on such an occasion had lost each other over the lines. Seeing no Germans, I passed my time hovering over the French observation machines. Lufbery found one, however, and promptly brought it down. Just then I chanced to make a southward turn, and caught sight of an airplane falling out of the sky into the German lines.

As it turned over, it showed its white belly for an instant, then seemed to straighten out, and planed downward in big zigzags. The pilot must have gripped his controls even in death, for his craft did not tumble as most do. It passed between my line of vision and a wood, into which it disappeared. Just as I was going down to find out where it landed, I saw it again skimming across a field, and heading straight for the brown band beneath me. It was outlined against the shell-racked earth like a tiny insect, until just northwest of Fort Douaumont it crashed down upon the battlefield. A sheet of flame and smoke shot up from the tangled wreckage. For a moment or two I watched it burn; then I went back to the observation machines.

I thought Lufbery would show up and point to where the German had fallen. He failed to appear, and I began to be afraid it was he whom I had seen come down, instead of an enemy. I spent a worried hour before my return homeward. After getting back I learned that Lufbery was quite safe, having hurried in after the fight to report the destruction of his adversary before somebody else claimed him, which is only too frequently the case. Observation posts, however, confirmed Lufbery's story, and he was of course very much delighted. Nevertheless, at luncheon, I heard him murmuring, half to himself: "Those poor fellows."

The German machine gun operator, having probably escaped death in the air, must have had a hideous descent. Lufbery told us he had seen the whole thing, spiralling down after the German. He said he thought the German pilot must be a novice, judging from his manœuvres. It occurred to me that he might have been making his first flight over the lines, doubtless full of enthusiasm about his career. Perhaps, dreaming of the Iron Cross and his Gretchen, he took a chance—and then swift death and a grave in the shell-strewn soil of Douaumont. . . .

IX—STORY OF PRINCE'S AERIAL FIREWORKS

Now and then one of us will get ambitious to do something on his own account. Not long ago Norman Prince became obsessed with the idea of bringing down a German "sausage," as observation balloons are called. He had a special device mounted on his Nieuport for setting fire to the aërial frankfurters. Thus equipped he resembled an advance agent for Payne's fireworks more than an *aviator de chasse*. Having carefully mapped the enemy "sausages," he would sally forth in hot pursuit whenever one was signalled at a respectable height. Poor Norman had a terrible time of it! Sometimes the reported "sausages" were not there when he arrived, and sometimes there was a super-abundance of German airplanes on guard.

He stuck to it, however, and finally his appetite for "sausage" was satisfied. He found one just where it ought to be, swooped down upon it, and let off his fireworks with all the gusto of an American boy on the Fourth of July. When he looked again, the balloon had vanished. Prince's performance isn't so easy as it sounds, by the way. If, after the long dive necessary to turn the trick successfully, his motor had failed to retake, he would have fallen into the hands of the Germans. . . .

After dinner the same scene invariably repeats itself, over the coffee in the "next room." At the big table several sportive souls start a poker game, while at a smaller one two sedate spirits wrap themselves in the intricacies of chess. Captain Thénault labours away at the messroom piano, or in lighter mood plays with Fram, his police dog. A phonograph grinds out the ancient query "Who Paid the Rent for Mrs. Rip Van Winkle?" or some other ragtime ditty. It is barely nine, however, when the movement in the direction of bed begins.

A few of us remain behind a little while, and the talk becomes more personal and more sincere. Only on such intimate occasions, I think, have I ever heard death discussed. Certainly we are not indifferent to it. Not many nights ago one of the pilots remarked in a tired way:

"Know what I want? Just six months of freedom to go where and do what I like. In that time I'd get everything I wanted out of life, and be perfectly willing to come back and be killed."

Then another, who was about to receive 2,000 francs from the American committee that aids us, as a reward for his many citations, chimed in.

"Well, I didn't care much before," he confessed, "but now with this money coming in I don't want to die until I've had the fun of spending it."

So saying, he yawned and went up to bed.

X—STORY OF THE JOURNEY TOWARD THE SOMME

On the 12th of October, twenty small airplanes flying in a V formation, at such a height they resembled a flock of geese, crossed the river Rhine, where it skirts the plains of Alsace, and, turning north, headed for the famous Mauser works at Oberndorf. Following in their wake was an equal number of larger machines, and above these darted and circled swift fighting planes. The first group of aircraft was flown by British pilots, the second by French and three of the fighting planes by Americans in the French Aviation Division. It was a cosmopolitan collection that effected that successful raid.

We American pilots, who are grouped into one escadrille, had been fighting above the battlefield of Verdun from the 20th of May until orders came the middle of September for us to leave our airplanes, for a unit that would replace us, and to report at Le Bourget, the great Paris aviation centre.

The mechanics and the rest of the personnel left, as usual, in the escadrille's trucks with the material. For once the pilots did not take the aërial route but they boarded the Paris express at Bar-le-Duc with all the enthusiasm of schoolboys off for a vacation. They were to have a week in the capital! Where they were to go after that they did not know, but presumed it would be the Somme. As a matter of fact the escadrille was to be sent to Luxeuil in the Vosges to take part in the Mauser raid.

Besides Captain Thénault and Lieutenant de Laage de Mieux, our French officers, the following American pilots were in the escadrille at this time: Lieutenant Thaw, who had returned to the front, even though his wounded arm had not entirely healed; Adjutants Norman Prince, Hall, Lufbery, and Masson; and Sergeants Kiffin Rockwell, Hill, Pavelka, Johnson, and Rumsey. I had been sent to a hospital at the end of August, because of a lame back resulting from a smash up in landing, and couldn't follow the escadrille until later.

Every aviation unit boasts several mascots. Dogs of every description are to be seen around the camps, but the Americans managed, during their stay in Paris, to add to their menagerie by the acquisition of a lion cub named "Whiskey." The little chap had been born on a boat crossing from Africa and was advertised for sale in France. Some of the American pilots chipped in and bought him. He was a cute, bright-eyed baby lion who tried to roar in a most threatening manner but who was blissfully content the moment one gave him one's finger to suck. "Whiskey" got a good view of Paris during the few days he was there, for some one in the crowd was always borrowing him to take him some place. He, like most lions in captivity, became acquainted with bars, but the sort "Whiskey" saw were not for purposes of confinement.

The orders came directing the escadrille to Luxeuil and bidding farewell to gay "Paree" the men boarded the Belfort train with bag and baggage—and the lion. Lions, it developed, were not allowed in passenger coaches. The conductor was assured that "Whiskey" was quite harmless and was going to overlook the rules when the cub began to roar and tried to get at the railwayman's finger. That settled it, so two of the men had to stay behind in order to crate up "Whiskey" and take him along the next day.

The escadrille was joined in Paris by Robert Rockwell, of Cincinnati, who had finished his training as a pilot, and was waiting at the Reserve (Robert Rockwell had gone to France to work as a surgeon in one of the

American war hospitals. He disliked remaining in the rear and eventually enlisted in aviation). . . .

XI—STORY OF THRILLING MOMENTS IN THE AIR

Dennis Dowd, of Brooklyn, N. Y., is so far the only American volunteer aviator killed while in training. Dowd, who had joined the Foreign Legion, shortly after the war broke out, was painfully wounded during the offensive in Champagne. After his recovery he was transferred, at his request, into aviation. At the Buc school he stood at the head of the fifteen Americans who were learning to be aviators, and was considered one of the most promising pilots in the training camp. On August 11, 1916, while making a flight preliminary to his brevet, Dowd fell from a height of only 260 feet and was instantly killed. Either he had fainted or a control had broken.

While a patient at the hospital Dowd had been sent packages by a young French girl of Neuilly. A correspondence ensued, and when Dowd went to Paris on convalescent leave he and the young lady became engaged. He was killed just before the time set for the wedding. . . .

In a few days every one in this Anglo-American alliance was calling each other by some nickname and swearing lifelong friendship.

"We didn't know what you Yanks would be like," remarked one of the Englishmen one day. "Thought you might be snobby on account of being volunteers, but I swear you're a bloody human lot." That, I will explain, is a very fine compliment. . . .

Considering the number of machines that were continually roaring above the field at Luxeuil it is remarkable that only two fatal accidents occurred. One was when a British pilot tried diving at a target, for machine-gun practice, and was unable to redress his airplane. Both he and his gunner were killed. In the second accident I lost a good friend—a young Frenchman. He took up his gunner in a two-seated Nieuport. A young Canadian pilot accompanied by a French officer followed in a Sopwith. When at about a thousand feet they began to manœuvre about one another. In making a turn too close the tips of their wings touched. The Nieuport turned downward, its wings folded, and it fell like a stone. The Sopwith fluttered a second or two, then its wings buckled and it dropped in the wake of the Nieuport. The two men in each of the planes were killed outright.

Next to falling in flames a drop in a wrecked machine is the worst death an aviator can meet. I know of no sound more horrible than that made by an airplane crashing to earth. Breathless one has watched the uncontrolled apparatus tumble through the air. The agony felt by the pilot and passenger seems to transmit itself to you. You are helpless to avert the certain death. You cannot even turn your eyes away at the moment of impact. In the dull, grinding crash there is the sound of breaking bones. . . .

In spite of their bombardment of open towns and the use of explosive bullets in their aërial machine guns, the Boches have shown up in a better light in aviation than in any other arm. A few of the Hun pilots have evinced certain elements of honour and decency. I remember one chap that was the right sort.

He was a young man but a pilot of long standing. An old infantry captain stationed near his aviation field at Etain, east of Verdun, prevailed upon this German pilot to take him on a flight. There was a new machine to test out and he told the captain to climb aboard. Foolishly he crossed the trench lines and, actuated by a desire to give his passenger an interesting trip, proceeded to fly over the French aviation headquarters. Unfortunately for him he encountered three French fighting planes which promptly opened fire. The German pilot was wounded in the leg and the gasolene tank of his airplane was pierced. Under him was an aviation field. He decided to land. The machine was captured before the Germans had time to burn it up. Explosive bullets were discovered in the machine gun. A French officer turned to the German captain and informed him that he would probably be shot for using explosive bullets. The captain did not understand.

"Don't shoot him," said the pilot, using excellent French, "if you're going to shoot any one take me. The captain has nothing to do with the bullets. He doesn't even know how to work a machine gun. It's his first trip in an airplane."

"Well, if you'll give us some good information, we won't shoot you," said the French officer.

"Information," replied the German, "I can't give you any. I come from Etain, and you know where that is as well as I do."

"No, you must give us some worth-while information, or I'm afraid you'll be shot," insisted the Frenchman.

"If I give you worth-while information," answered the pilot, "you'll go over and kill a lot of soldiers, and if I don't you'll only kill one—so go ahead."

The last time I heard of the Boche he was being well taken care of.

XII—STORY OF ROCKWELL'S LAST FIGHT

Kiffin Rockwell and Lufbery were the first to get their new machines ready and on the 23rd of September went out for the first flight since the escadrille had arrived at Luxeuil. They became separated in the air but each flew on alone, which was a dangerous thing to do in the Alsace sector. . . .

Just before Kiffin Rockwell reached the lines he spied a German machine under him flying at 11,000 feet. I can imagine the satisfaction he felt in at last catching an enemy plane in our lines. Rockwell had fought more combats than the rest of us put together, and had shot down many German machines that had fallen in their lines, but this was the first time he had had an opportunity of bringing down a Boche in our territory.

A captain, the commandant of an Alsatian village, watched the aërial battle through his field glasses. He said that Rockwell approached so close to the enemy that he thought there would be a collision. The German craft, which carried two machine guns, had opened a rapid fire when Rockwell started his dive. He plunged through the stream of lead and only when very close to his enemy did he begin shooting. For a second it looked as though the German was falling, so the captain said, but then he saw the French machine turn rapidly nose down, the wings of one side broke off and fluttered in the wake of the airplane, which hurtled earthward in a rapid drop. It crashed into the ground in a small field —a field of flowers—a few hundred yards back of the trenches. It was not more than two and a half miles from the spot where Rockwell, in the month of May, brought down his first enemy machine. The Germans immediately opened up on the wreck with artillery fire.

In spite of the bursting shrapnel, gunners from a near-by battery rushed out and recovered poor Rockwell's broken body. There was a hideous wound in his breast where an explosive bullet had torn through. A surgeon who examined the body, testified that if it had been an ordinary bullet Rockwell would have had an even chance of landing with only a bad wound. As it was he was killed the instant the unlawful missile exploded.

Lufbery engaged a German craft but before he could get to close range two Fokkers swooped down from behind and filled his aeroplane full of holes. Exhausting his ammunition he landed at Fontaine, an aviation field near the lines. There he learned of Rockwell's death and was told that two other French machines had been brought down within the hour. He ordered his gasolene tank filled, procured a full band of cartridges and soared up into the air to avenge his comrade. He sped up and down the lines, and made a wide détour to Habsheim where the Germans have an aviation field, but all to no avail. Not a Boche was in the air.

The news of Rockwell's death was telephoned to the escadrille. The captain, lieutenant, and a couple of men jumped in a staff car and hastened to where he had fallen. On their return the American pilots were convened in a room of the hotel and the news broken to them. With tears in his eyes the captain said: "The best and bravest of us all is no more."

No greater blow could have befallen the escadrille. Kiffin was its soul. He was loved and looked up to by not only every man in our flying corps but by every one who knew him. Kiffin was imbued with the spirit of the cause for which he fought and gave his heart and soul to the performance of his duty. He said: "I pay my part for Lafayette and Rochambeau," and he gave the fullest measure. The old flame of chivalry burned brightly in this boy's fine and sensitive being. With his death France lost one of her most valuable pilots. When he was over the lines the Germans did not pass—and he was over them most of the time. He brought down four enemy planes that were credited to him officially, and Lieutenant de Laage, who was his fighting partner, says he is convinced that Rockwell accounted for many others which fell too far within the German lines to be observed. Rockwell had been given the Medaille Militaire and the Croix de Guerre, on the ribbon of which he wore four palms, representing the four magnificent citations he had received in the order of the army. As a further reward for his excellent work he had been proposed for promotion from the grade of sergeant to that of second lieutenant. Unfortunately the official order did not arrive until a few days following his death.

The night before Rockwell was killed he had stated that if he were brought down he would like to be buried where he fell. It was impossible, however, to place him in a grave so near the trenches. His body was draped in a French flag and brought back to Luxeuil. He was given a funeral worthy of a general. His brother, Paul, who had fought in the Legion with him, and who had been rendered unfit for service by a wound, was granted permission to attend the obsequies. Pilots from all nearby camps flew over to render homage to Rockwell's remains. Every Frenchman in the aviation at Luxeuil marched behind the bier. The British pilots, followed by a detachment of five hundred of their men, were in line, and a battalion of French troops brought up the rear. As the slow moving procession of blue and khaki-clad men passed from the church to the graveyard, airplanes circled at a feeble height above and showered down myriads of flowers.

Rockwell's death urged the rest of the men to greater

action, and the few who had machines were constantly after the Boches. Prince brought one down. Lufbery, the most skillful and successful fighter in the escadrille, would venture far into the enemy's lines and spiral down over a German aviation camp, daring the pilots to venture forth. One day he stirred them up, but as he was short of fuel he had to make for home before they took to the air. Prince was out in search of a combat at this time. He got it. He ran into the crowd Lufbery had aroused. Bullets cut into his machine and one exploding on the front edge of a lower wing broke it. Another shattered a supporting mast. It was a miracle that the machine did not give way. As badly battered as it was Prince succeeded in bringing it back from over Mulhouse, where the fight occurred, to his field at Luxeuil.

XIII—STORY OF LUFBERY'S DARING FLIGHT

The same day that Prince was so nearly brought down Lufbery missed death by a very small margin. He had taken on more gasolene and made another sortie. When over the lines again he encountered a German with whom he had a fighting acquaintance. That is he and the Boche, who was an excellent pilot, had tried to kill each other on one or two occasions before. Each was too good for the other. Lufbery manœuvred for position but, before he could shoot, the Teuton would evade him by a clever turn. They kept after one another, the Boche retreating into his lines. When they were nearing Habsheim, Lufbery glanced back and saw French shrapnel bursting over the trenches. It meant a German plane was over French territory and it was his duty to drive it off. Swooping down near his adversary he waved good-bye, the enemy pilot did likewise, and Lufbery whirred off to chase the other representative of Kultur.

He caught up with him and dove to the attack, but he was surprised by a German he had not seen. Before he could escape three bullets entered his motor, two passed through the fur-lined combination he wore, another ripped open one of his woolen flying boots, his airplane was riddled from wing tip to wing tip, and other bullets cut the elevating plane. Had he not been an exceptional aviator he never would have brought safely to earth so badly damaged a machine. It was so thoroughly shot up that it was junked as being beyond repairs. Fortunately Lufbery was over French territory or his forced descent would have resulted in his being made prisoner.

I know of only one other airplane that was safely landed after receiving as heavy punishment as did Lufbery's. It was a two-place Nieuport piloted by a young Frenchman named Fontaine with whom I trained. He and his gunner attacked a German over the Bois le Pretre who drove rapidly far into his lines. Fontaine followed and in turn was attacked by three other Boches. He dropped to escape, they plunged after him forcing him lower. He looked and saw a German aviation field under him. He was by this time only 2,000 feet above the ground. Fontaine saw the mechanics rush out to grasp him, thinking he would land. The attacking airplanes had stopped shooting. Fontaine pulled on full power and headed for the lines. The German planes dropped down on him and again opened fire. They were on his level, behind and on his sides. Bullets whistled by him in streams. The rapid-fire gun on Fontaine's machine had jammed and he was helpless. His gunner fell forward on him, dead. The trenches were just ahead, but as he was slanting downward to gain speed he had lost a good deal of height, and was at only six hundred feet when he crossed the lines, from which he received a ground fire. The Germans gave up the chase and Fontaine landed with his dead gunner. His wings were so full of holes that they barely supported the machine in the air.

XIV—STORY OF A SURPRISE ATTACK ON THE BOCHES

The uncertain wait at Luxeuil finally came to an end on the 12th of October. The afternoon of that day the British did not say: "Come on Yanks, let's call off the war and have tea," as was their wont, for the bombardment of Oberndorf was on. The British and French machines had been prepared. Just before climbing into their airplanes the pilots were given their orders. The English in their single-seated Sopwiths, which carried four bombs each, where the first to leave. The big French Brequets and Farmans then soared aloft with their tons of explosive destined for the Mauser works. The fighting machines, which were to convoy them as far as the Rhine, rapidly gained their height and circled above their charges. Four of the battle planes were from the American escadrille. They were piloted respectively by Lieutenant de Laage, Lufbery, Norman Prince, and Masson.

The Germans were taken by surprise and as a result few of their machines were in the air. The bombardment fleet was attacked, however, and six of its planes shot down, some of them falling in flames. Baron, the famous French night bombarder, lost his life in one of the Farmans. Two Germans were brought down by machines they attacked and the four pilots from the American escadrille accounted for one each. Lieutenant de Laage shot down his Boche as it was attacking another French machine and Masson did likewise. Explaining it afterward he said: "All of a sudden I saw a Boche come in between me and a Breguet, I was following. I just began to shoot, and darned if he didn't fall."

As the fuel capacity of a Nieuport allows but little more than two hours in the air the *avions de chasse* were forced to return to their own lines to take on more gasolene, while the bombardment planes continued on into Germany. The Sopwiths arrived first at Oberndorf. Dropping low over the Mauser works they discharged their bombs and headed homeward. All arrived, save one, whose pilot lost his way and came to earth in Switzerland. When the big machines got to Oberndorf they saw only flames and smoke where once the rifle factory stood. They unloaded their explosives on the burning mass.

The Nieuports having refilled their tanks went up to clear the air of Germans that might be hovering in wait for the returning raiders. Prince found one and promptly shot it down. Lufbery came upon three. He drove for one, making it drop below the others, then forcing a second to descend, attacked the one remaining above. The combat was short and at the end of it the German tumbled to earth. This made the fifth enemy machine which was officially credited to Lufbery. When a pilot has accounted for five Boches he is mentioned by name in the official communication, and is spoken of as an "Ace," which in French aërial slang means a superpilot. Papers are allowed to call an "ace" by name, print his picture and give him a write-up. The successful aviator becomes a national hero. When Lufbery worked into this category the French papers made him a head liner. The American "Ace," with his string of medals, then came in for the ennuis of a matinee idol. The choicest bit in the collection was a letter from Wallingford, Conn., his home town, thanking him for putting it on the map.

XV—STORY OF THE LAST FIGHT OF NORMAN PRINCE

Darkness was coming rapidly on but Prince and Lufbery remained in the air to protect the bombardment fleet. Just at nightfall Lufbery made for a small aviation field near the lines, known as Corcieux. Slow-moving machines, with great planing capacity, can be landed in the dark, but to try and feel for the ground in a Nieuport, which comes down at about a hundred miles an hour, is to court disaster. Ten minutes after Lufbery landed Prince decided to make for the field. He spiraled down through the night air and skimmed rapidly over the trees bordering the Corcieux field. In the dark he did not see a high-tension electric cable that was stretched just above the tree tops. The landing gear of his airplane struck it. The machine snapped forward and hit the ground on its nose. It turned over and over. The belt holding Prince broke and he was thrown far from the wrecked plane. Both of his legs were broken and he naturally suffered internal injuries. In spite of the terrific shock and his intense pain Prince did not lose consciousness. He even kept his presence of mind and gave orders to the men who had run to pick him up. Hearing the hum of a motor, and realizing a machine was in the air, Prince told them to light gasolene fires on the field. "You don't want another fellow to come down and break himself up the way I've done," he said.

Lufbery went with Prince to the hospital in Gerardmer. As the ambulance rolled along Prince sang to keep up his spirits. He spoke of getting well soon and returning to service. It was like Norman. He was always energetic about his flying. Even when he passed through the harrowing experience of having a wing shattered, the first thing he did on landing was to busy himself about getting another fitted in place and the next morning he was in the air again.

No one thought that Prince was mortally injured but the next day he went into a coma. A blood clot had formed on his brain. Captain Haff in command of the aviation groups of Luxeuil, accompanied by our officers, hastened to Gerardmer. Prince lying unconscious on his bed, was named a second lieutenant and decorated with the Legion of Honour. He already held the Medaille Militaire and Croix de Guerre. Norman Prince died on the 15th of October. He was brought back to Luxeuil and given a funeral similar to Rockwell's. It was hard to realize that poor old Norman had gone. He was the founder of the American escadrille and every one in it had come to rely on him. He never let his own spirits drop, and was always on hand with encouragement for the others. I do not think Prince minded going. He wanted to do his part before being killed, and he had more than done it. He had, day after day, freed the line of Germans, making it impossible for them to do their work, and three of them he had shot to earth.

Two days after Prince's death the escadrille received orders to leave for the Somme. The night before the departure the British gave the American pilots a farewell banquet and toasted them as their "Guardian Angels." They keenly appreciated the fact that four men from the American escadrille had brought down four Germans, and had cleared the way for their squadron returning from Oberndorf. When the train pulled out the next day the station platform was packed by khaki-clad pilots waving good-bye to their friends the "Yanks."

The escadrille passed through Paris on its way to the

Somme front. The few members who had machines flew from Luxeuil to their new post. At Paris the pilots were reënforced by three other American boys who had completed their training. They were: Fred Prince, who ten months before had come over from Boston to serve in aviation with his brother Norman; Willis Haviland, of Chicago, who left the American Ambulance for the life of a birdman, and Bob Soubrian, of New York, who had been transferred from the Foreign Legion to the flying corps after being wounded in the Champagne offensive. . . .

(Here Jim McConnell continues to relate his adventures in the air, describing how France trains her air pilots. His book also contains many interesting letters from him. And, then, alas, he, too, fell from the clouds on that fatal day in March, 1917, and went to a hero's grave.—EDITOR.)

THE LOG OF THE "MOEWE"—TALES OF THE HIGH SEAS

The Adventures of a Modern Pirate

Told by Count Dohna-Schlodien, her Commander, and Translated by Eugenie Martin

Everybody has heard of the *Moewe*, the German auxiliary cruiser which on two occasions at least stole through the British blockade and roamed about the Atlantic, sinking ships and occasionally sending a prize like the *Appam* into port. Count Dohna-Schlodien, the captain of this latter-day privateer, is a popular hero in Germany. These tales are translations of the gist of his exploits, as told in the *Wide World Magazine*.

I—STORY OF THE GERMAN MINE-LAYERS

"To LAY mines along the enemy-shores and then make a cruiser-campaign." Such, briefly, were my orders when I was appointed commander of S. M. S. *Moewe* at the end of 1915.

It is easy to imagine my pride and elation.

To lay mines and injure the enemy's sea-borne trade! Neither of these duties was new to the German Navy.

The clamorous complaints in the daily newspapers, voicing the indignation of England, France, and Italy concerning the heavy losses sustained by their mercantile navy and cruisers, as well as against our interference with their over-sea connections, were sufficient testimony to the activity of our U-boats in the North Sea, the Irish Sea, the Mediterranean, and the Black Sea.

It fell to my share, however, to take a German cruiser successfully into the far world-sea, where, since the exploits of the *Karlsruhe*, the *Dresden*, the *Emden*, the *Ayesha*, and the auxiliary cruisers *Prince Eitel Friedrich* and *Kronprinz* the German flag had not dared to show itself owing to the overwhelming superiority of the enemy.

We Germans were sick of hearing England boast that her fleet had driven us from the highways of the ocean, and that her navy safeguarded the routes between Europe and the United States, Africa, and Australia.

When I got my orders, I realized fully that if my plans were to succeed, we must not count on daring and good luck alone, but that cunning must make up for what we lacked in strength.

Shortly before Christmas we made a few brief trialtrips. Then we busied ourseves with the final and not least important of our preparations—an attempt to give the *Moewe* the aspect of an inoffensive merchant vessel.

Beaming with pleasant anticipations, the crew set to work, and to such good purpose did they labor that within a few hours the *Moewe*, under her fresh coating of paint, was—outwardly at least—transformed into an ordinary merchantman. Not even the most suspicious English man-of-war would ever imagine for a moment what a dangerous cargo she carried. But all this labor of love was wasted. A heavy storm and a deluge of rain forced us to suspend our work, and the next morning the *Moewe* was in a sorry plight. The fresh paint had run in streaks, and made her look like a marine zebra. Fortunately, the weather remained dry the night before we were to start. The painting was done again, and the work was accomplished, this time with notable success, for as a result of the damp first layer of paint the final coating did not look too aggressively new.

We raised anchor and steamed out of port in a fog. Soon we exchanged farewell greetings with the German outpost boats, and, shortly after, reached the zone where at any moment we might run against an English destroyer or submarine. Everyone on board was strung up to the highest pitch. What would the next moment bring us? I recalled the remark of a friend who, on hearing of my appointment, asked: "After all, what do you expect to do? The very first day you will be captured!" From the moment we were in the open sea we were prepared for battle, and anyone who had attacked us, small or big, would soon have discovered that the *Moewe* was not quite so peaceful and tame as she looked. Nevertheless, I must admit that too premature an encounter would have been fatal to our object.

As luck would have it, the weather favored us; a thick fog encompassed us, and that first night was as dark as we could have wished.

I told the crew briefly what was expected from them, and pleasure showed in the face of every man when he heard we were out against England, for to wipe out the hated English foe is the dearest wish of every German sailorman.

At dawn, after successful evading all notice, we were in sight of Norway's snow-capped mountains, and we continued our route with a favorable wind.

The day was exceptionally fine, and the fact that the first difficulties had been so easily overcome filled me with confidence in the future. It depended now entirely upon me to lead my faithful crew and our good ship to the desired goal and injure the enemy wherever we might find him.

The last day of the old year turned out to be the hardest we had experienced hitherto. To get as close as possible to the English shores was our aim, but an angry west wind continually obstructed us and interrupted our course. I soon got sick of waiting and preferred to run the risk of fighting the wind. I had to reckon, however, with a specially furious sea. Drenched to the skin, I finally gave up the struggle, and allowed the ship to drift for hours.

In the afternoon the wind abated, and it was once more possible to take a southerly course.

At last, when the lead gave twenty-five fathoms, a powerful coast-light suddenly shed its radiance upon us. We now knew all we wanted to know, and we turned back, with the intention of steering straight for this spot on the following day.

Meanwhile, the new year had come in, minus the usual bell-ringing and songs! At seven o'clock in the morning I entered my cabin drenched and frozen.

The New Year began well.

We lay so quietly under the mild, westerly wind that, having still a couple of hours before beginning our mine-laying, we set to work painting the sides of the vessel, badly damaged by the weather.

Then, in broad daylight, we slowly steered for the English coast.

II—STORY OF MINES OFF THE ENGLISH COAST

Those were hours I shall not easily forget. Far and wide, nothing was to be seen on the surface of the sea. In spite of a brilliant sun and a remarkably clear horizon, we remained unnoticed. Nearer and nearer we drew to the coast. Evidently the English had no idea that this first day of the New Year was the dawn of a great holiday for us and that there was a *Moewe* which, instead of waiting for March and April, was determined, at this unusual season, to lay a few eggs along the English coast!

Mine-laying is not an easy task; the entire crew must take a hand in it. As a rule, the mines—egg-shaped black monsters, almost the size of a man—lie carefully stowed away in long rows in the hold. When the moment to use them arrives they are brought to the upper deck and there again arranged in rows. Shortly before they are laid they are provided with ignition fuses. This detail is attended to by a specially-trained *personnel*, under the supervision of torpedo officers. At the command "Throw!" each mine in turn receives a violent push and drops with a graceful dive into the water at a safe distance from the ship.

It was three o'clock in the afternoon when we began to dispose of the mines. To the accompaniment of hissing steam, the rolling of the mines between the lower and upper tracks continued without interruption. Above, on the bridge, joy reigned supreme, for the weather was splendid and we followed the coast-line without anything suspicious coming in sight. In my most sanguine dreams I could never have imagined that we would thus remain unchallenged and unmolested.

At four o'clock a brilliant light once more beamed on us from the shore. We could now see our exact whereabouts, but, anxious not to be overtaken by the dark, we almost immediately turned back.

The glass now began to drop suddenly; the wind rose, and it began to rain. Soon a perfect deluge was falling. So much the better—the worse the weather the better for us! We resumed our mine-throwing, after the necessary preparations.

Everything went well, though the storm raged more furiously than ever. At nine o'clock, still undetected, we turned to sea. Our dear cousins meanwhile remained blissfully ignorant of our friendly visit to their shores.

The decks were cleared, but there was still no rest for us. The storm was at its height, and the hour was full of danger. In front of us, in the direction of the wind, lay the coast and the blinking lights of the boats at anchor. Behind us were the mines we ourselves had dropped, and into which we would infallibly drift if we failed to maintain ourselves against the wind. Only at four o'clock did we go forward once more, when the first officer came to release me from my post after twenty-four hours' strenuous duty. On the following day I expressed my thanks to the crew for the good work they had done.

It was well that we had our task behind us, for in the days that followed we should have no opportunity of carrying out our designs. For a whole week we were battered about in the wildest manner, and had only one thought—to keep the ship head-on to the raging sea. There was no question of advancing. To avoid detection I would have willingly gone farther away from the coast, but this could not be done.

At last, however, the glass began to rise again and we approached the coast for the second time. In the feeble light of dawn a big steamer hove in sight.

At first, from her build, we took her to be a passenger boat; then, as she seemed anxious to follow in our wake, we began to have some doubts. When we saw that she was painted grey, we jumped to the conclusion that she was an enemy auxiliary cruiser, and one of the largest at that. What a catch for us!

All eyes were fixed on me. Every man was anxiously awaiting the command to fight. But the *Moewe* dare not think of fighting yet. She dare not expose her cards and reveal her next move, which was still mine-laying. Even were the issue of the encounter to our advantage, the wireless on board the other boat would betray everything. Our chief aim must first be attended to—all our mines must be laid—then only would the *Moewe* be free to act as she pleased.

With mingled feelings we watched the big boat get behind us. There was now some eight thousand yards between us—a good firing distance.

Suddenly she veered away from us, as if satisfied with her inspection. We could even hear her sending a wireless to the nearest shore station, possibly to signal our presence. Were this the case, painful results would certainly ensue for us. I altered my course as soon as the boat disappeared—it was better to avoid complications. At full speed we steamed for the point where we had decided to lay our next mines. This time the weather was calm and clear.

At eight-fifteen, as we threw the first mine overboard, some lights blinked into sight. They came from English fishing-boats, and we avoided them with care. But gradually the number of these boats grew to such an extent that we could no longer evade them. The mines tumbled into the water in their very midst, and though every instant we feared detection, we continued our exertions during the whole night without a hitch. Either they took us for one of their own patrol-boats, or else, after the way of good fishermen, they thought of nothing at all. At six o'clock, our task satisfactorily completed, we left the shores of England in dazzling sunlight, looking forward to a couple of days' much-needed rest.

The first day the men took things easily, and only the most indispensable duties were performed. The news which we received daily by wireless told us that an enemy man-of-war had run across a mine, and we would have given anything to know whether the mishap was due to one of the "eggs" the *Moewe* had laid. Subsequently we ascertained that such was the case.

Something like sixty nautical miles separated us now from the usual steamer-route.

III—STORY OF THE SHIP BOUND FOR BRAZIL

The next day, on January 11th, at ten in the morning, a cloud of smoke was signalled. We went slowly towards it. Presently, with glasses, we could make out the tops of masts and the funnels of our first victim. She must not escape us. Orders were sent to the engine-room to give us as much speed as possible. When, at last, we got a nearer view of the boat, we put her down to be English, and about the same size as the *Moewe*. As the distance between us diminished, a second cloud of smoke came in sight on our other bow, and grew rapidly larger and larger. Evidently a second victim was flying into our arms! If the captain of this second boat had been more considerate he would have waited until we had at least settled with Number One. Owing to his untimely appearance our task would be doubly difficult. But we did not allow our spirits to be damped. We simply slowed down in order to reconnoitre the second intruder. This boat also turned out to be English, of the same size as the first.

When she was sufficiently near, we hoisted the signal, "What is your name?" The answer came: *"Farringford."*

The time for action had arrived!

As we saw that the boat to starboard was slower than the *Moewe,* we first tackled the second intruder.

We signalled "Stop," and showed the German ensign, and—to let both our neighbors see that we were in earnest—we fired a shot. Both ships stopped immediately. The *Moewe* steered towards the *Farringford,* and, at a distance of fifty yards, I shouted: "Abandon the ship immediately.

My intention was to take the crew on board; then to approach the other boat and, finally, to sink both vessels.

But this was easier said than done. Owing to the high seas, the transfer of the crew of the first boat was somewhat difficult and took time; meanwhile, the other ship utilized the opportunity to disappear in a dazzling rainbow. I consequently gave up my first intention of blowing up the *Farringford*. Instead, I ordered a few shots to be fired at her. Two of these having struck the water-line, and her sinking appearing to be imminent, we were at liberty to pursue the fugitive at full speed. Overtake her we must, for if she escaped us our detection was a dead certainty. Presently the fugitive was once more in sight. I sent a shell through the air, and, with a great display of smoke, the steamer tried to increase her pace; but a second shell recalled the captain to his senses. He notified his intention to stop by showing all his lights and three red lamps, and after a two hours' pursuit we got alongside him.

A prize-crew of two officers and six men promptly went on board. The first thing to be done was to ascertain the owner of the boat and cargo. Then her papers had to be examined and their accuracy verified. Finally, the crew was reviewed and the cargo examined. The results were duly signalled to the *Moewe*.

We were thus informed that she was an English steamer, the *Corbridge*, three thousand six hundred and eighty-seven tons, taking a cargo of four thousand tons of coal from Cardiff to Brazil.

IV—STORY OF THE LIVERPOOL TRADERS

This welcome capture meant another two months' cruising for us! The *Corbridge*, therefore, was not sunk, but received the order to follow in our wake, after which we jointly returned to the spot where we had abandoned the *Farringford*.

In spite of a brilliant moon, there was nothing to be seen. Our shells had done their work well, and the ship was at the bottom of the sea. We felt justly elated at the success of our double capture on the very first day of our hunting expedition.

The next twenty-four hours brought us nearer to the usual shipping route, but nothing untoward occurred. The crew of the *Corbridge* was reinforced and put under special orders. Then she was released. I shall have more to say about her later on.

The second morning after the sinking of the *Farringford* another cloud of smoke was signalled. On this occasion, too, we commenced by acting very cautiously, for fear of the new-comer suspecting our *bona fides* and signalling our presence by wireless. Having ascertained that the boat had no wireless on board, however, we steered straight for her. The captain, however, seemed to have smelt a rat, and tried to evade us. Our intimation to stop, accompanied by a shell, soon convinced him of the futility of such an attempt. Sadly, he brought his ship to a standstill. From the prize-crew I sent on board we learnt that the boat's name was *Dromonby*, three thousand six hundred and twenty-seven tons, and that she belonged to the British Government, and was on the way to South Africa with a cargo of coal. The crew of fifteen men was transferred to the *Moewe*, and the ship blown up.

Another cloud of smoke being signalled, the *Moewe* got ready again.

This time also the boat was an "Engländer"—a specially fine steamer, *Author* by name, three thousand four hundred and ninety-six tons register, and worth three to four million marks. After the usual formalities, the crew, consisting of four Englishmen and forty-five Indians, was taken on board our ship. We also transferred sheep, chickens, and eggs, and our larder was thus renewed in a most satisfactory way. There were also many valuable race-horses on board, but unfortunately they had to be shot.

The weather remained calm. We worked busily, without any fear of interference, until still another cloud of smoke appeared on the horizon to the south. Completing the transfer as quickly as possible, we turned all our attention to the sinking of the *Author*. In the general hurry, a mishap occurred. Three patent life-buoys had inadvertently remained on board the *Author*, and, just as we thought all was over, these buoys caught fire from their contact with the water and suddenly exploded. Had this noise been heard by the approaching steamer, she would certainly have got alarmed, and might possibly have escaped us. We therefore pretended to be looking for a man overboard, and meanwhile secured the buoys. The boat came towards us unsuspiciously, and it is easy to imagine the painful surprise of her captain when he received the brusque order:

"Stop at once and abandon your ship!"

After a moment's hesitation he complied.

We ascertained, in the usual way, that the ship's name was *Trader*, three thousand seven hundred tons, and that she was bound with a cargo of raw sugar to Liverpool. We sank her in a quarter of an hour, by opening her valves and applying a few bombs. Practice makes the master!

I summoned the three captains of the sunk boats to the bridge, and made the seriousness of the situation clear to them. I impressed upon them that, provided the prisoners complied with all our regulations, they could count on fair treatment, but that the slightest insubordination would be followed by the severest punishment.

I must say that our prisoners observed my warning

in the most praiseworthy fashion, and in return they were allowed, on favorable occasions, to air themselves on deck, which they greatly appreciated, for the accommodation set apart for them, where a hundred and fifty men were huddled together, was insufficiently ventilated and altogether inadequate.

The housing of the prisoners presented at first considerable difficulties and caused the first officer no small trouble and perturbation. Finally, the space where the mines had been kept was set apart for the whites, while the Indians were accommodated in the stern. Fortunately we had sufficient wood to improvise makeshift tables, benches, and so on. Gradually things began to look more shipshape, but nevertheless we were very anxious to get rid of this superfluous humanity at the earliest possible opportunity, and before long the wish was gratified.

Though we were close to a much-used trade route during the whole of the following day, we did not catch sight of a single vessel, and we utilized the time to repaint once more the *Moewe's* sides, which sadly needed a fresh coating.

V—STORY OF SINKING OF THE "ARIADNE"

The next morning, at seven o'clock on January 15th, we met the British steamer *Ariadne,* three thousand tons, with a cargo of maize. In the most obliging manner she ran right into our arms.

The searching of the ship and the capture of the crew were again carried out according to the prescribed rules, and I decided to sink the abandoned ship in precisely the same manner as the *Farringford*—by shelling her—as this gave our gunners an opportunity of practising.

The chart house was chosen for a target, and immediately after the first shell the ship caught on fire. Enormous volumes of smoke filled the air. Glorious though the sight was, we found it most provoking, for we feared that the smoke might serve as a warning to some approaching vessel. We waited patiently, or rather impatiently, for fully half an hour, for the "passing" of the *Ariadne,* but as she showed no signs of sinking we finally decided to speed her on her way by sacrificing one of our torpedoes. No sooner said than done! Very shortly afterwards the *Ariadne* took her final plunge.

Almost immediately a cloud of smoke showed in the distance, heralding the passage of a fast steamer going north. We began preparations at once to hurry after her, and, if possible, waylay her. While feverish preparations were going on in the engine-room, we continued our investigations. The speed of the vessel was a capital point, for, assuming that we annexed her, her pace, provided it turned out equal to ours, would prove an enormous advantage. On the other hand, fast boats are generally provided with wireless, and we ran the risk of being signalled, in which case we would be compelled to resort to drastic measures, a course we would rather avoid with a passenger boat. Also, of course, the vessel might prove to be an auxiliary cruiser, or even a man-of-war. We approached her, therefore, very cautiously. The first officer, who went aloft with his glasses, informed us that the boat had only one funnel and very big superstructures. That meant that she could only be a passenger boat, or else an auxiliary cruiser. Still very cautiously we approached her, and soon were practically certain that we were in the presence of a passenger boat, though her nationality remained doubtful, as she carried no flag.

VI—STORY OF THE CAPTURE OF THE "APPAM"

At a distance of about two thousand yards, I steered in such a way that a collision was imminent, unless the ship got behind the *Moewe*. At last we caught sight of her name—*Appam*. Turning to the International Shipping List, we read: *Appam,* English steamer of the Elder Dempster Line, seven thousand eight hundred tons register; carries passengers and has a wireless. That such a big boat carried also a precious cargo we did not doubt for an instant.

Without more ado, therefore, we hoisted the signal, "Stop at once," and also showed our war-flag, in the hope that the ship would abandon all thought of resistance. But she disregarded our signal, and we had to follow it up with a shell as a warning to the captain and a reminder of what it means to ignore, in war-time, the orders of a man-of-war.

Our shell had the desired effect; the *Appam* slowed down considerably and, finally, stood still. A few seconds later, I was told that her wireless was operating. Immediately our own operators intervened in such a way that the enemy's message became indecipherable. At the worst, any ship hovering in the neighborhood could only have been able to make out that something unexpected was taking place. But even that was to be avoided at all costs.

I therefore ordered a shell to be aimed at the wireless on the *Appam's* bridge. It silenced the apparatus at once, and the *Moewe* then got behind the English boat. I next saw English man-of-war sailors in uniform in the act of directing upon us small, quick-firing guns. Had they really fired on us, it would not have been an act of courage, but cold-blooded folly and reckless audacity, for surely they must have known that their small guns would have been quite inadequate against our far better equipment.

It would have been, moreover, a distinctly criminal act towards their passengers, for if we retaliated the unarmed passengers would most certainly have come to grief.

To end the critical situation, I quickly fired a second shell over the heads of the firing brigade. We saw the men scurry away, and then return to their posts and resume their preparations for firing. This made my blood boil and I ordered a few well-directed shells to be fired straight into their midst. Then, at last, their thick heads understood that we were in earnest. I promptly dispatched two boats to the *Appam,* for we now could see on board quite a number of English naval uniforms. Her deck was getting more and more crowded with people, who, in great excitement, were equipping themselves with life-belts and moved in all directions like a swarm of bees.

A striking contrast to this scene was presented by a group of people leaning on the taffrail and making joyful signals in our direction. We soon unravelled this mystery. These people were our own compatriots—twenty-one civilians, with three women, and eighteen prisoners of war from the Cameroons police. They had all been arrested in Duala, at the beginning of January, and put on the *Appam* to be interned in England. Their joy at their happy and quite unexpected release is indescribable, and we naturally reciprocated and shared in their delight.

I ordered them to be transferred at once to the *Moewe,* and they joined us with shining eyes and smiling faces. We celebrated the occasion by drinking to the health of His Majesty the German Emperor.

More and more satisfactory tidings came from on board our capture. The ship was laden with a precious cargo, which would compensate us amply for the risk we had run in attacking a vessel provided with wireless. Specially welcome was the news that the *Appam* was carrying a million marks in gold. Without losing a minute we transported this treasure to the hold of the *Moewe*. It was comparatively light booty—eighteen cases in all; sixteen cases of them contained fourteen bars of gold apiece, and two gold-dust.

So far everything had gone splendidly. What, however, was to be done with the four English officers, twenty sailors and marines, and the hundred and sixty passengers on board the *Appam?* To transfer them to the *Moewe* was out of the question, every available corner being occupied.

After some deliberation, I dispatched Reserve Officer Berg, with a prize-crew of twenty men, to the *Appam*. The released Germans were told to consider him as the master of the ship and on every occasion to back him up. That being settled, we hurriedly departed, for the *Moewe* still feared the possible consequences of that interrupted wireless message of the *Appam*.

Our next act was to ascertain what provisions the *Appam* had on board, for my intention was to send our captive into some port only after a considerable time, for with our parting from her the secret of our existence would naturally come to light.

At nightfall we stopped the ship, and I summoned the captain, officers, and crew of the *Appam,* also the four officers and sailors belonging to the British Navy. By all laws and rights they were prisoners of war, and had to join their friends below.

VII—STORY OF THE COLONIAL PRISONERS

The passengers of the *Appam*, our officers told me, were literally trembling for their lives. I decided, therefore, to have an interview with the two most representative passengers, the Governors of the English colonies of Sierra Leone and Nigeria—Sir Edward Merewether and Mr. James. These two gentlemen, on being conducted to my cabin, had the situation fully explained to them. Fortunately for them, the German Colonials on board the *Appam* had already informed me that both these men, in striking contrast to the usual English official, were not rabid German-haters, and had in the prosecution of their official duties treated Germans comparatively well.

I consequently informed them that, in spite of their official capacity, I had no intention of detaining them as prisoners on the *Moewe*. (The fact that, had I done so, they would have been very much in our way, I, of course, kept to myself.) I clearly saw that both these gentlemen of high standing had expected a very different fate, for their expression brightened at my words. They passed a night on the *Moewe* and were conducted back to the *Appam* the following morning, after breakfast, with instructions to tell their fellow-passengers that the *Appam* would eventually be brought into a certain port under German command. Every passenger could keep his belongings, but every eligible man had to sign an undertaking not to bear arms in this war against Germany or her allies. So long as the orders of the German officer in charge were obeyed, everyone would be well treated, and everything would be done to ensure the safety of the ship. At the slightest sign of opposition or insubordination, however, the vessel would be blown up.

The *Appam* remained with us for the time being, as the stocktaking of the coal and provisions lasted a considerable time. The ex-captain had originally informed us that his ship was only provided for another five days. After some persuasion, he admitted that there was sufficient fuel and food to last double that time. Consequently, the ship could be taken to the United States of America, the only country where we could berth our prize.

VIII—STORY OF THE FIGHT WITH THE "CLAN McTAVISH"

The following afternoon a cloud of smoke appeared on the horizon. At closer quarters, we recognized a fast steamer, provided with wireless, but without high superstructures. We therefore jumped to the conclusion that the vessel was an important cargo-boat.

It was already quite dark when we overtook her, and I made use of the Morse lamp to ask for her name. Her answer came promptly: "First tell us yours."

One name is as good as another, so I deemed it advisable to usurp that of the sunk steamer *Author*.

After some hesitation, the stranger signalled with the Morse lamp: *"Clan McTavish."*

Delighted to be again dealing with an "Engländer," I ordered, without losing a second:

"Clear for battle to starboard."

The guns took aim, and I shouted:

"This is a German cruiser. Stop at once!"

"We have stopped," came the answer, but, though four hundred yards divided us, we heard them working with all their might to set their ship in motion. I fired a shot, whereupon I was told that the enemy vessel was using her wireless.

Without wasting another second, I gave the order to aim at the wireless, and the first shell silenced it. Almost immediately, a streak of light pierced the darkness and something hissed over our heads. At first I thought I had made a mistake, but as a shell dropped into the water quite close to the *Moewe,* there could be no doubt that the Engländer intended to put up a fight.

We opened fire, and shot after shot rang out. But the Engländer was tenacious. Her shots answered ours— strangely enough, without once hitting us. That seemed to exasperate her only the more, and thick smoke enveloped us. Then, suddenly, the enemy ship slowed down and she signalled:

"We have stopped completely."

Soon we were able to ascertain the damage caused by our firing. Afterwards, the captain told us that our first shell had killed a Lascar. The second shell went through the cabin of the second officer, creating havoc in that part of the ship. The third shot hit the captain's bridge. Other shells killed seventeen Lascars and wounded five. A shell having hit the water-line and another the engines, the captain had at last given up further useless opposition.

While the prize-crew went on board, I summoned the *Appam* to help us. She had watched the fight from a distance, and it is easy to imagine with what feelings.

The *Clan McTavish,* five thousand eight hundred and sixteen tons, was bringing a considerable cargo of wool, leather, skins, and india-rubber from Australia, worth about ten million marks. How splendid if we could have taken all that wealth home with us! Unfortunately, we had damaged the engines of the *Clan McTavish* beyond repair. All thought of the cargo had therefore to be abandoned, especially as we were in a hurry to get away—pursued, as usual, by the fear of a possible surprise.

So, two hours later, the *Clan McTavish* disappeared into the deep sea, and, once more, we feasted our eyes on the rare and suggestive sight of a sinking ship, rendered even more attractive by a brilliant tropical moonlight night.

Her crew consisted chiefly of Indians, who meanwhile had been transferred to the *Moewe*.

One of our shells had hit a boat and killed fifteen poor fellows. Three men, severely wounded, who had been rescued from the water by the *Appam*, died during the night.

When the captain reported himself to me, I took him severely to task and pointed out to him that, by ignoring my orders and entering into a useless battle with us, he had unnecessarily caused the death of eighteen men.

By way of excuse, he replied that he had no idea that our boat was a man-of-war; he had taken the *Moewe* to be an armed merchantman, and thought his and our chances were about equal. Moreover, he declared himself free of all responsibility in the matter; his orders had been to bring his ship to England. To that end he was provided with a gun, and it was his duty to make use of it when the occasion arose.

Frankly, I liked the loyalty with which this old Scotch sea-bear defended his case. I shook hands with him and admitted that, most probably, in his place, I would have acted exactly in the same way.

Still in company with the *Appam*, after the sinking of the *Clan McTavish*, we proceeded westwards. At last, however, there came the day when I thought it was opportune to part from Lieutenant Berg. He was instructed to make for a port in the U.S.A., and I entrusted to his care the civilian passengers of the seven ships we had sunk up to now. Naturally, I would have preferred to leave them in safe custody in Germany, but the situation precluded this altogether.

Our primary object being to sink more ships, we needed all our available space for future guests. So we only retained on board the three officers belonging to the English Army, twenty man-of-war sailors and marines, the crew of the *Clan McTavish*, and a hundred Indians.

Before parting with them, I once more summoned the captains of the seven captured boats and impressed upon them that it was their absolute duty to preserve peace and order on the *Appam*. They replied by assuring me emphatically that the German commander would be obeyed as strictly as they themselves had been.

Thus reassured, I let them go, yet it was not without misgivings that I watched the *Appam* disappear below the horizon. And, truly, it was no trifle to bring the boat safely through the lines of the British cruisers in the Atlantic, to the coast of the United States. Yet I knew full well that Lieutenant Berg, like all the officers of our merchant navy, was a master of his craft, able to handle the most difficult situation. We learned with great satisfaction about a month later, through a wireless message, that the *Appam* had reached Newport News exactly at the appointed time, without any undue complications.

The secret of the *Moewe* had been preserved!

Among our guests on board, the Indians were undoubtedly the most interesting. Picturesque to a degree, not only by their brightly colored attire, but even by their demeanor, which possessed a rare dignity, their presence was very welcome to me on board my ship. Yet, naturally, I did not retain them solely for these æsthetic reasons, but because I knew they could be very useful. In the neighborhood of the Tropics there reigns an intolerable heat, with intermittent downpours, and in the interior of the ship the temperature exceeds the limits of endurance. In such conditions Indians are invaluable.

We employed them principally as coal-heavers, for it was impossible to use them in any other regular capacity, as they only worked willingly when their customs and religious ceremonies are not interfered with. Punctuality in meals was an equally important point with them; in the middle of their work they would throw down everything and start cooking their mutton and rice, or rice and mutton. No other food seemed to exist for them, and our European fare they appeared to regard with loathing. Sarang, the oldest among them, told me that, so long as they had rice, they were willing to do any work; but if rice failed them, they would all die, without the slightest resistance. In consequence, every ship we captured after this was thoroughly searched for rice before it was sunk. Unfortunately, we never found much of it, so that the rations of the poor Indians grew more and more meagre. Yet, I am glad to say, Sarang's sombre prophecy was not realized; every one of the Indians survived this skimpy diet. Their good will was invariable, no matter what they were told to do. Our crew was now less numerous, as a good number of men had been taken away to form two prize crews, and the work was pretty hard, the cleaning of the ship and the upkeep of the war material being no small matter, and the Indians' help was invaluable.

IX—STORY OF THE "EDINBURGH" ON VOYAGE FROM INDIA

The time had now arrived to renew our coal reserves, and so we went in quest of our first prize, the *Corbridge*, which the reader will remember was in charge of a prize-crew, and had parted from us on January 12th. We expected her now to have reached the appointed spot where we intended taking over her cargo of coal. Late in January we met a three-masted sailing-ship, the *Edinburgh,* one thousand four hundred and seventy-three tons, on her way from India to Liverpool, carrying two thousand tons of cattle food in the shape of rice-flour. This ship, whose unlucky star placed her in our way, had already been twenty-one months at sea, and for an incredibly long time had lain becalmed in windless latitudes, waiting for a propitious breeze. Now, when the wind had actually risen and the *Edinburgh* could at last escape from the broiling heat and the inexpressible dullness of endless waiting, the *Moewe* appeared and shattered all her hopes!

We pitied the poor old captain, who was sixty-seven years old; but war is war! He and his crew had to take up their quarters with us, and their ship had to bid a hasty adieu to this world. The cattle will wait for their food in vain.

The following day, on January 28th, precisely at the appointed time, the *Corbridge* loomed in sight and joined us where we were lying at anchor. The transfer of the coal took fully three days. Heat, noise and coal-dust were everywhere; there was no getting away from it. But it was glorious to watch the zeal with which the crew toiled away. The unloading of a cargo of coal is never a small affair, and the *Corbridge* lacked everything that might have made the task easier. Every moment we were confronted with new difficulties, but they were always solved by some obscure inventive genius from among the crew. Ingenuity coupled with good will can achieve much. Night and day the men labored unremittingly, until the precious black stuff was stored carefully in every available corner on our boat.

As a last souvenir of the *Corbridge* we appropriated

the pigeons and the pigeon-house erected on the bridge. Subsequently, these delightful birds helped us to while away many a pleasant hour, when, on perfectly calm days, they fluttered about the ship.

As for the *Corbridge,* we had got out of her all we wanted, and she was presently sunk in the usual way.

Now that the *Moewe* had once more a supply of coal we felt like different beings, and pined for fresh deeds.

Yet we had to be more cautious than ever, for, surely, the disappearance of so many vessels within a few weeks would serve as a hint to our enemies that all was not as it should be in the Atlantic.

That this was so was proved to us, if only by the fact that the game we were hunting was now conspicuously rare. In vain did we search the zone usually overrun by ships. Not a single cloud of smoke came in sight! At last we decided to leave the beaten track and seek for our quarry elsewhere. After much patience, and a certain amount of good luck, we finally succeeded in making fresh victims. As ships were evidently taking every precaution against us, and were attempting by all possible means to evade us, we retaliated by resorting to new stratagems—the continual repainting of the *Moewe,* in order to vary her aspect as much as possible, being the most frequent one we adopted.

X—STORIES OF SHIPS ON BOTTOM OF THE SEAS

Our first capture on this occasion occurred on February 4th—a Belgian boat, the *Luxembourg,* four thousand three hundred and twenty-two tons register, with a cargo of five thousand nine hundred tons of coal, the property of a railway company in Buenos Ayres. Considering the high price of coal and freight, this cargo alone was worth about a million marks. Yet cargo and ship promptly disappeared into the depths.

The crew of the Belgian ship consisted of the most varied types of humanity. The majority were neutrals, chiefly Greeks and Spaniards, and their transfer to the *Moewe* was rather a comical affair. They were hampered by the most unnecessary paraphernalia—mandolins, parrots, zithers, monkeys, dogs, and so on.

On February 6th we captured another vessel, the English steamer *Flamenco,* four thousand six hundred and twenty-nine tons register. She met our advances by using her wireless. We retorted with a few well-directed shells, and this quickly brought her to her senses, especially as she had caught on fire. The crew rushed to the boats, one of which upset, and about twenty men fell into the water. This is no joke in this region, where sharks abound, and we were genuinely pleased when our prize-crew succeeded in fishing all, save one man, out of the waves.

While preparations were being made to sink the *Flamenco,* I summoned her captain and remonstrated with him for having used his wireless, an act which had provoked us into firing. He replied that his duty was to thwart our plans, just as much as mine was to capture his boat. One of the neutrals transferred on board the *Moewe* confirmed our suspicion that we were being tracked. He told us that the English cruiser *Glasgow* had overtaken them the previous day and had warned them of the danger of an encounter with the *Moewe*.

At first we were inclined to doubt the story, for up to now we had neither seen nor heard of this cruiser. On developing some photographic plates seized on board the *Flamenco,* however, we made the acquaintance of this English cruiser. We must have unwittingly passed each other in the night.

We continued our voyage in splendid weather, though the heat was insufferable. Good luck was slow in coming. But one afternoon, shortly after five, we caught sight of a vessel, and quickly went in pursuit. She proved to be the Norwegian *Estrella,* so we let her go. On this occasion we once more changed the aspect of the *Moewe*.

For days after that we only saw flying-fish, water, and passing clouds. But on Sunday, after having the whole day in vain searched the horizon, towards evening we perceived a cloud of smoke.

We hurried forward, but, unfortunately, it was quite dark before we overtook the steamer.

Our request for her name remained for a time without an answer. Then came the reply: *"Heraclide."*

This was disconcerting, for Lloyd's Register contained no such name. We repeated our question and received the same answer:

"Heraclide."

"What nationality?"

"Good friend."

"What line?"

Deep silence.

Now we knew how to act. If the boat had claimed to be a neutral, I should have let her go unmolested. On the other hand, a neutral would never have given such an equivocal reply, so, of course, she could only be an "Engländer."

I ordered her to stop.

While we slowed down, the steamer suddenly accelerated her movements in an evident attempt to escape. That put an end to my patience. We sent a shell in her direction, and I heard the captain ironically inquire:

"What did you shoot at?"

He must have realized, though, the seriousness of his

position, for he forestalled a second shell by signalling with the siren that he had stopped. The boat's name now became apparent. She was English, and, as we had rightly surmised, the *Westburn,* a comparatively old boat of three thousand three hundred tons, with a cargo of coal and a speed of only seven knots.

That Sunday our hopes were destined to be fulfilled a second time. While the crew of the *Westburn* was being transferred to the *Moewe,* a white light showed on the horizon. We swiftly got ready, and, adapting ourselves to the course of the *Westburn*—which was in tow —we steamed towards the new-comer.

At six o'clock in the morning we ran alongside of her. She proved to be the steamer *Horace,* three thousand three hundred and thirty-five tons, with a particularly rich cargo of spirits, grain, wool, meat, and antimony—all things that Germany is in great need of. Yet it was out of the question even to attempt to send this prize home, as she was deficient in coal. There was nothing for it but to sink her and all she contained.

XI—STORY OF THE EXPLOSION ON THE "WESTBURN"

We had now so many mouths on board to feed that it was imperative to get rid of them. The *Westburn* was requisitioned for this purpose, and all our guests, with the exception of those whom we considered prisoners of war, left the *Moewe.* There were some hundred and fifty in all, and they were anything but comfortable in the old boat during their enforced voyage to Teneriffe, where the prize-commander—the officers' orderly, Badewitz—was instructed to conduct them. The prize-crew consisted this time of only eight men. On this occasion, too, I summoned the captains of the six captured ships and impressed upon them that, at the slightest sign of insubordination, or attempt at mutiny, Commander Badewitz had my orders to blow up the ship.

Later, I learned from the papers, that the *Westburn* arrived in broad daylight at Santa Cruz, in Teneriffe. A few hours earlier, the big English ironclad *Sutlej*, twelve thousand two hundred tons, had dropped anchor in the harbor. When the German war-flag, proudly fluttering at the stern of the *Westburn*, was noticed by the *Sutlej*, the *Westburn* was already inside the three-mile zone in Spanish waters, and her arrival could not be hindered. It was arranged with the harbor authorities that the prisoners should remain on board until the following morning, and the prize-commander gave them once more to understand that, at the slightest offence against discipline, he would blow up the ship. So, in spite of the presence of the English warship, the prisoners had the sense to remain quiet. The next morning they were partly landed and partly taken on board English ships, while, early in the afternoon, the *Westburn* left the harbor to avoid being detained by the authorities.

Outside, the *Sutlej* was lying in wait, eager to pounce upon her presumed prey the moment she left the three-mile zone. Hardly had the *Westburn* steamed out of the harbor, however, than she was seen to be surrounded by a white flame. The ship swayed to one side, while the crew rushed to the boats.

According to the papers, one of the boilers, all of which were in a wretched condition, had burst. Whether true or not, this incident played into our hands. It was very considerate of the ill-fated boiler to explode just at the precise moment when the *Westburn* was liable either to be seized by the Spanish authorities or pounced upon by the English vessel. It was far better for us that the cargo of four thousand tons of coal should go to the bottom of the sea rather than that it should be utilized by an English ship.

The very next day after parting from the *Westburn* we caught sight of another steamer. After a four hours' pursuit we ascertained that she was a neutral, and we slunk away in the darkness, hoping we had not been recognized.

XII—STORY OF THE "MOEWE'S" PREY—AND RETURN HOME

Our next encounter was with a big, stately passenger-ship, which, unfortunately, we could not waylay.

The time was now fast approaching when it became necessary to think of returning home. The nights were growing shorter, and the season of winter storms being at an end, we ran a greater risk of being captured.

On reaching more northerly latitudes, we received glad tidings from home more and more frequently by wireless. A special joyful occasion was when news reached us that fifty men of our crew had been granted the Iron Cross.

On February 24th one more valuable prize fell into our hands—the Frenchman *Maroni*, three thousand one hundred and nine tons, with a cargo of wine, on its way from Bordeaux to New York. Thirty-three Frenchmen were transferred on board the *Moewe*, but the ship, of course, was sunk, and with her—much to our chagrin—a thousand cases of Pommery. We could not get at them quickly enough, for they were packed away securely in the hold. But we carried away innumerable eggs, fine French cheeses, and many other provisions we had long been obliged to do without.

A specially welcome find on the *Maroni* was the newspapers. Our cruising-campaign had inspired many indignant articles, and we perused them with much zest. "Pirate" was the mildest of the terms applied to us by the French press.

Still further pleasure we derived from the reading of the English and American papers seized on the next and last boat we sank—the British steamer *Saxon Prince*, three thousand four hundred and seventy-one tons, carrying a cargo of wool, grain, and explosives from America to England.

We learnt from these papers of the great impression produced on the marine insurance companies by the disappearance of the first boats we captured. Many conjectures were made, but not one of them approached the truth. The possibility that a German cruiser had broken through the British lines in the North Sea did not occur to anyone, until the *Appam* reached the United States and her passengers gave authentic accounts of that quasi-fabulous bird of prey called the *Moewe*.

Long-winded articles told us how Lieutenant Berg had loyally and conscientiously fulfilled his share of the joint task by retarding as much as possible the bringing of his ship into port.

It is easy to imagine with what pleasure we welcomed the good tidings concerning our adopted daughter, the *Appam*, and how gratified we felt when even the enemy paid tribute to Lieutenant Berg's energetic and tactful handling of the situation.

After that the *Moewe* made straight for home, her good star once more enabling her to get safely past all obstacles. As a reward for their services, every member of the crew was given the Iron Cross of the Second Class, and the Commander was summoned by the great War Lord himself to come and tell him all the details of the sinking of the hated "Engländers."

PRISONER'S VOYAGE ON GERMAN U-BOAT UNDER THE SEA

Comfort, Even Gayety, Aboard Craft

Told by (Name Withheld by Request)

Much of the mystery and rumor surrounding German submarine methods is cleared away by this narrative of a steamship officer who spent many days as a prisoner on one of the powerful new U-boats. His story was written for the *New York Times* on condition that his name be not disclosed. Treated with great consideration by his captors, he had an opportunity to learn how the officers and crew lived, to study their attitude and manners, their work with torpedoes and deck guns, their system of attack and defense, and their science of navigation. It is reproduced here by permission.

I—STORY OF THE MYSTERIOUS CAPTURE

This is a true record of actual experience as prisoner on board a German submarine. The ship I left may be called the *Wanderer,* and to the submarine I will refer as the "U-boat."

All went well till one day the first intimation of any danger around was hearing a shot fired, and in a few seconds a shell hit the water a little distance from the ship. The weather was good and sea calm and no craft was discernible, though lookout men were watching—and I draw attention to this to show that, in spite of precautions, it is difficult to recognize a submarine on the surface, with her conning tower painted the color of the water, at a range of three to four thousand yards. Very shortly a second shot was fired, whereupon through the glasses a conning tower became visible and also men standing on the deck, so we became aware that a submarine, evidently a big one, was on our track. We then stopped, return fire being impossible and to run away useless, as we would soon have been overhauled.

Presently a flag signal was hoisted from the periscope, which read: "Send an officer here with your ship's papers." Pushing off in a small boat, I was soon aboard the submarine, where I was at once taken down below and questioned by the commander as to the name of the ship, owner's name, nationality, where from, where bound for, and nature of cargo. After a few minutes' conversation a young officer hurriedly entered the cabin and informed the commander that he thought a patrol boat was in sight. The commander promptly ordered some other prisoners to be brought up, placed in the *Wanderer's* boat and pushed off. Presumably this was done at once, for presently I could hear what sounded like hatches on deck being quickly lowered and a buzzing sound, which I knew afterward was due to the lowering of the periscope.

In a few seconds all was still, and we had submerged. The whole affair happened so quickly that I could scarcely realize I was now a prisoner in a submarine, and as I thought of my shipmates my only consolation seemed to be that the *Wanderer* was safe enough, for the present at least. Left alone to myself in a small cabin, I wondered what was going to happen next and what was going to be the end of it all. Being told not to leave my cabin, I obeyed and, as I felt somewhat dazed and confused, took off my coat and lay down on my bunk.

Thoughts crowded through my head, and I had an almost irresistible impulse to get out of the inclosed narrow space and speak to some one, no matter who. This was denied me for two hours, (which seemed like as many days,) when the commander called me into the saloon, was quite cheery, told me not to be frightened, that we were a long way from the original scene, that we were on the surface, and that we were all safe again. To me the consolation sounded strangely ironical, but he was evidently in earnest and wished to put me at my ease.

"Where is the ship?" I had to ask.

"Don't trouble," he replied. "She has gone off all right and there is nothing in sight."

Presently two more of the U's officers entered the saloon and we sat down to our first meal, which consisted of preserved meat, biscuits, butter, tinned tomatoes, marmalade, coffee with milk, and a glass of port wine to finish. My appetite was not good, but the fare was wholesome enough, and my hosts, knowing I could understand German, conversed cheerily. For the most part I answered only when spoken to, asking no questions lest I might be thought inquisitive, but taking in everything. Here let me say that officers and crew set out from the start to make me comfortable and feel at home; were hospitable, courteous, and kind in every way, and put no special restrictions upon me.

The commander frankly told me to ask him any questions I liked about the boat, and that if he sometimes made no reply that I was not to take further notice of it.

"Perhaps," said he, "there are one or two things I do not want you to see, but you must not mind that, and as to the war or what is going on, we will not talk of it."

So that what I saw or heard aboard passed the censor, so to speak, so far as the U officers were concerned, and I formed no opinion that they willfully gave me any false information. I am not clear yet as to their motive in taking me prisoner at all, as I was of no use to them and only took up room and consumed food. Nor could it have been worth their while to "terrorize" one individual like myself. Of course, I carefully refrained from touching on this point, nor did I ask what they intended to do with me if we got safely to port, preferring to remain silent and patiently await developments.

When on deck for fresh air I saw no land anywhere, nor did I expect to be allowed to see it, and probably if I had I should not have been any the wiser. Nor was I shown any charts or allowed to make any periscope observations, although on some occasions I was asked to retire to my cabin, mostly around noon, when navigation was being worked out. The course we took I never knew, and the only clue I had to position was one day when, to my relief, I was informed they hoped to land within twenty-four hours.

First, as to the U-boat herself: She was about 250 feet long, had a crew of about 35 men, carried two 4½-inch guns, could steam 18 knots on the surface and 11 below if required, and had a range limit of 3,200 miles steaming at 12 knots on the surface.

Leaving Germany she was stored for a twelve-weeks' cruise; when I joined her she had provisions only for a few more days as prisoners previously captured had consumed some of them, hence their anxiety to get rid of the remaining ones sent off in a hurry in the *Wanderer's* boat. The original stores were preserved pork and beef, vegetables, tinned soups, fruit, raisins, biscuits, butter, marmalade, milk, tea, and coffee. Prior to sinking one ship they had commandeered eggs, fresh meat, butter, vegetables, and some liquor to afford variety to the larder; so that the bill of fare was varied and there was no stinting of rations. Any cooking was done on an electric stove.

II—STORY OF LIFE ON THE SUBMARINE

The U was driven by petrol, but they said colza or benzoline or any kind of machine oil not too thick could be used, and if this could be replenished from any captured ship so much the better. I would have liked to know about any of the supply ships which undoubtedly have a secret rendezvous with these submarines, and also about land bases in some of the neutral countries so-called, but this information was, of course, denied me.

The living quarters were small but comfortable, officers having separate small cabins and the crew bunks with narrow alley way in between. Ventilation was surprisingly good, pipes for the purpose running all through the boat, foul air being extracted by exhaust and fresh air driven in four or five times a day for half an hour at a time while on the surface.

More than once I remained below for more than twelve hours and did not suffer from headache or symptoms due to bad air. Sometimes we were submerged for four hours, sometimes longer, once for close on fourteen hours, but I felt little inconvenience. The officers stated that up to twenty-four hours of continual submersion they were fairly comfortable; after that, for six hours, it was uncomfortable, and subsequently became intolerable, due to the "sweating" from the framework of the boat, which rendered the clothing damp. To obviate this, leather suits were worn mostly during prolonged submersion, and this process was perhaps the most disagreeable experience of all. For purposes of ventilation, therefore, and in order that the crew might remain in good health, as well as for necessary locomotion, the U remained as much as possible on the surface both day and night.

The idea that most of the submarines come inshore at

night and lie at the bottom in bays is quite a wrong one—perhaps at the beginning of the war, when the boats were smaller, they may have done so; but the larger ones for choice avoid the shallower water and keep out in deeper channels. Safety to themselves prompts such procedure, for they are quite alive to the danger of nets and explosive bombs dropped from the air and surface of the water. When homeward bound and nearing their own shores they often lie at the bottom all night and wait for daylight before proceeding for fear of encountering English patrols or destroyers. With their own war craft they have special flag signals by day and Morse flashes by night. The larger U's have wireless installation by which in code they can communicate with each other, but their range of transmission is short.

The sanitary arrangements below were good and much the same as on any liner. A petty officer was in charge of the sanitation, who also was first aid ambulance man, had charge of the medicine chest, and when required acted as a gunner—quite a handy man. There were two good lavatories on board, effete matter being expelled by force pumps at any time. Other than drinking water there was scarcity of fresh water for domestic uses, so there was no chance of a fresh water bath, another of the drawbacks experienced, although sponging off in cold salt water is at all times refreshing.

There was a variety of books to read, comic and other papers, among them two English papers nearly three weeks old; a gramophone and several records, so that we had music, singing, and occasionally dancing for exercise' sake, but no smoking below, which was strictly forbidden and was perhaps the greatest hardship of all.

There was thus a little gayety on board to relieve the monotony, although, truth to tell, I found the voyage an exciting one and my shipmates seemed merry enough.

In fact, I was surprised at myself getting used so quickly to the new life, and am bound to confess that I was no more worried about what was going on above the surface of the water than I had previously been on my own boat about what takes place at any minute from under the water.

III—STORY OF THE HALE AND HEARTY CREW

The crew on board were quite self-composed, jocular for the most part, serious enough in what they were out to do, but not worrying much about the risks thereof, nor did they seem to regard their calling as any more hazardous than on any other war craft in dangerous waters. Being all young men, full and fond of adventure, the incitements seemed stimulating to their nerves, and victims they looked on as legitimate prey and with no feelings of remorse. The reports I had heard that men in Germany had to be forced into the submarine service seemed to amuse them immensely. On the contrary, they declared there was any number of volunteers for the work, and that many young officers were willing and glad even to pay a premium to get on a "sub" in preference to other war craft, where they said the routine was harder and more irksome.

What their pay was I did not hear, but I gathered it was good, and that provision in the way of bonuses for "good work" and pensions for their dependents were allowed. The idea, too, that at the end of a cruise they were all so nerve-racked that they needed a long rest they declared was too absurd. Many U-boats, they said, made consecutive voyages after a short spell in port to store up, and their "rest depended entirely on the emergencies of the moment."

I must say that on parting with them I saw no signs

of any breakdown, either physical or mental, although all of them looked for a holiday, which is a sailor's privilege. Sailors, we are told, are proverbial for their modesty and the unassuming way they talk of themselves, but this trait I failed to discover in the U-boat officer, who was boastful enough of the great work he was doing for the Fatherland and quite callous as to the methods employed in so doing.

I saw little or nothing of the actual manipulations during submersion, but they were probably on the usual lines known to all such boats and about which there is no particular secret. Every foot of submersion is indicated by a handle turning around on a disk as on the face of a clock, the chief care being not to sink too deep. I gathered this boat could easily be out of sight in less than ten seconds, and steam 11 knots at 60 feet below the surface, 7 knots at 90 feet, and was tested to sink to 200 feet, below which depth there was danger of the sides of the boat being driven in from pressure of the water. At 50 feet below the surface, while in motion, there was little movement or vibration to be felt; at 80 feet practically none at all, and the stillness became monotonous.

During the voyage one ship was torpedoed, but they prefer shelling for economy's sake, although they had plenty of shells aboard and did not stint them in attacking one sailing ship. During the torpedoing process I was surprised how little concussion was felt below—in fact, beyond a slight "bumping" sensation I might not have known it at all.

IV—STORY OF THE TORPEDO ROOM

Of torpedoes on board there were eight "large" and eight "small," as they called them, which when dis-

charged liberate their own propeller and shoot along at
some ten feet below the surface at a rate of up to forty
knots an hour, occasionally "breaking surface," i.e., coming up higher and throwing jets of spray in their course
and then submerging again.

It appears that 55 per cent, or more than half, of the
torpedoes fired miss their mark, and with this average
they seem satisfied. Once they let go at a ship two torpedoes at 3,000 yards' range, and both missed, the range
being too long; but they did not care to come any nearer,
as they believed the ship to be well armed.

They prefer to fire at 500 to 700 yards, which means
that at this range the track or "wake" of a projectile
would be discernible for, say, twenty-five to thirty seconds—not much time, indeed, for any ship to get out of
the way. At 100 yards' range or less they do not care
to fire unless compelled to, as the torpedo is nearly always discharged when the submarine is lying ahead of
the object, i.e., to hit the ship coming up to it; it follows
that a gun forward is more useful than one aft, the gun
aft being of real service when a submarine starts shelling, which she will do for choice from aft the ship rather
than from forward of her, where she would be in danger
of being run over and rammed.

Owing to the big expense of wasted torpedoes it had
been planned to build special larger U-boats, two-deckers carrying larger guns for shelling purposes—hence the
sooner all merchantmen are well armed the better for
them.

Talking one day of the number of submarines lost, the
officers declared that the Allies' reports of their captures
and sinkings were much exaggerated. Naturally they
would say so, but the truth is probably best known at
headquarters, where such figures are checked up. Once
or twice when on the surface we were fired at at long

range and quickly submerged, although the U crews recognize they are a difficult target to aim at, let alone hit, as I, too, knew from experience.

The periscope is about seven inches in diameter and moves up and down like a piston rod in a cylinder, accompanied by a buzzing kind of sound, which became familiar after a day or two. If required it can reach seventeen feet above the surface and may be used as a flagpost for signals. At its summit is a mirror, three to four inches in diameter, from which images are reflected to a larger mirror below used by the observer.

When a ship is first sighted the chief point is to determine her course, which may be easy if she is going in the same direction, but more difficult if not. The next point is to determine as near as possible the speed of the object ship, the size and general lines being considered, and deductions drawn. Next, the distance away of the approaching ship has to be noted.

Under ordinary circumstances on board ship the nearer one standing on deck is to the water the more limited will the horizon be, and likewise the higher from the water, as in the "crow's nest," the bigger the horizon. Standing on deck, seventeen feet from the surface of the water, the horizon, on a clear day, would, roughly speaking, be three miles. The same rule practically applies in periscope work, which, as it can extend seventeen feet in the air, will give a three-mile horizon vision. Therefore, according as is the position on the horizon rays, so will the distance away of the object ship be gauged.

The course, speed, and distance off being calculated, the U has then to manoeuvre to get into position for firing, taking care to avoid the actual track of the approaching ship and to get nearly "broadside on" to her. Hence there is nothing worries them and upsets their calculations more than when the ship alters her course frequently—this manoeuvre being called zigzagging—and which accounts largely for the high percentage of misses registered. The more often the alteration of course takes place, the bigger and more uneven the zigzag, the better for the ship.

Daylight is most suitable for torpedo firing, but there is nothing to prevent its being accurate enough during moonlight, even so far as minor work is concerned. As the torpedo can be discharged from the surface as well as when submerged, the precaution of having every light on the ship extinguished is a necessary one. It is remarkable how few collisions at sea have taken place during the war, even though the ships are running without any navigation lights and even during fog no whistle is sounded. The periscope being in those days a "familiar object," it is believed that some of the later U-boats have another device in the shape of a small hatch opening upward which can be opened by the observer on the submarine, enabling him to look around the surface of the water.

Ordinary navigation on the U-boat is done on usual lines, i.e., sextant and compass and bearings from landmarks by day and observation by stars and of lighthouses by night, but the reckoning of distances by dead reckoning, that is, on the log, has to be dispensed with. The compass used is a gyroscopic one, so there is no deviation due to magnetic influence, and the courses are all therefore "true courses."

There were no signs of any soundings being taken while submerged, but of course they were frequently taken from the surface while approaching land. While on the surface, if the sea was at all rough, the U rolled considerably and the officers, in oilskins, were lashed to the nearest stanchion to prevent being washed overboard. On the for'ard deck on either side of the bow was a small anchor about the same size as used on a 500-ton ship.

The personnel of the U-boat consisted of a commander and three officers, a commander engineer and three officers, several petty officers and ordinary crew, all of whom were young men. Each department had its own section to look after, a full log was kept of all that went on aboard as in peace times, and discipline throughout was excellent.

So much for my cruise in the U-boat, which was satisfactory enough as an experience and certainly on the lines of all's well that ends well. With my queer underwater shipmates I parted on quite good terms, impressed not a little with their general courage and mostly with their coolness under conditions which required steady head and hands and observation which called for considerable cunning and resource.

Compared with a small submarine of the early type I found this U-boat so vastly improved that it was hard to realize so much advance had been made in so short a time; and if it be true that practice makes perfection, there is no knowing what further developments are in store for this class of war craft.

. . . . . .

Before concluding I must refer to certain cruises made by U-boats across the Atlantic to America. Much fuss was made about these and the performances were called "marvelous," "astounding," and so on. From experience I fail to see anything wonderful about them. Once the submarines navigated clear of the north of Scotland, the rest of the voyage was plain sailing for the modern U-boat as I saw it—and, in fact, the voyage for those on board must have been simply a restful and pleasant holiday run.

THE DARKEST HOUR—FLEEING FROM THE BULGARIANS

Our Experiences in the Great Serbian Retreat

Told by Alice and Claude Askew

A vivid narrative, by eye-witnesses, of the supreme tragedy in the history of gallant little Serbia. Mr. and Mrs. Askew went to the country as members of a Field Hospital, and, with the Staff of the Second Army, took part in the terrible retreat across the mountains into Albania. "Little we thought," write the authors, "that it would prove to be the Via Dolorosa, the stony road to Calvary, of an entire nation." Original stories told in the *Wide World Magazine*.

I—STORY OF THE FLIGHT FROM PROKUPLJE

WE WERE surprised when we were told by one of our friends on the staff of the Second Army that we must prepare to leave Prokuplje that very evening.

"Why," we cried, "only a few hours ago we were told that the Bulgarians have had a bad set-back!"

"So they have," was the quiet rejoinder. "The Bulgarians won't get here in a hurry. But the Germans may."

Which goes to show that at this period the Serbian Army was putting up a gallant fight against foes that were bearing down upon it from all sides. What was the good of beating back the Bulgars when the crushing force of the Austro-Germans, with their heavy artillery, had also to be reckoned with? If it had been only the Bulgars!

As a matter of fact, the immediate source of danger was not so much that Prokuplje would fall as that the road to Prishtina—the only route open to the retreating army—might be cut. Koshumlja was threatened, and if Koshumlja were to be taken we should all be caught like rats in a trap.

We had come to Prokuplje from Nish, and all the time we were there—over a week—there was heavy fighting. Had the promised assistance come even then, at the eleventh hour, the tide might have been stemmed, the tables turned, for the Serbian successes were by no means to be despised. The famous Morava division of the Second Army had covered itself with glory in a tough battle at Mramor, Lescovatz had been retaken, and the Bulgarians had been driven out of Nish. The latter victory, however, proved useless, for the Germans immediately stepped in their place.

And in spite of all this, Prokuplje must be evacuated.

We liked Prokuplje—it is a pleasant little town very picturesquely situated. Moveover, we had comfortable quarters in what we were frequently told was the "finest room in the town."

We were always being envied our luck in finding accommodation. Generally speaking, it was abominable beyond description, but the man who sleeps in the open air will envy him who has a roof over his head, and he who lies upon bare boards may be excused if he covets his friend's mattress.

A friend of ours, coming to visit us at Scutari, was stopped by an acquaintance in the street and asked where he was going. He mentioned our name.

"Oh, those are the lucky people who did so well for themselves at Plavnitza," was the grudging comment.

Had we been asked we should not have agreed that we did well for ourselves at Plavnitza; indeed, the night we spent there was not far off being the worst in all our varied experience.

II—STORY OF OUR NIGHT AT PLAVNITZA

In the first place, we had no desire to stay there at all. We were waiting for a steamer to take us to Scutari, but a violent storm had arisen and the steamer failed to appear. Furthermore, we were not actually at Plavnitza, but upon the quay, the best part of half an hour's walk from the village along a sort of embankment that was swept by wind and rain and where the mud was so deep and sticky that it needed courage to face it.

There were many people in the same plight as ourselves, but when it became a matter of certainty that the steamer was not going to show up they returned to the village and sought accommodation there for the night. No doubt a large number were disappointed.

For ourselves, we stayed where we were—on the quay. We had found shelter of a kind, and we were not disposed to give it up to someone else on the remote chance that after ploughing our way through the mud again we might find something better at the village.

There was only one building on the quay, a storehouse for goods delivered by the steamer. Just now there was nothing doing, and the doors were locked. There was, however, a small room, with a dirty narrow bed in it; it was occupied generally by the watchman, but he happened to be absent that night. He had left his son in charge, a sickly, pale-faced boy of fourteen or fifteen, who never ceased smoking cigarettes, and who had the manners and conversation of a grown man.

It was in this room that a crowd of us sought refuge from the storm, and here, when most of the others took their departure, we elected to remain. Our small host was very kind—he gave up his bed to us—but it was quite beyond his power to make the general conditions anything but disgusting in the extreme. We shiver still at the recollection of them.

Our young friend had been lavish in his hospitality, and so we shared the room with some half-dozen men—excellent fellows, but whose habits could hardly commend them as companions for the night. The fact that there was a lady in the party made no difference to them at all.

Oh, the atmosphere of that room! It was redolent of stale fish, cigarette smoke, and the smell of foul garments sodden with rain. The storm that raged outside made it quite impossible to open door or window.

It was very cold, and we, like the rest, had been drenched to the skin, but, of course, we could not think of removing any of our wet clothes. We were faint for want of food, too; expecting to reach Scutari that night, we had brought but little with us, and that we had consumed at midday. But in that fœtid atmosphere we could not have eaten much, however richly supplied we might have been.

Our little host sat on a box and smoked and talked with his other guests for the best part of the night. It was the same with them all. When they were not smoking and spitting they were eating dried fish and cheese, the order of which was sickening to sensitive nostrils.

The boy was bare-footed, and his clothes hung about his wizened, deformed body in rags. They were palpably verminous, and, knowing this, we shuddered for the bed upon which we lay. Nevertheless, the poor little fellow was so cold when at last, like the rest of the company, he stretched himself out on the filthy floor to sleep, that we were impelled to give him one of our coverings, ill as we could spare it.

We had but a small fragment of candle, which spluttered to its end somewhere in the early hours of the morning. After that we lay, sleepless, in total darkness, listening to the moaning of the wind outside and the contented, unconcerned snoring of our companions. And there was a great fear upon us—that the coming of day might not bring us relief, for if the storm continued, as was by no means unlikely, the steamer would be indefinitely held up, nor could any rowing-boat venture forth. If there had only been a road to fall back upon! But there was none.

We shall not easily forget our night upon the quay at Plavnitza, and it certainly never occurred to us that we were likely to be envied the experience!

III—STORY OF THE LAST HOURS BEFORE RETREAT

But to return to Prokuplje, where we occupied "the finest room in the town"—which meant that it possessed a fairly comfortable bed, carpet, curtains, and abundant decoration upon the walls in the way of Berlin wool-work and cheaply-framed photographs. We were sorry that we had to leave it in such a hurry, though, perhaps, we should have regretted our comfortable quarters still more had it not been that our host had elected to slaughter three large pigs that day in the yard just beneath our window, and so all the resultant processes were thrust upon our unwilling view.

The administrative staff of the Second Army were leaving Prokuplje that evening, so we were told; the operative staff would take its departure early the following morning and probably, for strategic reasons, follow a path across the hills instead of the main road. There would be room for us in one of the cars, and we were to be informed by the orderly of our friend, Captain Gworsditch, aide-de-camp to the staff—who himself would be absent till late that night—at what time we were to hold ourselves in readiness. No doubt it would be about six o'clock, certainly not later than seven. With luck it should not take us more than twenty-four hours to make Prishtina, whither we were bound, but the road in places was very bad, and so we must allow for longer, and if we had not provisions enough in hand for the journey, it would be wise to lay in some more.

We reviewed our stock. We had bread, cocoa and tea, a bottle of Greek brandy, sugar, and three tins of sardines. Thinking things over, we calculated that if we had a good dinner before we left we should require nothing more; if all was well we should dine the following night at Prishtina.

We did not know that we were shortly to be under famine conditions. True, we had had difficulty with our meals at Prokuplje, but this was not so much due to a shortage of supplies as to the fact that we had no one to cook for us. The young woman of the house was extremely lazy, and used to protest that it was as much as she could do to look after her father and the children. Nevertheless, she spent half her time gossiping in the street, for which, not unfrequently, her father would thrash her, and, as, in retaliation, she would bully her little brothers and sisters, the whole house used often to resound with ear-splitting and most discomforting howls. So it happened that our food, which was brought to us every morning, uncooked, by Selam, Captain Gworsditch's orderly—we did not have our own orderly till later—might, or might not, be attended to; if it were, it was usually so badly cooked as to be uneatable; if it were not, we had to do the best we could with it ourselves, which was generally even more fatal in the result. Eventually, however, we found a cook who was quite clever in spite of the poverty of material at her disposition.

But we were very remiss in failing to purchase supplies while they were still to be got, and we suffered for it—not only upon the journey to Prishtina but afterwards, for Prokuplje was the last town upon our route at which preserved foods, chocolate, biscuits, and suchlike necessary articles of consumption were to be purchased. And even at Prokuplje they were getting scare; the last tin of sardines we bought came from the private store of the chemist; all the other shops were sold out.

We waited patiently that evening for the arrival of Selam, who was to take us to our car, and we did not worry till eight o'clock struck and he had not arrived; even then we were not particularly concerned, for we concluded that the staff must have postponed their departure. But that was not so; Selam had mistaken his orders, and we were left behind!

We learnt this when, about nine o'clock, Captain Gworsditch himself appeared, having found out that there had been some mistake. He was terribly worried for it was absolutely necessary for us to get off at once—yet what was to be done, since the cars had already started, all the carriages were requisitioned and at that time of night and in the pressure of flight it was impossible to arrange for horses? There was one at our disposition, our beloved charger Pigeon, but we were two people and we had some luggage as well. It seemed as if we must walk or travel by ox-wagon, but anything of the sort was decidedly dangerous as it was imperatively necessary to pass Koshumlja with the smallest possible delay.

For two hours, with Captain Gworsditch, we beat the town in search of a conveyance, and at last luck befriended us. We found some motor vans that were going to Prishtina with a heavy load of petrol, and the officer who was arranging the consignment happened to be a cousin of Captain Gworsditch. It was arranged that we should travel in one of the vans, and so we were hurriedly packed in with some half-dozen other refugees, and by midnight we were off. It was by no means comfortable, and sleep was impossible because of the jolting of the car on the rough road, but we comforted ourselves with the reflection that we should not have another night of it. We were traveling at a fair rate—not till the following day did we realize that that was because we had started late and the great mass of traffic was in front of us.

IV—STORY OF JOURNEY TO KOSHUMLJA— AND THE KING

We reached Koshumlja at about eight in the morning and remained there for a couple of hours. We had fondly imagined we should find an inn of sorts where we could obtain some breakfast, but there was nothing of the kind, nor could we purchase any food or wine, as we had relied upon being able to do. We were, however, most hospitably entertained by the family of the local chemist, whose shop we had merely entered to make some small purchase. They gave us bread, cheese, sausage, and coffee, had our muddy boots cleaned for us, and generally provided for our comfort before we started off again. They were genial, kindly folk, true Serbs, and later on we had frequent occasion to contrast their hospitality with the rough and money-grabbing methods of the Montenegrins.

They told us a lot of interesting things, among others that a few days earler they had been asked by the local authorities to prepare a meal for a couple of distinguished travellers. No names were mentioned. They had done as they were bid, and were now quite sure that it was the King himself whom they had entertained.

On leaving Koshumlja that morning we ourselves saw the King. He was riding with a small retinue, hardly an assumption of state, and to one of us particularly the little calvacade had something about it that was infinitely pathetic. A brief quotation from one of our diaries will explain why:—

"At Koshumlja to-day we saw the King. Curiously enough this is the first time that I have come across him since I have been in Serbia, though Alice saw him at Tarpola. He is a fine old man, and trouble, sickness, and age have not bowed him. And meeting him thus my mind goes back—how many years it may be I should be afraid to guess. I was a small boy spending my holidays with my people at Vevey, on the Lake of Geneva, and at the hotel we struck up an acquaintance with Prince Peter Kara Georgevitch. He was then in the prime of life, tall, dark, handsome—not yet married. He used to talk to us quite unaffectedly of his hopes and ambitions. King Milan was, of course, the prime enemy.

"'One day I shall come into my own.' I can quite well remember him saying that.

"And it was true. Destiny—call it what you will—gave him the coveted throne. And now, a dozen years later, he has lived to see a fresh shuffle of the cards. How they will fall it is still for time to show."

We made but poor progress that day, and it was not to be wondered at. The congestion of traffic was amazing. It would hardly be an exaggeration to say that from Koshumlja to Prishtina there was an unbroken stream of vehicles of the most varied kinds, though the ox-wagon predominated enormously. With these were soldiers and civilians on horseback; soldiers and civilians on foot; oxen laden and unladen; pack-horses; buffaloes, donkeys, and mules; dogs on the leash or running with their masters; men, women, children, and beasts jostling each other in the confusion of hurried flight. It was not so much the retreat of an army as of a whole nation.

Yet all was orderly and in the main good-tempered. The soldiers were kept to their respective "trains," and were well under the control of their officers. There were as yet no ghastly roadside sights, but now and again came presages of what was to be—the fall of a tired horse, the overturning of a cart, and once we were sickened by seeing a couple of frightened oxen, with wagon attached, precipitate themselves over the low parapet of a bridge into the torrent that flowed below. There was little or no excitement, and the empty space was rapidly filled up; it was not well to fall out of rank, if one could help it.

We soon gave up hope of reaching Prishtina that night. Midday to-morrow, the chauffeur promised us. In this confidence we consumed two of our tins of sardines during the day—it was not much for lunch and dinner—leaving the third for breakfast. And therein lay a catastrophe, for when we came to open the tin, hungry after another wakeful and uncomfortable night, the contents proved to be hopelessly bad! We made a meal off dry bread, and it did not improve our tempers to see our companions devour a pig's head between them. There was something revolting in the way they picked the bones.

That day progress was slower than ever; we did not seem able to make any headway at all. By midday we could scarcely have advanced half-a-dozen miles. It became increasingly clear that we should have to spend a third night among the petrol-cans—if not a fourth and fifth. That was bad enough in itself, but what about food?

Our companions did not seem to mind a bit. They were in no hurry and, considering that they had lost practically all they possessed in the world, wonderfully cheerful. But we were anxious to get to Prishtina and rejoin our friends who might be concerned about us; we were nervous on their account, too, since, though there had been no attack upon the main road, we had heard a great deal of firing going on among the hills, and we knew that the route by which they proposed to travel came at times—especially at the old Turkish frontier which we were approaching, very near our own.

V—STORY OF WHAT THE BULGARS DID

It was near the frontier, as we learnt afterwards, that the staff had a very ghastly experience. They came, quite unexpectedly, upon the mutilated bodies of some fifty men—Serbs, not regular soldiers, but transport-bearers and drivers—practically unarmed. They had been massacred by Bulgars, a skirmishing party that had been shown a path across the mountains by some treacherous Albanians, and which had fallen unawares upon the unfortunate Serbs. The brutality of the Bulgars upon this occasion—brutality as to which there can be no doubt whatever—was on a par with all the other stories that have percolated through.

They tied their unfortunate victims—defenceless men, be it remembered—hand and foot and then proceeded to slash them to pieces with their swords. Having perpetrated these murders and secured all the booty that they could carry off, they escaped by the same way that they had come.

No punishment could be meted out to them, but it is good to know that the treacherous Albanians were caught and promptly shot, while their houses were razed to the ground—a more drastic punishment still, according to local views.

No wonder we heard firing among the hills!

About midday we determined to abandon the lorry and to make our way on to the next village—some dozen miles—on foot. We did not feel disposed to face another night of discomfort, but what put the finishing touch was the introduction into the car of a little live pig that was destined to be a new travelling companion until such time as he should be killed, cooked, and eaten. We had no food left of our own, but we felt that we could never regale ourselves upon that pig.

We found an officer friend who gave us a couple of soldiers to carry our baggage, and we set out to thread our way through the stream of traffic; but we did not walk very far, for coming presently across a carriage, empty except for a load of forage, we determined to commandeer it. The driver informed us that he belonged to a cavalry division attached to the First Army, and if his commandant had no objection to our intrusion he, for his part, had none either.

Presently the commandant himself came along. He knew us by repute, as did most of the other officers, and the result was that we were cordially invited to ride with the division and offered hospitality and refreshment for the night.

It was, however, well after seven o'clock and dark by the time we had crossed the old frontier and descended upon the broad plain of Kossovo. Having practically had nothing to eat or drink all day—and very little the day before—we rejoiced when at last camp was reached and we found ourselves sitting beside a huge wood fire—it was bitterly cold—waiting for our supper to be cooked for us and for our tent to be pitched.

We did not reach camp, by the way, without some excitement. Out of the darkness there suddenly came the sound of shooting uncomfortably near. Our friend the commandant was riding by our side at the moment; he apologized and galloped off sharply. Then came more shooting. We learnt afterwards that it was a case of Albanian snipers, and that due punishment had been meted out.

Our supper consisted of "confection," as the tinned meat provided to the army is called. When cooked it is quite good, as each tin, besides the meat, contains an ample supply of soup. We had Nestlé's milk, too, and now for the first time we learnt to appreciate this commodity at its true value. What we should have done without Nestlé's later on it would be hard to say. Our friend was very apologetic about the entertainment he was able to offer us, and kept repeating that it would have been very different in other circumstances; but we were able, wth absolute truth, to assure him that we had rarely enjoyed a meal so much.

We might have added: "or slept so well." We were accommodated in a little "dog-kennel" tent, but there was a comfortable mattress and plenty of wraps, and though the rain fell in torrents during the night, it did not affect our rest. We only felt a sense of rejoicing that we were no longer wedged in among the petrol cans, cold and uncomfortable, and in unavoidable proximity to uncleanly companions—not forgetting the pig. As a matter of fact, had we remained in the lorry we should have been another three nights *en route*.

Our kind friend's hospitality did not end with the night. The carriage was placed at our disposition the next morning, and starting at six o'clock we reached Prishtina by noon. There was no breakfast in camp for anybody, but we were provided with *peksimeat,* as the hard army biscuit is called, water, and cognac as we drove along.

And as we came to Prishtina our spirits revived, and we told each other that, after all, there was still hope for Serbia. There would be a concentration of the three armies upon the historic plain of Kossovo, and perhaps, if things were well in the south, a junction might yet be established between the Serbs and the Allies. It would be a grand thing, we argued, if Kossovo should once again be the scene of a tremendous battle—Kossovo which is already the centre of all that is best in Serbian legend and story—and if at Kossovo Serbia should vindicate her honour and re-enter into possession of her own!

Perhaps at Prishtina our flight would find its end! Alas, for such sanguine views; our stay at Prishtina was destined to be short, and when once again we set out upon the weary road of retreat it was to find the wayside scattered with dead oxen, dead horses—and dead men. At Prishtina Serbia entered in earnest upon her road to Calvary.

A MAGYAR PALADIN—A RITTMEISTER OF THE HUSSARS

Along the Road from Poland to Budapest

Told by Franz Molnar, Celebrated Hungarian Dramatist

The character sketch is from the pen of Franz Molnar, the celebrated Hungarian dramatist and correspondent in the field of the *Budapest Az Est* and the *Vienna Neue Freie Presse*. This war has been a war of anonymity. Its vastness has submerged individuals and individualities. It is the more interesting, therefore, to catch now and then some impression of personality and to find some figure standing out clearly and picturesquely from the mass. In Rittmeister Farkas, Molnar has drawn from life a character which epitomizes the romance of the war. This story is translated, and the introduction prepared by William L. McPherson in the *New York Tribune*.

I—STORY OF THE GUERILLA WARRIOR

ONE evening I notice in front of the General Staff Headquarters some General Staff officers in conversation with a little officer, two heads shorter than any of them. The little officer wears a dark hussar's jacket; his breast is covered with decorations, conspicuous among them being the Iron Cross. The diminutive but well set-up hussar is continually being embraced and patted affectionately on the back. He talks loudly and merrily. I hear that he has visited headquarters in the interest of one of his fellow hussars.

"You must stay here for supper!"

He stays. I sit opposite him and take a good look at him, for I have already heard much about him. The Army Corps Hoffmann is very proud of him; he is our guerilla leader, a legendary hussar type—Clemer Farkas de Also-Takach. Formerly he was Rittmeister of the 14th Hussars. Now he is commandant of the cavalry detachment of the army corps, the "Detachment Farkas." He has as many cavalrymen as an Oberst has in peace time. Therefore, his hussars call him "Herr Oberst Rittmeister." He has hussars, uhlans, dragoons, Ukranian volunteers—altogether a most daring collection of riders and fighters. Nearly all the cavalry regiments of the monarchy are represented in it. The organization is a good counterpart of the Hoffmann Army Corps, which has been constructed in a somewhat similar fashion.

The Rittmeister has a marked resemblance to a peppercorn. He is very small, very hard and very strong. A handshake with him is an athletic exercise. His glance is clear and open, like that of a ten-year-old boy. You can hear him laughing over the next hill. He cannot tell stories; nor will he. All that he told me was that his veterinary had saved the life of a little girl, taking twenty-three splinters of a Russian shell out of her body, and that thirty-six members of his family were in the field.

Rittmeister Farkas won his fame in Galicia. A Cossack sergeant rushed at him and tried to spit him with a lance. Farkas broke the lance under his armpit and then crushed the sergeant's head with the butt of a revolver. He gave the lance to the Heir Apparent. That was his first exploit. Then came his first "action." He is posted one day in Russian Poland with his hussars as support behind the artillery. A heavy Russian shell explodes in his neighborhood, and as it throws up the earth it uncovers a telephone wire. Farkas notices the wire, takes hold of it and follows it. The hussars dig up the ground over it and find that it leads to a farmhouse. They dig no further and conceal themselves.

Near the farmhouse is a well. Every few minutes a

Russian peasant comes to the well, works the draw pump and calls something down into the depths. They seize the peasant and he turns out to be a Russian soldier in disguise. Farkas takes his favorite sergeant, Galambos, and three hussars, gets a long, stout rope and slides, with his four men, down into the well.

A yard above the surface of the water he finds a stone shelving and under the shelving an opening, which leads into a dark tunnel. Now everything is cleared up. This region was once an artillery practice field; no wonder that it is so nicely fitted out. They push into the tunnel and come to a telephone cell, in which three Russians sit by candlelight before a modern field telephone. From there the Russian field artillery is directed according to the information shouted down the well.

Farkas throws his revolver away. One of the Russians, knife in hand, hurls himself upon him. Farkas seizes the wrist of the Russian and breaks it, for he is a master of jiu jitsu; he instructs his men constantly in Japanese ring methods. Two Russians are killed. The one with his wrist broken confesses that the telephone cell is a signal station and that the little detachment is a signal patrol. He also delivers to Farkas a textbook containing the A B C of more than 300 light signals. Light signals are given with lamp groups, which consist of two, five or eight lamps. They can send almost any kind of news.

Farkas clambers up out of the well and makes good use of the book. With his hussars he goes every night on the hunt for light signals. Whenever at night the combination of two, five or eight lamps is in use signal patrols are killed or captured. It is plain that the Russians, before the war, must have instructed 30,000 to 40,000 people for this service. Many of these people worked in peasant clothes behind our lines in Russian territory. Farkas hunted down these signal devices in farm houses, windmills, in the midst of swamps and in the tops of trees. With ten to fifteen hussars he soon made 140 of them useless. In this region the Russians lost all interest in signal giving. Farkas had many times done his work on horseback; oftener he had crawled on his stomach. To his comrades he said that he had at last got some profit out of the many pictures of daring adventure which he had seen in the kino shows.

II—TALES OF FARKAS—THE HUSSAR

The Herr Rittmeister has taken a pledge; while the war lasts he will not drink, gamble or hunt. Of these three hunting is his only real passion. He would hate to be a bad shot. In the wall of the Nyiregyhazy barracks he shot his monogram with a pistol: thus, C. F. They made him pay for the damage to the wall. Rittmeister Farkas is therefore the only man in the country who has ever, out of his own pocket, built part of a barracks.

Once from a local train, which was running through the hunting preserve of a friend, he saw a deer. He pulled the emergency signal, shot the deer and then said: "Now go ahead!" For that he was put under arrest in the barracks for thirty days. Now, however, every one of his bullets belongs to the Fatherland, and his iron will, his daring, his mobile spirit, his technical skill, his great, romantic heart, encased in his small steeled body, belong, all, all to the Fatherland.

The Rittmeister wept when he heard that the Russians stood before the Bereczke Pass. He did everything in his power to get to that threatened point. So he became attached to the Group Hofmann, which in the fall of 1914 drove the Russians out of Berog and Marmaros.

About Christmas time in 1914 he is fighting in the Carpathians. On December 19 he climbs, with his hussars, the Vehikzi Brh Mountain, 1,600 metres high, and at night descends with them, in snow up to the arm-pits, to Firelopfalva, on the other side. He leads the march and kills the Russian outposts. The Russians are driven out of the village, losing 150. He cannot bring away the Russian weapons, so he collects them in a pile and burns them.

The Russians, who know him well, send three battalions of infantry and four companies of Cossacks against him. Three days long, until December 22, he stands off, with a few hundred cavalrymen, all their attacks. Then he sends his people back, remaining the last one on the spot. He keeps a uhlan sergeant with him to hold off the Russians until his troop has crossed the mountains. The two hide behind a rock. Farkas takes up his Mannlicher, with a telescopic sight. Suddenly the sergeant receives a bullet in his calf. Farkas would gladly retire, but he cannot carry the sergeant with him and will not leave him in the lurch.

About 10 a. m. the Russians begin to climb in skirmish line up toward him. At 10 o'clock Farkas, from behind his rock, shoots down his first Russian; at 4 o'clock in the afternoon his sixty-seventh. Up to the neck in snow, without a bite to eat, he keeps all assailants at bay. At 5 o'clock it is pitch dark. Farkas goes away, returns in a sled and carries off the wounded sergeant.

The Germans he likes very well, and they like him. A German general said to him: "Explain to me, please, what the rôle of Hungary is in this war."

Rittmeister Farkas showed his outstretched hand.

"Excellency," he said, "if this war is a box on the ear which we are giving the enemy, then in this five-fingered box on the ear Hungary is not the least important finger."

He is assigned for six weeks to the German Guard and receives into his detachment some Prussian cavalry. Between Uzok and Bereczke he climbs with them over the mountains and holds for six days, with 500 cavalrymen, a line southeast of Turka against 5,000 Russians, with seven cannon and ten machine guns. His cavalry troops form on the hill surrounding the Russian position. Farkas stands in a church tower from which he can see the enemy. He has three small flags—a green one, a yellow one and a red one. When the Russians develop to the left he puts the green flag out of the tower window. Then the cavalrymen on the hills to the left fire. He waves the right wing flag and other troopers fire from the right. The Russians turn about and then the yellow flag is hoisted and the fire comes from a third direction. Thereupon the Russians intrench themselves in a half circle at the entrance of a narrow pass; for they believe the enemy menaces them from three directions. While Farkas plays his tricks with the Russians the Prussian Guard accomplishes its work.

Farkas may now retire. On the way he meets a German sergeant major with fifteen or twenty infantrymen. He halts them.

"Listen," says Farkas, "I have been here for six days covering the Prussians so that they could march quietly. Reciprocate, please, and cover my troops."

"Glad to do it," answers the German.

So he develops a line with his twenty men in order to hold the Russians back, while Farkas withdraws his troopers.

For this Turka exploit the latter gets the Iron Cross.

The commandant of the Prussian Guard, General Baron Marschall, says goodby to him in a personally written letter and calls him a "brilliant Hungarian hussar officer."

He has already three slight bullet wounds, the tuft has been shot away from his shako, his pistol holster has three bullet holes (I am almost embarrassed to write this down, for it sounds like a copy of a romance of Dumas), his Attila is pierced in three places. There are two holes in his breeches, his shako is split from the top by a sabre stroke and one of his spurs has been shot away. Otherwise, God be thanked, he is unharmed. I am not confident that the reader will believe all of this. But it is sufficient that several thousand men here know that it is true and that I also know that it is.

III—THE KNIGHT OF THE ARMORED TRAIN

Rittmeister Farkas is a little wonder of the war; he is so unique, original and incredible in his way that I had to examine many documents and official reports before I was absolutely convinced of the truth of the stories about him. In November, 1914, he receives from Peter Hoffmann, who loves him like his own son, a gift especially suited to his adventurous character—two armored trains. Then he is happy. Naturally he steams with both behind the enemy's front, lets one run through a tunnel and stop near its exit, so that nobody can attack it, and starts back with the other to a certain factory building in which a Russian regiment is quietly enjoying a mid-day meal. With his single cannon he shoots off the factory chimney, which falls into the crowd of diners below. The regiment is panic-stricken. Then the armored train fires with four machine guns into the regiment, plants seven shells in the officers' quarters and creates such a confusion among the Russians that they arrive at Bereczke a week later than they had planned to arrive. Then he returns the armored trains to His Excellency with thanks.

A little sadly he looks after them; for they were "as if made for him."

Meanwhile he constructs machine guns and creates a machine gun section and a section of mounted pioneers. Now his detachment has machine guns and pioneers. He looks out for all technical details and understands them all.

"In geography I know nothing," he says; "I know only thirty kilometres in front of my nose, but I know those kilometres well."

His pride is that he has never eaten before his men have. Once, however, he ate nothing after his men had eaten. On the crest of the Carpathians the Russians shot one of his horses. He let the cook make goulash out of it for the men, but he ate none of it. "Not because I couldn't stomach it, but because I loved the horse when he was alive." He preferred to remain hungry.

I talked with his troopers. They never speak his name without standing at attention. Out of curiosity I ask:

"Why are you so fond of him?"

They look at me and smile embarrassedly—old Landsturm men, with big mustaches, fathers with many children.

"We are everlastingly fond of him."

At last one of them gives this explanation:

"He leads the fight well."

So I learn that once in the Carpathians, when everything came to a standstill because the Russians delivered a terrible fire and there was no cover, he lay on the ground before them and cried:

"Here I am—as cover for you. Lie on your stomachs and fire from behind me!"

Complaints, which I sometimes hear, are directed not against him, but against his business management. At the first he paid twenty-nine kronen for each Cossack captured and five kronen for each Russian infantryman. The troopers, whom he has led in almost 200 fights and skirmishes, brought the Russians in so eagerly that prices fell—and fell very sharply. A Cossack went down to four kronen and an infantryman down to one kronen. Not because the Cossack is worth four times as much, but because he has a horse.

To-day, at noon, Rittmeister Farkas left us. God knows when I shall see him again. Tiny, clever, good-hearted, brave Rittmeister Farkas, mathematician, marksman, bridge builder, locomotive driver in one person, doctor, chaplain, letter writer and brilliant commandant of lonely, middle-aged soldiers, daring Herr Oberst-Rittmeister Farkas—a little red hussar's cap which becomes smaller and smaller in the dust of the road—you give me so many things to think about that at night I can hardly go to sleep.

Who is able to explain these men to those for whom they have been fighting for more than a year?

OUR ESCAPE FROM GERMAN SOUTH-WEST AFRICA

Told by Corporal H. J. McElnea, late of the Imperial Light Horse, South Africa, and set down by J. Christie

An echo of General Botha's brilliant campaign in German South-West Africa. Captured by the Germans during a skirmish, the author gleaned some information concerning the intentions of the enemy. Night and day he schemed to get away in order to give his superiors the news. Finally, with three companions, he essayed the task of escaping from the military prison at Franzfontein and making his way for over two hundred and fifty miles through a terrible region of uninhabited mountains and desert to Swakopmund, where the British forces were in occupation. Lack of food and water, suffering of body and mind, blistering heat and extreme cold—the author experienced them all during his nightmare journey, which he related in the *Wide World Magazine*.

I—STORY OF THE IMPERIAL LIGHT HORSE

MY SQUADRON of the Imperial Light Horse, which had been operating for several months with Luderitzbucht, German South-West Africa, as a base, finally left on 13th December, 1914, with the Natal Carabiniers and two machine-guns. We went to Rooikop, where we camped for the night, and the following morning marched on to our advance camp at railhead. Here we found some infantry and mounted men belonging to the Kaffarian Rifles and Nesbitt's Horse. The force marched out from railhead at sundown, trekked all night, and arrived at Tchukaib at two o'clock in the morning. About half-past seven in the evening of the same day, after having watered our horses, we marched out, having left all spare kit, greatcoats, mess-tins, and so on, in camp. We travelled until about one o'clock in the morning, when we off-saddled, linked horses, and lay down to rest. In about two hours' time we got orders to up-saddle and move on. Strict orders were given not to strike matches, or make any unnecessary noise. We arrived within sight of Garub Station just before daylight on December 16th, 1914, and halted behind some kopjes for about half an hour or so.

During this halt most of us discarded our tunics and strapped them on our saddles. We then marched on, keeping to the north of the railway line, until about a mile beyond the railway station, where we passed the pumping-station, which had been completely destroyed by the enemy.

My troop (No. 2, D Squadron, Imperial Light Horse) now got orders to trot up in front of the column. We crossed the railway line and proceeded back towards the station, on the south of the line.

We were next instructed to march towards the kopjes to the southeast, and my section was sent in front, scouting. I rode on about six or seven hundred yards in front of the troop, and then I noticed some other men being sent forward, so I took the right flank with my section. We now crossed three sand-dunes. In crossing the third I noticed some fresh spoor, which indicated that the enemy had passed shortly before towards the kopjes in front. Just as we neared the top of the fourth dune a single shot rang out, and almost immediately after the Germans opened a murderous enfilading fire from rifles and machine-guns. I gave orders to my section to retire, and we galloped towards our troop, but had only covered about a hundred yards or so when my horse got hit and I fell heavily on my head.

How long I remained senseless I am unable to say,

but when I regained consciousness I found I was not alone. Trooper Joyner, belonging to my section, lay about five yards from me, and nearer the enemy. I asked him if he was hit, but got no reply. I tried to raise myself, but felt a severe pain across the small of my back. My first thought was that I had been hit there, and I put my hand round, but could discover no indication of a wound. I then dragged myself forward towards Joyner, but when I got alongside him I saw that he was dying and quite beyond human aid. I decided the best thing to do was to get hold of my rifle, which was lying about seven yards to my rear.

Having secured the rifle, I banked up some sand with my hands and made a small sangar, behind which I took up my position. All this time heavy firing was going on, and bullets were continually dropping in the sand all around me. Our men had now got a Maxim in position immediately behind where I was lying, and there seemed to be a duel going on over my head between it and one of the enemy's machine-guns.

The Germans were very well concealed, and I could see little to shoot at, but I had an occasional "pot" at anything I thought was moving on the kopje. I afterwards found out that there were about two hundred Germans, some of whom were on the top of the sand-dune, which was only two hundred and fifty yards away. Some of the enemy must have seen me from their position, for presently I got a bullet right through my hat, which made me sit pretty tight. Needless to say I promptly removed the injured headgear and put it beside me.

The firing continued for nearly three hours, during which time I did not know what was happening, as I could not see our men. I then heard a loud cheer from the direction of the enemy's trenches, and soon afterwards the fire seemed to die away, and I could distinctly hear voices in front. Next I saw five men galloping towards me from my right flank. At first I thought they were my own men, but as they came closer I discovered they were the enemy. I then realized, for the first time, that our fellows had retired, and that I was surrounded.

I lay where I was until the Germans came up to me, and they proceeded to disarm me by taking away my rifle, bayonet, and bandoleer, which they examined carefully for dum-dum bullets. They also took my haversack, which contained my rations, and my field-glasses. Two of them then assisted me towards the station, where I found a large number of the enemy off-saddled. These men were reinforcements from Aus, and it was their arrival that had caused our force to retire. They numbered about a thousand, with two Maxim guns. As I approached the station a German officer came riding past. He pulled up his horse and frowned at me. "You are Imperial Light Horse, D Squadron," he growled. "You were at Kolmaaskop. You —— dog!" Then he rode on.

II—ON A PRISON TRAIN IN SOUTH AFRICA

I was now taken to a room at the back of the station, where there were a number of German officers and a German doctor sitting around smoking and laughing, apparently well pleased at having driven the British back. The doctor examined my back, and told me I was not seriously hurt, but that the muscles were strained. I remained in this room, under a guard, for several hours. All this time the enemy appeared to be blowing up the railway in the direction of Tchukaib, as I could hear the explosions. Presently one of the German officers came in and gave me some bread and water.

He could speak English, and was apparently seeking information, as he asked me how many men had come to Garub that morning, which question I refused to answer. After several further attempt to get information about our troops, and finding it useless, he left me. Towards evening I was taken from the station to a train which had arrived from Aus. On the way I was jeered at by several German soldiers. One, I remember, asked, "Well, how do you like the German-West, old chappie?" When I arrived at the train I found that I was not the only prisoner, as there was a Carabinier standing there under escort. Immediately I saw him I beckoned him to one side and told him, as I was an older soldier than he, that either that evening or the following morning we should be taken in front of the German intelligence officer, and that he was to be very careful what he said. This Carabinier was Trooper Martins, who was sent with a despatch to General McKenzie from his officer commanding. When within about two hundred yards of the kopje where he expected to find the general the enemy opened fire on him. He turned and galloped off, but his horse was shot before he had gone far, and he was unable to get away. Some Germans came down and took him up to their trenches. This man and I were close companions right up to the night of my escape.

We were now placed in a truck which contained two horses and a native, and two armed guards got in with us. After waiting for a couple of hours the train proceeded to Aus, where we arrived after dark. Here we were marched straight to the German guard-room. The guards placed us in a dark cell, measuring about ten feet by five, with a wooden bench to sleep on. The cell had small portholes for windows, and a heavy door, which was locked and barred. A sentry remained on guard all night.

Next morning one of the guards brought us some breakfast, which consisted of black coffee without sugar, some black bread, and a little fat. After we had eaten this food we were taken from the cell, and brought to a building where there seemed to be much military activity. My mate was taken inside a room, and I was sent away to the rear of the place with my guard. While I was waiting several German soldiers came out, and some of them asked me various questions.

After waiting for about an hour and a half the Carabinier was brought out, and I was taken inside. Here I found a German officer who could speak most perfect English. He sat with large rolls of paper in front of him, and started off by asking me my name, where I had come from, what my nationality was, my religion, and how long I had been in South Africa. I then told him that I had no objection to answering questions concerning myself or my people, but he must not ask me anything about the force I belonged to. He then reminded me curtly that I was a prisoner of war.

"Yes, I *am* a prisoner of war," I said, "and I expect to be treated as such." I added that, a short time previously, I had been one of a party who captured some Germans, including an officer, and I did not think our O.C. brought any undue pressure to bear on them. This seemed to cool the German down a bit, and he actually started to give *me* information—of a sort. He asked me if I knew that there were twenty-five thousand rebels in the Orange Free State under De Wet and Beyers, also if I was aware there was a rebellion in Egypt and India, and that numbers of our Dreadnoughts had been sunk by the German fleet? Fortunately I knew that all this was false, so I was not dispirited. He next proceeded to ask me questions concerning the forces, which, of course, I refused to answer. Finally, with my mate, I was sent back to the cell.

Here we were given some food, which consisted of boiled meat and greasy water, intended for soup. When we asked for knives and forks the guard said we could not have any, "as there was a danger sometimes of prisoners committing suicide." I happened to have a penknife, which I had managed to conceal from my guards the previous day when asked to turn out my pockets, and so we managed somehow.

My mate told me that he had been given to understand that if he would go back to his regiment and try to induce the Boers to go over to the Germans he could have his freedom. This he refused to do.

The morning following, after breakfast, we were allowed to use water to wash ourselves. Later on in the day we were taken separately in front of the German commandant at Aus, and questioned once more. I informed the commandant through the officer interpreter that I had nothing to add to what I had said the previous day. After several vain attempts to obtain information we were sent back to our cell, where we remained until the following day, when we were taken by a guard and put on the train in a cattle-truck going east.

All the way along the line, wherever the train stopped, German soldiers and women came and stared in at us. One soldier remarked amiably that it would have been better for us if we had been drowned before landing in that country.

We arrived at Keetmanshoop at about 9 p.m., and were met by a fresh guard, who took us to a military barracks. Here we were given some food and blankets, and obliged to sleep in a little room with a light burning all night. A German officer visited us through the night. During the time we were in Keetmanshoop several of the soldiers became very friendly, and some of them were inclined to talk a lot. From one of them we learnt what I considered to be very important information, of most vital interest to our forces, and that night I could not sleep, puzzling my brains as to the best way of getting this news to them. The following morning I suggested to my mate that if they made him the same offer as they did at Aus he had better accept it, so that he could carry this information. I also told him to tell the Germans they could hold me responsible for any breach of faith on his part. The offer, however, was not renewed. We remained at Keetmanshoop until December 24th, and were then taken under a strong guard to the railway station, and placed in the train going north.

While here we were joined by five other prisoners, one of whom had been in a hospital suffering from a wound. The other four were Dutchmen living in German South-West who had been arrested because they refused to fight for the Germans.

We arrived at Marintal about sundown, and here the train remained for the night. We were allowed to get out of the carriages and sleep on the ground, alongside the railway line. The following morning one of our guards "stood" us coffee in the hotel, as it was Christmas morning—a decidedly merry Christmas for us!

III—BEHIND THE BARS IN WINDHUK PRISON

Finally, after a tedious journey, we reached Windhuk, where we were taken straight to the jail, and all seven of us placed in a small cell. Immediately after entering it we heard voices calling us in English from surrounding cells, and, looking through the bars of the windows, we saw many anxious faces. All the men were shouting to us to know where we came from, what regiment we belonged to, and if we could give them any news how the war was going.

During our stay in Windhuk prison we were rather badly treated, not being allowed out of the cell for more than ten or fifteen minutes, morning and evening, and never allowed to communicate with the other prisoners. On the sly, when the warders were not watching us, we sometimes managed to get a few words with them through the windows, but that was all.

About a day or two after Christmas, while I was looking through the bars of my cell window into the jail yard, one of the political prisoners—a British subject taken in German South-West after the war broke out—whispered to me that there was great excitement amongst the Germans down town owing to the receipt of news that a British force had landed at Walfish Bay and had occupied Swakopmund. I might here explain that the political prisoner referred to enjoyed the privilege of going down town under escort for the purpose of making purchases for those prisoners who were fortunate enough to have money or banking accounts. His information was very useful to me, as this was how I first discovered our forces were at the northern German seaport.

The prison food here was very bad. It consisted of a quarter-loaf of bread (to last all day), a cup of black coffee in the morning, without sugar, and the same in the evening. At midday we got an enamel basin with some dirty-looking meat and mealie soup, and sometimes a little rice or macaroni. We were given to understand that this was the same food as the Kafir convicts got. There were from thirty to forty Britishers in the prison, mostly "politicals"—British subjects taken in German South-West Africa after the war broke out, the balance being soldiers belonging principally to the Union Defence Force. There was also in this prison a captain of the Royal Fusiliers named Limfrey, who had been on a shooting trip in the country, and who was arrested by the Germans as a spy. Not being able to prove anything against him, however, they kept him as a prisoner of war.

On January 8th we were taken from the prison with fourteen other prisoners, making seventeeen in all (the four Dutchmen being left behind), and marched through Windhuk to another prison at the military barracks, where we remained for the night. The following morning we were given some kit, consisting of a shirt, blanket, mess tin, knife, fork, spoon, and towel, and then taken to the railway station, where there were a large number of people congregated to look at us.

From Windhuk we went to Karabib and Okanyande, and were then told to prepare for yet another journey.

On the day following—January 16th—all the soldier prisoners, forty-seven in all, including six officers, left in four ox-wagons for Franzfontein. We travelled by night, and slept by day. Water was very scarce *en route*, and was obtainable only from boreholes on the farms, which were few and far between.

The escort consisted of German soldiers on each wagon; also a mounted party under the charge of an officer.

We arrived at Outju, a large and important military post, on January 19th. Here we found nearly all of the officers of the Union Forces who were prisoners. We remained for a couple of hours, and I had the opportunity of speaking to several of them, and amongst them Captain Turner Jones. With him I discussed the possibility of the information which I had gleaned at Keetmanshoop being conveyed to our forces, but he told me that he did not think there was the least chance of anybody getting away. However, I gave him the information in case anybody managed it. We then proceeded on our journey, having left the six officers behind and taken up three men.

IV—UNDER A GUARD OF HOTTENTOTS

We arrived at our destination on the morning of the 24th. Franzfontein is a military post of some importance, in direct telegraphic and telephonic communication with Windhuk and about a hundred and fifty miles from the railway. On arrival here we were told off in messes of ten, one man being in charge of each mess. We were then marched into the barbed-wire enclosure, where we found two hundred and ninety-three other prisoners. They had all been there for about four months, and represented eighteen different regiments.

The first thing we did on arrival in the camp was to rig up a "bivvy" for shelter from the blazing sun, and to sleep in at night. This was done by fastening a blanket and waterproof sheet together, and with two sticks, and stones for anchors, we made a little tent large enough for two people. Cadman, of the S.A. Mounted Rifles, and myself were the inmates of our particular "bivvy." Martins and Lawford, our other mates, slept under a tree alongside. We then fixed up a fireplace. Most of the men had already built little ovens, so we were soon as comfortable as circumstances would permit.

The enclosure was of a triangular shape, about a quarter-acre in extent, and had a stream of water running right through from fence to fence. Outside the barbed wire there was a thick thorn-bush hedge built up to form a sort of stockade. We were obliged to parade each morning at 6 a.m., afternoon at four, and every evening at six, when the man in charge of each mess reported if his ten men were on parade. This report was conveyed through the sergeant-major to the German officer who was always present. Rations were drawn each morning by the men in charge of every mess. The only amusement in camp was bathing in a pool which the prisoners had constructed by widening the stream, with an occasional open-air concert at night-time, which always concluded with the National Anthem and "Rule Britannia," everyone present standing to attention. At the base of the triangle was the guard-house, which was fitted with a large alarm-bell. Two soldiers were always on sentry outside the triangle, night and day.

The garrison consisted of twenty-five to thirty soldiers, and a number of Hottentots. The Germans were also reputed to have several bloodhounds, and special native trackers. I also heard that they had a Maxim gun in the barracks.

From the time we left Keetmanshoop until we arrived at Franzfontein my sole thought was the best way of escape, and I discussed this matter with several men on the journey. My first idea was to go north towards Portuguese territory, through Ovamboland; but I found I should have to travel through a fever-stricken country inhabited by hostile natives. Immediately on my arrival at Franzfontein, one of the first things I noticed—which appeared to me to be rather extraordinary—was that most of the men appeared to be in possession of water-bottles. I could not understand why the Germans had not taken these away.

Soon after our arrival in camp I received a message from Dr. Dawson—a prisoner who acted as medical officer to the prisoners—stating that he would like to see me. I found him in a rather dilapidated house close to the base of the triangle. He told me that he had heard that I had been caught on the Luderitzbucht side recently, and wanted to know all the recent news.

After having talked with him for some time, I came to the conclusion that I was speaking to a man who could be a good friend, and whom I could trust, so I asked him what he thought of the chances of escaping. He told me that several men had been discussing it, but he was afraid it was hopeless, as he considered it a physical impossibility for anyone to carry sufficient water to maintain a human being during the time it would take to reach Swakopmund, the nearest point occupied by our forces.

Life in the camp during the next few days was very monotonous, and food appeared to be daily getting getting scarcer. They gave us flour, which we mixed with our mealie meal porridge to make it "pan out," as we found making bread not at all economical. Sometimes the meat was very bad, and once or twice the doctor ordered us not to eat it. We received firewood every evening, and of this there was no scarcity, on account of the surrounding country being composed of thick bush.

All the time the problem of escape worried me.

V—THE NIGHT ESCAPE IN THE STORM

On February 3rd, about 2 p.m., I met Dunbar, of the Transvaal Horse Artillery, and asked him if he could introduce me to any man in camp who knew the road to Swakopmund. He told me that nobody had ever been in that part of the country before, so that no one knew the road. About an hour later he informed me the doctor wished to speak to me. On entering the room where Dr. Dawson was, he told me to close the door and sit down. Looking out of the window, to make sure that there were no German soldiers about, he said, "I am informed that you are anxious to escape. Why is that?"

I told him I possessed what I considered to be valuable military information, which I was anxious to communicate to the authorities. He then asked me if I had thought of the difficulty of reaching Swakopmund across something like two hundred and fifty miles of mountainous desert country. I replied that I had seen a map, had a fair idea of the distance, and was prepared to take my chance. Dr. Dawson next inquired if I thought I was strong enough to stand the journey, as it could not possibly be done in less than seven days, and anyone attempting the task would have to carry at least four water-bottles and two water-bags.

"If you are going to escape," he added, "it must be to-night, between eight and nine o'clock. There are three other men going at that time, and you can join them."

He inquired what preparations I had made with regard to food and water on the road, and I told him none.

"I can supply flour to make fat cookies," he said, "but you will have to see to the water-bottles and water-bags yourself."

Then, in confidence, I told the doctor what I had heard at Keetmanshoop, and he agreed with me that the news was most important, and that I must go at all costs.

Soon afterwards the doctor sent for the other men who were to be my companions in the attempt to escape. They were Sergeant Mackenzie, of the Upington commando, a Scotchman; Trooper Maritz, of the South African Mounted Rifles, a Boer; and Trooper Franzen, of the Veteran Signalling Corps, a Norwegian. When they entered the room he formally introduced me to them, and told them that I wanted to accompany them on the journey. After having discussed our plans for getting away from the camp, and the route we were to take, we parted, having arranged to meet again at 8.30 p.m. under a specified tree close to the fence. Needless to say, I was very excited, but I started to collect water-bottles and bags, and by 7 p.m. had everything prepared for the journey. One of my messmates, Trooper Cadman, kindly gave me his boots, as he thought they were in better condition than my own for our long desert trek. Another, Trooper Martins, gave me his socks, water-bottle, and water-bags. Trooper Lawford gave me his haversack and tunic. The tunic I was not inclined to accept, as it was the only one he had, but the generous fellow pressed me to take it. Trooper Dunbar, of the Transvaal Horse Artillery, gave me his belt, containing a pair of wire-cutters, which he had concealed from the Germans. These were the only cutters in the camp, all others being taken away.

At about 8 p.m. I said good-bye to my own messmates, all of whom wished me the best of luck, and requested me to communicate with their relatives if I was fortunate enough to get through.

I then made my way to the appointed spot, where I met the other three men, also the doctor and a few of our comrades who were "in the know." Here I received fifteen or sixteen "fat cookies," which I placed in my haversack, together with a half-bottle of rum. The doctor had previously given us a small compass, and each of us had a "first field dressing" in case of wounds, also some boracic powder and a tin of ointment, which we found very useful on the journey.

And now came the business of the escape. One man was placed at the point of the triangle, as shown in the sketch, and another at the base, to signal to us when all was clear. The signal arranged was the striking of matches. All four of us, after having shaken hands with our benefactor, the doctor, crept down alongside the fence. It was very dark, and there was a slight drizzle of rain. The other prisoners in camp were attending a concert which had been arranged by the doctor to avert suspicion. As we lay there, waiting breathlessly for the signal, we could hear the two German sentries talking outside the fence, only some ten yards away from where we lay. We had to remain motionless for about half an hour, and needless to say the suspense was very great. At last, however, the sentries moved, going in opposite directions around the triangle, and soon afterwards we saw the eagerly-awaited signal. Franzen, one of my three companions, immediately got out underneath the wire and through the bush on the outside. The dogs at the farmhouse about a hundred yards away promptly commenced to bark, and we had to remain where we were for about ten minutes, dreading discovery all the time. Maritz, another of my companions, then followed Franzen; Mackenzie went next, and I followed. Getting underneath the fence was a rather difficult task, as we had to lie flat on our bodies and drag ourselves through, each hand being fully occupied holding a water-bag. When I got outside the fence I rearranged the bushes to cover the gap we had made, and then made tracks in the direction of a large tree some fifty yards from the fence, going from here to an old kraal wall where we had arranged to meet. On arrival there, I found that I had lost one of my precious water-bottles and the half-bottle of rum in getting through the fence, but we decided we must go on without them.

"Well, this is the first part of the business finished," said someone, and then, shaking hands, we set out.

VI—FLEEING ACROSS THE AFRICAN WILDS

We travelled all night over flat country covered with thick thorn-bush, going in a southwesterly direction until 6 a.m. the following morning, when we rested for an hour. Then we pushed on again; we wished to put as great a distance as possible between us and the camp, as we thought there was a danger of the Germans finding the missing water-bottles and the half-bottle of rum at daylight. Even if they did, however, we knew the native trackers would have a difficulty in picking up our "spoor," as it had been raining during the night, and the rain would have obliterated our footprints.

About noon we saw a herd of whitish animals, like mules, which I understood were quagga. We also saw several herds of zebra. We halted again at 1 p.m., rested for another hour, and then walked on until 9 p.m. The country here was hilly, with patches of thorn-bush, and the veldt offered fair going. We rested until 11 p.m., walked on until three next morning (February 5th) and rested until five. From 5 a.m. we walked all day over sandy, flat country covered with thick bush. Here I got separated from the others for about two hours, but was in no danger, as I carried the compass at this time. I afterwards saw my companions about a mile away, and we exchanged signals and soon came together again. I then handed the compass back to Franzen, and between him and Mackenzie it was carried for the remainder of the journey.

About 7 p.m. we got some water to drink from crevices in the rocks, by sucking it up. It was a laborious business, but we wanted to conserve our scanty supply as much as possible. This was about 9 p.m. Soon after dark it commenced to rain very hard, and we got wet through, having no shelter and all being in shirt-sleeves (I had discarded the tunic given me by Trooper Lawford and buried it in the sand the previous day). We moved on again at midnight, but were only able to proceed slowly as it was still pitch dark, and the ground very rocky. However, we struggled along until 4 a.m.

We started off again at daybreak, feeling frightfully cold and miserable, our clothes being soaked through. We managed to fill four water-bags from pools in the rocks, crossed a sand flat, and halted about noon at a small kopje in the middle of it. While resting there we saw a Klip Kafir coming from a north-westerly direction. He passed without seeing us, and returned at about 3 p.m. with a companion. We had to remain hidden until 5 p.m., owing to the proximity of these natives, as they would have been dangerous to us. They are quite uncivilized and wild, use poisoned arrows, and are generally shot by the Germans at sight. They had four dogs with them, and we were lucky the animals did not scent us.

We were obliged to sit tight for some time after these savages passed, as they disappeared down an old river-bed, and we were not sure whether they had remained there watching us or not. However, luckily for us, it was the last we saw of them, so at about 5 p.m. we resumed our journey, and continued walking until 7 a.m. the following morning (Saturday, February 6th). During the night we suddenly came upon a few native huts at the bottom of a cliff, close to an old river-bed, but we passed as quickly as possible and none of the inmates appeared to have heard us. Probably these huts belonged to the natives we had seen earlier in the day.

We had now arrived at the "Blue Mountains," which we could see so plainly from our prison camp at Franzfontein. We were obliged to keep to the north of this range, as we looked upon it as being one of our "danger-points." We had heard that the enemy had a signalling-post on the highest peak, which communicated with Omarura. Since then I have been informed that they not only had a signalling-post, but a whole company stationed on top of these mountains, so our luck was again "in."

Having rested from 7 to 11 a.m. we moved on once more. The country now became very broken and hard to walk over. Deep kloofs and huge boulders were much in evidence, and we had to do a lot of climbing. To make matters worse, my boots were giving way fast, and had it not been for the wirecutters given to me by Dunbar, I don't know what I should have done, as with them I managed to pull out the nails and repair the boots with a piece of wire I had in my pocket. My feet were now getting very sore, and the climbing began to tell, for each hill seemed to be steeper and higher than the previous one, and the ground got steadily worse and worse.

About 2 p.m. we suddenly came on some running water, which gave us great encouragement, as we thought it was the Omarura River, and we rested here for an hour. Our "fat cookies" were now running low, and we only dared eat half of one for each meal, when we could easily have demolished six or seven and still felt hungry. At 3 p.m. we resumed our journey for about two hours, but as we found the stream was bearing too much to the north-west we reluctantly decided to leave it. Filling up our water-bottles and sacks, and taking a good drink, we again struck off in a south-westerly course across a high mountain. The stream we had just left might only exist for a day, being caused by the recent rains in the mountains. It was the first running water I saw in German South-West, with the exception of the small stream at Franzfontein.

We continued walking until 7 p.m. and then waited for the moon to rise.

It made its appearance at 11 p.m. and we again resumed our wearisome tramp and continued marching until 5 a.m., passing through a broken, hilly region. We rested for about half an hour, and then "trekked" on once more, continuing the whole day until 6 p.m. over frightful country. I thought we should never come to the end of these terrible mountains, and my poor feet were not improving. We rested from 6 till 10 p.m. and moved on again till 1 a.m., when we halted for three hours, all of us feeeling very tired and exhausted. This was Tuesday, February 9th. We started again at 4 a.m., got out of the hills about 7 a.m., and continued walking over fairly flat country until 11 a.m., when we were obliged to halt and rest, as the heat was unbearable. At 3 p.m. we "trekked" on. Our troubles seemed to be on the increase, for presently my boots gave out altogether. One of my comrades, Maritz, manufactured a pair of sandals for himself from my leggings, using his sheath knife, and gave me his own *veldt schoons**. His feet were in good hard condition, as he had been going without boots for some considerable time. The *veldt schoons* he made himself whilst a prisoner, from raw hide, and I found them very useful, although a little on the

---

*I should like here to put on record my admiration for my three companions. No man ever had better "mates." Had it not been for Maritz's noble act in giving me his own shoes I could not possibly have reached the sea; it was a splendid piece of self-sacrifice. Mackenzie was our leader. His optimism and cheeriness kept heart in us all through that weary trek, and all three of them showed the utmost good-fellowship and pluck.—H. J. McElnea.

small side. I was obliged to cut a piece off the toe of each, which afterwards handicapped me, as the sand worked in and made blisters on my feet. I used the pugaree from my hat and the bandages from my "first field dressing" to prevent this, but with very little benefit.

We continued walking until 9 a.m., when we halted for two hours. Our food was now running out. I had one "fat cookie" and Mackenzie had a half of one. I shared mine between Franzen, Maritz, and myself. The two men at first seemed reluctant to accept their portion, but I insisted on it, saying that we might just as well all die together. At 11 p.m. we again resumed our interminable journey, and walked on till 3 a.m., when we rested for one hour, and continued until daybreak. We could now distinctly hear the roar of the sea, and also see the fog along the coast. This gave us great encouragement, and we went ahead with renewed energy. About 10.30 a.m. we struck some wheel-tracks leading south-west, which we decided to follow. This was Wednesday, February 10th.

VII—LEFT BEHIND TO DIE IN THE DESERT

I now found it very difficult to keep up with the others, owing to my feet being so bad. The heat was terrific, and, to make matters worse, our precious water was almost finished. Early in the afternoon I found that I was unable to continue at the same pace as the rest, so I told them to go on. I would follow as best I could, I said, and if they reached Swakopmund they could send back assistance. My own idea was that it was better for one man to die than all four, as the others could not be of any assistance to me by remaining. As they moved on Franzen waved a cheery good-bye. "We will wait for you at Swakopmund," he shouted. I now took off my *veldt schoons* to attend to my blistered feet, and remained for a few hours resting until it got a bit cooler. I divested myself of all superfluous articles, left two of my water-bottles and the wirecutters behind, and walked on alone. By this time I could distinctly see the waves beating upon the shore and soon afterwards reached the beach, where I followed the coastline south.

Towards evening I sighted some buildings, which I thought were the outskirts of Swakopmund. This gave me great encouragement, so I continued as fast as circumstances would permit, and reached the buildings after dark. To my disappointment I found only several broken-down shanties, without any signs of life. I afterwards discovered that this was a sealing station, and the name of the spot Cape Cross. The buildings had been destroyed by the Germans, and the people who worked there, being mostly British, were taken prisoners. Cape Cross is ninety miles from Swakopmund, and had I known this fact then I should probably have thrown up the sponge. My only thoughts at the time were of our own pickets, whom I feared might shoot me. Several times I fancied I heard the challenge, "Halt! Who goes there?" to which I replied "Friend!" in a loud voice; but each time the only answer I received was the mocking echo of my own voice. Presently I noticed a tramline, which I followed for a mile or two, when suddenly I heard a peculiar noise, resembling pigs grunting and lambs bleating. I went in the direction of these animals, as I supposed, and suddenly found myself right in the thick of a herd of seals, some of them much bigger than myself, who started jumping all around me. I "cleared" for all I was worth, as I had nothing to protect myself with. This must have been about 11 p.m., and soon afterwards it began to rain heavily, so I dug a hole behind a mound to protect myself from the piercing wind. It was bitterly cold, and I was soaked to the skin in a very short space of time. My bags were empty, and here were tons of life-giving water going to waste, so I devised a plan to catch some of the precious liquid, by cutting the side and top seams of my water-bags, spreading them out on the sand, and then making an impression in the centre which formed a cup-shape. When the rain ceased I got out of my burrow, and had a good drink of the water which my sack had caught. This was the last fresh water I had until the following Saturday afternoon.

Feeling miserably cold and weak, I moved stiffly on through the darkness. At daybreak, to my concern, I found that I was nearly surrounded by the sea, but the water on my left was not very deep. Here I saw thousands of pelicans and other birds, so I looked for eggs, but could not find any. Taking off my *schoons,* socks, and riding pants, I waded across the water to dry land. Here I noticed a few wagon tracks going north and south, so I decided to follow them, wherever they led. After wandering along for some hours I saw some rocky ground on my left and went towards it in search of fresh water. I found a little in the crevices in the rocks, but unfortunately it was brackish. However, I filled my remaining water-bottles, as it was better than nothing, and continued on my journey along the sea coast until the heat became unbearable. I then halted and took off my shirt, and with the assistance of some large whale-bones, with which the beach was strewn, and the remains of an old deck-chair which had been washed up on the shore, I rigged up a shade and remained under it until it got cool, when I again moved on. This time I walked until it got quite dark, when I dug a hole in the sand behind a mound and got into it. By this time my hopes of reaching Swakopmund had almost completely vanished, and

I wondered if I should ever wake again. I felt quite indifferent to my fate; in fact, as I scooped out the hole, the thought occurred to me that I was digging my own grave. After getting into it I saw two wolves, or wild dogs—I don't know which—but they only looked at me and trotted off. If they had attacked me I should have fallen an easy victim.

I slept well that night, and did not awake until daybreak, when I again got on the move. Several times during the day I must have been quite delirious, for once I found myself sitting on a rock cleaning out the salty sand from a hole, so that when it rained again the water there would not be salty, and some poor traveller might get a drink! About noon I crossed a riverbed, and found some more water, which was also brackish. Later on I crossed yet another channel, which, I understand, was the Amuroro River. There was a little vegetation here, but no water. However, I found a large wild-fig tree laden with green figs, so I thought I was in clover; but to my dismay found the inside of them perfectly dry, and full of insects. I did manage to eat some of the outside peel; then I lay down under the tree and slept for a couple of hours. When I awoke I found four arrows quite close to me, and tied them together with a piece of calico. Looking around the tree, I found four more. They were all cleverly made, with feathers at the end, and I took them with me and moved on.

I have no recollection of what happened during the night of that day, but I must have been wandering on all the time. The following day I saw a mountain away on my left, so I thought of going towards it, as there might be a chance of getting water. I went about a mile, but finally decided it was no good going any farther. I then commenced turning up all the stones I could find, so that if it rained I might catch a little water to drink.

The fluid in my bottles was now getting putrid. I had been taking a mouthful at a time, not allowing any to get down my throat, as I feared that if I swallowed the awful stuff it would drive me mad. I was now asking myself which was the best and easiest way of putting an end to my misery; I had no hope of getting out alive.

I believe if it had not been for the valuable information which I possessed, and which first prompted me to attempt to escape, I should have committed suicide, but a reluctance to let my news die with me kept me going. I now seemed to be having recurrent spasms of delirium, for once I remember suddenly coming to my senses and finding I was laughing. I imagined then my end was pretty near. It did not seem to worry me; in fact, I felt a sort of happy feeling, and thought to myself, "Well, I am going to meet my old friends who are dead."

VIII—DIGGING MY OWN GRAVE— THE REUNION

I tied my water-sack to a piece of the deck-chair which I had been using for a walking-stick, to represent a flag, and propped it up in the hope that it might be seen by some passing ship or a patrol. It would also mark the place where my body would be found. I then lay down and went to sleep for a couple of hours. Soon after I awoke I noticed three figures walking along the beach, about half a mile from me. I stood up and signalled to them, and they stopped, looked towards me, and then moved on.

"Whoever you are," I thought, "I am going to follow you." So I picked up my flag, arrows, and water-bottles —I must have looked a regular Robinson Crusoe—and went towards them. They sat down and waited for me. When I got up to them I thought they were natives, as they appeared to be black, and it was only after Mackenzie spoke that I recognized his voice, and knew that they were my own mates, whom I had lost three days previously.

"Good heavens, Pat!" cried Mackenzie. "How have you lived? Where did you get water?"

By way of reply I handed him my water-bottles. He took the cork out of one, smelt it, and threw both away; they smelt horrible. He then gave me some water, and I may say that I never tasted anything so sweet in my life before. I only took a little at a time, but each mouthful seemed to give me fresh life, and my tongue, which was swollen, got back to its normal size, and the horrid dry feeling in my throat went away. We remained here about an hour, during which time my mates and I compared notes as to what had happened since we parted on the Wednesday.

It was now February 13th, and a Saturday afternoon. They told me that on arrival at the sealing station, the evening we separated, they turned into a house and fixed up a lamp with some seal oil which they found. They left the lamp burning at the window so that I could see it, and being very tired, all of them went to sleep. The lamp, however, must have gone out. In the morning, finding that I had not turned up, Franzen and Maritz went back to see if they could find me. In the meantime Mackenzie hunted for shellfish among the rocks, and managed to find enough for two meals. There was a plentiful supply of water, as the previous night's rain had half-filled several old tanks. After going back a few miles Maritz and Franzen found the lid of a small tin box which they knew I had been carrying in my haversack. From this they realized that I had passed their sleeping-place during the night, and was probably somewhere in front. To make quite sure, however, they waited all that day, and resumed the journey on Friday morning. They noticed my "spoor," but had lost it some hours previously.

Mackenzie advised me to throw away the arrows I had been carrying, as one of us might easily get scratched and poisoned with them. I was now feeling much refreshed, so we all "trekked" on together. We had not gone very far when we saw a white sea-bird, with red on its bill, standing on the sand. It looked sick, so we gathered round it, and I gave Maritz my piece of deck-chair to kill it with.

We then set about collecting firewood, there being any amount of driftwood scattered about the beach, and with the aid of flint and steel, which Mackenzie carried with him, we lit a great blazing fire. In the meantime Maritz had skinned the bird, and Franzen had got some salt water in a kettle they had picked up at Cape Cross. After boiling our bird for about fifteen minutes we tackled it, my share being the liver and one of the legs. It did not taste at all bad. We then sat by the fire for some little time, feeling a good deal better, and again resumed our journey. We walked until 3 a.m., and then tried to sleep, but found it too cold. At daybreak we resumed our tramp. It began to drizzle, and about nine o'clock we came to some flat, rocky ground, where I borrowed a water-bottle from Franzen, and managed to fill it. We walked on until about 3 p.m., when we sighted what appeared to be tall chimney-stacks in the distance. Franzen asked me what I thought they were, and I said, "Perhaps some abandoned place, like the one we passed up the coast."

"I think it's Swakopmund," he said.

This I ridiculed, for I had quite given up hopes of seeing the town. I was feeling very weak now, and my feet were frightfully sore on account of the sand getting through my *schoons*. The others decided to push on as fast as possible, and, if the place turned out to be Swakopmund, to send back help. Before long they were out of sight, and I was alone once more. However, I "trekked" on, and just as the sun was going down I saw, to my huge delight, smoke emerging from a chimney-stack. I knew then that it must be the place we were looking for, and this made me plod on with fresh energy.

IX—SAVED AND READY FOR THE FRAY AGAIN

When I was about a mile and a half from the smoking chimney I saw three men coming towards me leading a horse. I signalled to them, and sat down to await their arrival. They turned out to be men of my own regiment, attached to the police of Swakopmund. They had been ordered out to meet me, my mates having reported that I was following on behind them. I was put on the horse, and on the way into Swakopmund was met by hundreds of men of the garrison. Some brought brandy and others tea, and one party had a stretcher. They let me have a little brandy, and removed me from the horse to the stretcher, and in this I was conveyed to the hospital.

The men of the garrison cheered again and again, and all of them seemed greatly excited. I suppose our arrival was something new for them, as I understand that duty at Swakopmund had been very uneventful.

I was taken to the Antonios Hospital, which was under the charge of Major Moffatt, and he and everybody else was most kind and attentive. My pulse on arrival read thirty-eight, and the nursing sister put me on the scales the following day, when I found, to my great surprise, that I had lost twenty-nine pounds in weight. Very soon, however, I began to regain strength, and in a few days could move around. After spending ten days in hospital I was brought before a board of officers, who inquired into the cause of my capture, and returned a verdict "that I became a prisoner through the fortunes of war, and through no fault of my own."

The same day I was sent to Walfish Bay, and the following morning joined the S.S. *City of Athens* for Cape Town, on a month's sick leave.

There were seven or eight Germans on board who had been made prisoners. I was told that they refused to believe that four men had escaped from Franzfontein Camp. They said that such a thing was quite impossible.

I have since been informed on good authority that we were almost recaptured within a few miles of Swakopmund. Since the surrender of German South-West I have ascertained from a released prisoner from Franzfontein Camp that our escape was "given away" by one of our fellow-prisoners just three days after we left. The Germans promptly gave chase, and must have been very close behind us at Cape Cross.

The Germans, however, returned and reported us dead, and as proof of their statement they produced my hat, which I had lost on the night of my encounter with the seals, south of Cape Cross. Some of our men had little difficulty in identifying the hat, as it was punctured by a bullet in the action at Garub, and had an "I.L.H." badge on it, which they knew by sight. When the officer commanding the camp first heard of our escape he laughed and said we could not get through, and that we were mad to try it. We did pull through, however, by the mercy of Providence, and are now again ready for the fray.

In conclusion I would like to state that I am quite convinced that, if they had had the chance, there were many other men amongst the prisoners at Franzfontein who would have accompanied our party. My own part in escaping from the enemy and bringing what I believed to be important information to our own forces I consider was nothing more or less than my duty, and what nine out of every ten soldiers would have done in similar circumstances.

WHAT AN AMERICAN WOMAN SAW ON THE SERBIAN FRONT

How I Viewed a Battle from a Precipice

Told by Mrs. Charles H. Farnum of New York

Mrs. Farnum was decorated by Prince Alexander for her relief work in Serbia. Here she tells how she stood for six hours at a military observation station on October 11, 1916, and watched the successful fight of the Serbians to regain the village of Brod at the beginning of their advance against the Bulgarians. Her story is told in the *New York Sun*.

I—STORY OF A DINNER WITH PRINCE ALEXANDER

HAVING conducted hospital work with the Serbian armies in two Balkan wars it was out of the question for me to go anywhere but to Serbia when the present conflict started. I love Serbia and the Serbian people, and when I have told my story perhaps you will, too.

After serving through one campaign, a disastrous one for Serbia, I came to America, and with the assistance of Miss Catherine Burke raised $38,000 for the American unit of the Scottish Women's Hospital. I was only too eager to accept when it was suggested by the Serbian Relief Committee that I return to the war zone to see that the money was properly administered.

This explains how I came to be in Ostrova on a certain evening last October, seated at dinner next to Prince Alexander of Serbia, whose generosity of heart led him to overestimate my service to his nation.

"Would you like to go to the front?" he asked me.

I had been behind the battle lines, and I wanted to tell my countrymen just how the Serbs were fighting.

"I would like nothing better," I said, "but, of course, it is impossible."

The Prince smiled. "Madam," he replied, "nothing that you may wish is impossible."

I thought at first that it was merely his innate politeness, but with the least possible delay Prince Alexander delivered me into the care of Col. Sondermayer, chief of the medical service of the Serbian army.

"She is to go wherever she wishes to," was the command delivered to the Colonel.

And so we started out in a somewhat rattly automobile and went upward into the mountains, passing a continuous stream of soldiers—French going to Kisova and Serbians to Dobrpolje. Ammunition trains and convoys of wounded rumbled over the roads day and night. They were the back currents, the eddies of the war we were traversing.

As we passed a stone post at the side of the wheel-rutted road one of the officers said: "We are now in Serbia. This soil has been wrested from the conqueror."

I cried, "Stoy!" which is to say "Stop."

The chauffeur brought the car to a standstill and I jumped out. The men followed me and we knelt and kissed the soil we all loved. I do not think their emotion could have been stronger than my own.

Shortly after this Major Todorovitch pointed into the sky and said, "See the aeroplanes. They are our scouts."

I looked in the direction he indicated, but all I could see was a series of puffs of white. It was shrapnel from the Bulgarian guns bursting so close to the Serbian planes that the round puffs of smoke were drawn out into streaks by the suction of the fast flying machines.

Occasionally we could see the sun flash on the wings

of the aeroplanes just as you can sometimes see the approach of a canoe by the flash of the sunlight on the paddles before you can really distinguish the craft itself.

At Vrbeni I met Gen. Vassitch, the *"voivode mishitch"* (commander-in-chief) of all the Serbian forces. Col. Sondermayer explained that I wished to go to the front.

"How far forward do you wish to go?" asked the General.

"As far as your officers can go," I replied.

The General shrugged his shoulders as though to say, "There is no place for these women in war," then seeming suddenly to realize that I was in earnest, he bowed and said, "Madam, you should have been one of us—one of our Serbian soldiers."

Calling his aide-de-camp, Major Todorovitch, he directed him to obey my orders and take me wherever I wished to go, so we again got into the rattly automobile and began to climb still further up into the mountains.

In the distance I heard the roar of the big guns. As their noise grew louder the strumming of the machine guns mingled with it and their staccato was always distinguishable even amid the ear crushing thunder of the high explosives. Then came the rat-a-pat of rifle fire, foolishly insignificant in point of noise compared to the cannon, but cruelly deadly, as any one who has seen war knows.

Artillery is terrifying, but after all it is cold steel in the hand-to-hand, bestial fighting that slays.

II—THE WOUNDED ON THE SERBIAN ROADS

The ammunition wagons almost jammed one side of the road now and the other side was jammed with the carts bringing back the wounded. On their scant beds of straw they lay, some groaning, some shrieking in delirium, some grinning, but almost all of them contented and uncomplaining if they had a cigarette.

Your wounded Serbian prefers his cigarette to an anæsthetic, and I have seen the most painful, shocking operations performed in the field hospitals with no other sedative for the patient than a cigarette. In Serbia no one begs. It is considered almost a crime, but there is one temptation the soldiers cannot resist, especially the wounded ones. That is to ask for a cigarette.

During one of our halts I spoke to one poor fellow whose lips were blue, eyes dim and breath coming in short, painful gasps, almost sobs. I knew that before he reached the field hospital his body would be taken from the cart and laid at the roadside for burial.

Although the words almost killed him he managed to gasp, "Little Sister—for the love—of mercy—a cigarette."

I gave him one. I saw him take one blissful puff, blow from his mouth the smoke, which was no bluer than his lips, and die. So small a thing as a cigarette had sent one man who died for his country before his God with a smile upon his lips, despite his suffering. Was this not worth my whole trip?

We passed the Serbian artillery and to the summit of Dobrpolje. Here in the crevice of a great rock we ate lunch, which had been supplied by officers at the very front. There were pancakes, raw onions, bread and Turkiss coffee, and a meat stew. I know something about fare at the front, and there is no doubt in my mind that these same officers went on short rations for many a day to make up for the repast they set me. There was more sugar in the coffee than a soldier in Serbia gets in four days.

In our crevice in the rock we were 500 yards in advance of the Serbian guns. The panorama of the battle was spread out before us. The great projectiles from the masked Serbian artillery, which was being fired over a range of hills, swept diagonally in front of me from a line behind. They exploded in the village of Brod and on the hill in the rear of it were the Bulgarian trenches. Through binoculars I could see into the Serbian trenches and sometimes men in the Bulgarian trenches.

The enemy's guns were firing from behind the hill on which stood the village of Brod, but they did not have the range of our artillery, and most of their fire fell on a village a quarter of a mile in our rear. At times, however, a big shell exploded in the Serbian trenches and I saw monstrous mushrooms of earth and debris hurled high into the air.

In the debris were many fragments. Some were of timber and some were of human flesh and bone.

Stretching away directly in front of us was a wide plain, at the far extremity of which against a hill was Monastir, resembling a great cluster of pearls against the dark mountain. The French from the heights of Kisova were shooting down into this plain.

It was terrible; it was grand. It was cruel; it was sublime. My emotions almost overcame me. Major Todorovitch, noticing my agitation, thought I was unstrung and wished to return to the rear.

"Do you not feel well?" he asked me.

"I feel—I feel like a man," I said.

It was the only way I could express myself. I understood now how men fought and died, and were willing to fight and die innumerable times if it were possible for their country. If some of my sisters who cry for peace at any price could have seen the grandeur of this war in a just cause I am sure they would feel as I did.

Major Todorovitch leaped to his feet and grasped both my hands. I thought he would crush the bones.

"Come," he cried, "you are one of us. You shall have the greatest honor of us all."

Dragging me to the edge of the precipice, where had a Bulgarian officer seen him a burst of shrapnel would have greeted him, he planted his feet firmly against a solid rock.

"Lean over!" he cried enthusiastically.

Holding to his hands, my arms straining behind me, I leaned far over the edge of the precipice. I seemed suspended over the very heart of the battle. It seemed for a moment as though the spirit of the war had caught me up and flown with me where the whole fabric of the world conflict was being woven beneath my feet.

"Now," cried the Major, "you are further into Serbia —Serbia reconquered—than the bravest of our brave have been. No Serbian fighting man has yet been so close to Monastir."

The fineness of his compliment could not have been excelled.

I had been told that I might remain upon the summit of Dobrpolje an hour, but the scene fascinated me so and my soldier escorts were so chivalrous that they gave in to me and it was not until nightfall that they dragged me away to the rear, although we had reached the summit about midday.

Once more we were in the backwash of the battle. The roads were lined with stretcher bearers and in the stretchers lay men whose blood dripped through the canvas and stained the dust of the roads—the dust for which they were fighting and dying and suffering the tortures of the damned.

From the *postes de secours* they were taken to the rear in carts, and the steady rumble of the heavy wheels reminded me of the passing of the tumbrels in the "Tale of Two Cities."

At one point we passed about 800 Bulgarian prisoners and they did not seem at all unhappy at being out of the fighting. It is a commentary on the nature of the Serbians that they gave cigarettes to the prisoners, although the Bulgars have committed nameless atrocities against their foes and have devastated thousands of acres of prune trees, thus destroying a lucrative and immense Serbian industry.

That night Brod fell to the Serbs, but nevertheless I had been that day further into Serbia than any of her fighting sons at that time.

III—A WOMAN OFFICER OF THE CAVALRY

I do not know what silly things Major Todorovitch told Gen. Vassitch, but the General, before all his staff, made me an officer of the First Cavalry, which is the crack Serbian regiment, and a uniform has been sent to me and is on the way to the United States, although there is not enough cloth in Serbia to clothe her own troops. Perhaps when I go back I can use it, for although many an officer offered me a horse, none proffered me a pair of trousers to ride in.

When I was back in Salonica Prince Alexander sent for me and with his own hands pinned on my breast the Order of St. Sava, which is the most coveted of all the Serbian orders.

When I asked him if he really thought I merited it, he said, "I know of no better friend to Serbia than you." I had already held the Kossova medal, which is given only for personal attendance to the wounded, and the Royal Order of the Serbian Red Cross.

Through the kindness of Col. Sondermayer another

woman and myself were smuggled into a dinner given to Venizelos, at which no women were supposed to be present. During the course of the dinner Venizelos suddenly turned his head so that he happened to see me and started, as might be expected at a dinner where women were excluded. I also was covered with confusion and could not help showing it.

The next day Col. Sondermayer called with an invitation to visit Venizelos. When we reached his office he was overwhelmed with work, but he rose from his chair and said kindly, "Have I not seen your face before?"

"Yes," I replied, "last night at the dinner when you turned your head and I lost mine."

He laughed, and we were engaged in conversation for an hour. Venizelos entrusted me with a message for the Greeks in America.

"Tell them," he said, "that we need them. If they cannot come to fight they can send money, and it will be used to take care of those who are fighting and those who are left alone after the great battles."

I might refer here to the attitude of the women and even the little children of Serbia and Greece. It is true that the hardest, most cruel burdens of war fell upon the women and the children who are left widows and orphans or who suffer while the men are at the front. It has always been so, but as in every patriotic nation the women are suffering and doing their share as bravely as the men. The soldiers are glad and proud to die for their country, and their women folk and children are proud to have them, despite the sorrow and privation.

It should be a lesson to us in America. Our men and our women and children would be as ready and as willing to bear their burdens, but now in peace and prosperity we should prepare against the time when we may have to take up our burdens so that they may fall no more heavily than is necessary.

Venizelos is above all a Greek.

"I do not care for myself or for what may become of me," he said. "I am working and living and will die for Greece. Greece must live and live in glory and integrity."

Salonica seemed to me the concentrated essence of life. It is a kaleidoscopic scene. You come across the uniform of pretty nearly every nationality, and every known language seems to be spoken. There are soldiers and refugees, Turks and Christians, Greeks and Jews, and the town hums like a beehive day and night. Troops are coming and going, not only white men but negroes, Sudanese, Congoese, Annamese and many others.

When I was in Serbia I had scooped up a handful of earth and had treasured it and brought it back with me to Salonica, where I showed it to some Serbs. Tears came into their eyes and they gazed upon it with a reverence worthy of a sacred relic.

One man thrust his hand into it and said, "You have had the honor and the joy, which, alas, I have not had, of setting foot on Serbian soil freed from the invader. But I swear to you by this sacred earth that I will not die until I have kissed the soil of my country. After that——" he shrugged his shoulders.

By now this man, who was a soldier, may have fulfilled his vow, and if so he is happy, though his kiss may have been a dying breath.

"KAMERADS"!—CAPTURING HUNS IN THE ALPS WITHOUT A FIGHT

An Extract from the Diary of a Lieutenant of Alpine Chasseurs

Set down by Henri Viard

A racy story told by a young French subaltern, showing how six Alpine Chasseurs bluffed three hundred Huns, with eight officers, into surrendering without a fight.—In the *Wide World Magazine*.

I—STORY OF SCOUTING IN THE ALPS

At 5 a.m. on a certain day orders were received for an attempt to drive the enemy from certain strong entrenchments.

To baffle observation, we went forward through the woods. Connection between units was very awkward to maintain, and, many a time, the direction would have been lost were we not guided by the sound of the guns. Nothing but the distant booming of Fritz's cannon and the occasional explosion of a shell broke the forest hush. In Indian file, with scouts some distance ahead, we scrambled through the undergrowth, our feet frequently caught by roots and all kinds of clinging impedimenta, our faces lashed by brambles. We were eager and silent. When exasperated by obstacles, the men swore in dumb show. The orders were to keep mum; so mum we kept.

One's imagination was at work, though, and this warpath-treading business was to me a sort of reminiscence. Had I not lived it before? When a boy, reading Fenimore Cooper and similar authors, I sometimes played at "Pathfinder"; now as a man I felt as if I really was a "paleface" leading a surprise partly through virgin backwoods after redskins. Of a truth, the savages that had come upon us from the northern prairies were far worse than Sioux, Cheyennes, Hurons, or Kickapoos. They had sung the She-go-dem, they had sent out the tomahawk and yearned for our scalps. Well, we'll have theirs instead.

At last, the two leading companions, Captain B——'s and my own, reached the edge of the woods and espied the village, four hundred yards away, all bright in the morning sun. The bulk of the battalion had not come up yet. Captain B—— turned and asked, "What next?"

"*Allons-y!*" we replied; "the others will follow suit." Accordingly we massed up quickly in two columns, just outside the cover, and then, "Forward!"

A rush, a pounce—we were intent on catching them. Whew! Caught a crab! The hornets had flown—the nest is empty. Where are the brutes? We meant to surprise them, but, by Jove, they gave us an eye-opener.

The solitary thoroughfare descending to the bridge was enfiladed by four machine-guns ambuscaded on the other side of the water. The moment we got into this beastly funnel the hose was turned on and torrents of bullets splashed by. I leapt to the right, my comrade to the left side of the street, and we fell flat into whatever recesses the walls offered. So long as those deadly jets continued the road was impassable. We could only communicate by shouts, but fortunately our vocal chords are sound. The guns made an infernal din. The bullets ricocheted with vicious hisses—pish, whizz, zizz—striking sparks from flints, zigzagging about, grazing the roadway, raising clouds of dust that hung like a fog overhead.

I squatted my Chasseurs behind the church buttresses, and from these shelters they made faces at their comrades over the way and exchanged banter.

"Put your hand out to see whether there is a draught!" yelled one.

"Can't hear. Come and tell dad, ducky," came the retort.

Irrepressible boys! Danger seems to sharpen their wits.

Presently an order reached me—Heaven knows how—to look out and select whatever "combat position" I could for my men.

But what position was I to select? I couldn't see much of a panorama from my hole. I must go out and reconnoitre.

I called for a volunteer, and every man in the platoon answered, "I, sir! I, sir!" Nearest, best heard. A glance at the fellow next to me. It was Pierrat, a brick. He would do. So, my steps dogged by this hardy terrier, I began to play hide and seek from enclosure to enclosure, dodging down towards the river. Now a back yard, now an orchard, had to be negotiated. They were tricky places; you never knew whether you wouldn't come to a dead stop before you were half-way through. From time to time, whenever a fresh bit of shelter is reached, without looking back, I called out to Pierrat: "Keeping on?"

"*Oui, oui,*" he answered, and it was a comfort to be sure that my faithful shadow was still at my heels.

II—A DASH ACROSS THE DEATH ZONE

When we were almost at the bottom of the declivity I descried near the bridge, but on the other side of the road, the railway station. A nice position, this—quite my fancy. Suppose we occupied it! But it must be investigated first, and—well, it was on the other side of the road. My rifleman and I took a long look at the building, and calculated the distance between it and us, and cast a wistful look at each other.

"Rum job, sir," Pierrat agreed. Then, after a moment's consideration, he blurted out: "But I've an idea. Let us make the dash together. The odds are that one of the two will get over."

"Quite so," I told him. "Yet, if I'm the one who does not, will *you* take command of the fellows?"

He hesitated for a second, took another look at me, and then answered, resolutely, "Why not, sir?"

I shook hands with my new-found successor and, in two leaps the seven-league-booted ogre would have been proud of, we were across the death-zone. Thence, crawling through some gardens, we reached the station unscathed. I got into what had been the waiting-room and the station-master's tiny office. Broken chairs, topsy-turvy tables, lacerated prints, smashed telephone and telegraph fixtures, and empty bottles galore strewed the floor. Wherever Teutons have been, "dead" bottles are certain to be found.

"Drunkards!" grumbled Pierrat, probably feeling very dry.

While I was observing the bridge and mill through the waiting-room's glass door, a stray bullet came crashing in to frame my head in a star of cracks, just under a clean round hole. A fig for aureoles! I'm not a saint yet, nor a hero—which fact I demonstrated instantly by a most unheroic back-start. The place was unhealthy; I would have a look elsewhere. Accordingly I went out on the platform. The part for passengers was too exposed —only fit for express despatch into the other world— but what of the goods department? Merchandise has a knack of lingering on local lines, so provident authorities build weather-proof accommodation for it. This goods depot was a splendid specimen of the sort, with stout, breast-high walls, formerly glass roofed. The glass being already smashed, it would not crash down on the men; but the walls stood, a strong parapet from behind which an efficient fire could be poured into hostile trenches.

I had got my combat position!

The trouble now was to man it. How many of my fellows would live to cross that bullet-swept road? Well, we should see. The first thing was to try and fetch them.

Leaving Pierrat with strict injunctions to keep under cover and have a nap if he liked, but on no account to attract the enemy's attention, I sneaked back somehow to my platoon and ordered a move. "Every man will shift for himself," I told them. "Rendezvous this side of the road opposite the station." I knew Chasseurs could be trusted to find their way through anything. My only doubt was whether I should not be outpaced. As a matter of fact, I was by no means the first in, yet not the last.

When everybody had joined but those whom it would be no use to wait for, I bade them crouch behind me in a line on the verge of the bullet stream, ready to plunge ahead the moment they heard the word.

Presently there came a lull. "Over, lads!"

And over we went. Some did not reach the other side. There are tombs opposite the station, each marked by a little wooden cross with a tam-o'-shanter on top, which will be tended so long as any one of us is left. How many? There was no time to count them just then.

At last we were in the station.

Here I concealed the men behind the parapet, with instructions to cut loopholes and amuse themselves by potting at whatever was worth a shot. At first they did not make much practice. Little by little, however, they spotted places where the Huns offered a target, and then there was sport.

Whenever a silhouette jerked into view, all my Chasseurs giggled for glee. They arranged a sort of rotation between the best shots, and no one would give up his turn to snipe. Pending developments, the more indifferent marksmen watched their comrades' practice, and at each "bull's-eye" a murmur of approval came from the spectators. One of them, a youngster, could scarcely control his excitment. He had a quick eye and, being often the first to catch a glimpse of something, yelped like a boy on his first morning out after grouse. "Here's stuff!" he cried. "Here's stuff!" His neighbour, a steady, unerring killer, suspected of poaching propensities in civilian life, used unconventional language under his breath at each exclamation. At last, as the tyro uttered a shout a little louder than usual, he gave him a vicious kick, bawling, "Hold your row!" The contrast between the advice and the stentorian way in which it was imparted made everybody smile—even the kicked one, who retorted, good-humouredly, "Keep your nerve, mate, or you won't shoot straight!"

Noon. Upon my word, this little game seemed as if it could go on indefinitely, for the Germans, their attention concentrated on the village, which they kept riddling with bullets, had not "registered" us yet.

I contemplated the bridge with longing, greedy eyes, for I felt mad to get to the other side of it. At last I ventured to send a suggestion up to my C.O. Back came the reply: "What's the sense of risking a bearer's life to transmit unnecessary messages? Pocket your pluck and stay where you are."

The time dragged awfully. What would introduce novelty into the situation? I was just "fed up" with it.

III—THE PLATOON AT THE CASTLE WALLS

About 4 p.m. the scene changed. From somewhere, like bolts from the blue, six-inch shells began to shower down, not on us, but in front of us. It made all the difference.

It was our own guns, firing at the Huns, and the first shots, somewhat short, fell in the river, sending up superb water-jets which the now oblique sun illuminated with all the colours of the rainbow. At times, spray splashed down right upon us and, though there is nothing particularly nice about a shower-bath when one is not in the undress for it, we laughed at the quip the sprinkling elicited from a Parisian: "Well spouted, Versailles waterworks!"

But our gunners soon found the exact range, and houses and enemy trenches and their contents began to play fireworks, with stones and pebbles and heads and limbs for stars and rockets. The Huns did not seem to like this; we could see them reel back. After each *rafale*, my men were so elated at the ensuing stampede that most of them popped up in full view over the parapet, cheering like mad, and forgot to shoot.

Presently our C.O. came down to the station and decided that the town should be entered. I had been the first to get near the bridge, and no one disputed my right to be the first across. "Fix bayonets and forward!" My men, highly-strung by protracted tantalization, rushed headlong into the village. I expected the Germans to counter with cold steel, but nothing of the sort happened. Where were the beggars? We searched the buildings. In the mill I found only three blanched Bavarians hidden away behind sacks of flour, and holes were promptly driven through the lot, sacks and all.

I formed my platoon up in two small columns, with

orders to advance crouching along the dykes on both sides of the road, which was still swept by machine-guns. Suddenly the *crécelles* ceased rattling, and I perceived against the enclosure wall of the castle a man signalling to us. I did not know for a moment what to make of his gesticulations, but I could see that he wore red trousers. It was "Come on!" that he was signalling. On, then, and the Evil One take the hindmost!

I heard later that the fellow was a prisoner and risked everything to give us a useful hint.

Pardieu! he did. He rendered the battalion an invaluable service that eventide.

The instant I realized the red-trousered signaller's meaning I guessed that something out of the common must be taking place within the castle. With my sergeant and four men, revolver in hand, I bounded at the double ahead of the platoon and threw myself against the entrance door. It crashed open, and I tumbled against six feet of grey-coated "Kultur."

Blood and fury! My left hand flew at his throat, clutched it, and gave it a violent twist, while my right tried to level the shooting-iron between his eyes. They met mine, and something in them made me shout in German, "Do you surrender?" He seemed to hesitate for the fraction of a second; then he gasped in pure French, "That was my intention." I relaxed my hold, and he added, calmly, *"La guerre est une chose effroyable. Je me constitue prisonnier."*

Very civil, I am sure. I felt I ought to bow, for classical language like this knocks a fellow a couple of centuries back. It knocked every glimmer of passion out of me. I recovered self-possession in a jiffy and—to make amends for whatever bad form there might have been in my recent exhibition of excitement—turned round majestically and surveyed the situation with lordly composure.

Jove!

In the huge yard were some three hundred Huns. The sight gave me a start, but I showed no emotion. Why didn't they shoot, though? They looked puzzled.

"I ask for the lives of my men," said the well-bred voice behind me. The tall jackanapes, it appeared, was their *Hauptmann* (Captain). Was he, then, surrendering the lot as well as himself?

I couldn't believe it, but I acted as if it was a matter of course.

"Granted," I growled, without turning a hair, "but arms down and hands up!"

"Ground arms!" bawled the German's voice. Scarcely had the command rung out when, like clockwork, forward bent three hundred automatons, down went three hundred rifles, and up again to attention stood three hundred disarmed boobies.

"Hands up!" Up went six hundred paws, and three hundred hoarse voices chorused "Kamerads! Kamerads!"

Ripping! I could have yelled with joy at the sight and shouted "Bravo!" But not a sound escaped my lips. Instead I folded my arms and remained motionless, looking very fierce, I dare say.

Wouldn't there have been a hullabaloo if somebody had guessed what thoughts were passing through the poor brain inside that stern figure?

IV—A DARING RUSE—AND SURRENDER

Presently, seven officers stepped out, marched up, fell in behind my prisoner, and extended the hilts of their swords to me. "Keep 'em," I ordered, dryly; "you'll give 'em to my C.O. Now let's move off, and be sharp!"

"May I beg leave to tell my men they will not be shot?" the Captain asked.

"Very well," I told him; "but don't be long about it."

He went towards his docile crowd and gave them the welcome assurance. Evidently they had been taught that the French give no quarter. I wished he would make a speech, for the whole point for me was to gain time so that supports might arrive. Back he came, and I was in a sweat with the perspiration oozing from my temples. When was he going to see that there were only four men, one N.C.O., and my anxious self on the premises?

Having placed my quartette of Chasseurs and the sergeant on guard at the ward end of the archway, so as to prevent any of the rats in the trap peeping out, I went with a thumping heart to the outer door and took a glance up the road. Hurrah! My platoon had crept up along the ditches. "Up with you!" I shouted, and, screening myself round the corner of the gateway, added, in a lower tone, "Do not look surprised." Then, aloud, I yelled: "Prisoners' escort! About—turn!"

It would never do to give the German officers a chance of realizing how enormously their men outnumbered mine, so I quickly returned to where the *Hauptmann* and his subalterns stood in a disconsolate group.

"You remain with me, gentlemen," I told them. "Make your men form fours and file out."

"Right! Fours! March!"

When the last four passed out—the whole of the idiots leaving their rifles and bayonets in the yard, of course— I ordered "Halt," and with the eight specimens of Hunnish officerdom swinging behind me in step, moved deliberately to the head of the column.

The enemy being now disarmed, I could afford a little more bluff; besides, through an extraordinary piece of luck, there were just enough survivors of my platoon left to make up the exact regulation number for a prisoners' escort.

"Quick march!" I ordered.

Off we moved, the Captain by my side, the lieutenants following respectfully three paces behind.

On the way towards the bridge, I thought I detected from the corner of my eye the *Hauptmann* giving me, once or twice, a sidelong glance. I pretended, however, not to see, looking steadily in front, watching anxiously for my supports. Here they are! The Colonel has caught sight of us and is advancing rapidly at the head of the battalion.

I heaved a deep sigh, which did not escape the Captain's attention, for he turned to me inquiringly.

"Allow me to introduce you to my commanding officer," I said, with a graceful smile, the full irony of which he probably did not fathom.

I do not think that particular Bavarian has made out to this day how it all came to pass. Let him try and tackle the mystery on the sunny Mediterranean shore, where chivalrous France affords captive officers ample and comfortable leisure.

So far as I understand it, the man thought superior forces had surrounded the castle, leaving no chance of escape. Feeling entrapped and labouring under the delusion that any further attempt at defence would be futile, his anxiety to save his men became uppermost in his mind. As to the men themselves, when they saw their captain surrender and heard no officer order anything, discipline made them remain inactive. The moment the Captain's command to "ground arms" rang out, discipline caused them to lay their rifles down without further thought or ado. One of them, whom I asked what induced them to throw their hands up, replied, as if astounded at the question: "Why, we were ordered to."

But what about the seven subalterns? Of course, they could not see through walls, and discipline, I imagine, made them "follow their leader" like the men.

If so, discipline be hanged! It is a comfort to think that had a French officer been weak enough to behave as their chief did in similar circumstances, there would have been someone there to blow his brains out and lead the company to a sortie. But what is the use of moralizing? Leopards do not change their spots. Besides, a gift horse should not be looked in the mouth, and the *Hauptmann* did me, at any rate, a good turn.

Before taking leave of him that evening I inquired what he thought of Alpine Chasseurs. His reply is worth recording, the first words so unexpected from one of the inventors of "frightfulness," the last ones eulogistic, after all.

"To begin with," he declared, "your artillery is diabolical. The use of such weapons ought to be prohibited. It is murder! As to your men, they are extraordinary. The way they creep along is inimitable. Hardly has one got a glimpse of them than—*houp-là!* they are on the top of you."

Then, after a pause, he added, emphatically:—

"They are wild-cats!"

LIFE ON A FRENCH CRUISER IN WAR TIME

"*Les Vagabonds de la Guerre*"

Told by René Milan

Translated from the admirably written papers published under the title "Les Vagabonds de la Guerre" in *Le Revue de Paris* for *Current History*. Especially interesting is M. Milan's account of the part played by wireless telegraphy in the war.

I—STORY OF WAR ON THE ADRIATIC SEA

At last, on the curve of the waves, is marked the outline of the enemy! Alas! They are only torpedo-boat destroyers! Swift and powerful destroyers, I admit, but Austria might very well have offered us an adversary of our own class. But let us be satisfied with the windfall. Too many days have been thrown away against invisible adversaries. These at least are real, living and full of ardour. They gallop toward us, torpedoes pointed; we point toward them our big guns, which cannot yet reach them; the game is equal. Like us, they have run up the battle-flag, and the *Waldeck-Rousseau*, driving over the waters like a thoroughbred, drags with her her cruisers and her two squadrons of torpedo boats to the adventure in which some one must die.

A few minutes pass, packed with anxious silence. The men shut up in the hidden vitals of the ship strain their ears to catch the muffled sound of the first salvo; they may be killed in a moment, if some well-pointed torpedo should touch the cruiser, but they give their whole souls of bronze to their apparatus and their machines, so that nothing may go wrong in this marvelous crisis. Through their range-finders, the gun-pointers watch the distance vanishing by a kind of miracle. Twenty thousand yards —eighteen thousand yards—fifteen thousand—fourteen thousand. Two thousand yards more, and the storm of our artillery will break over our adversary. In three parallel lines the Austrian destroyers pour forth torrents of smoke; they are in solid formation; each line glides over the blue water like a gleaming boa constrictor. Alongside of us our torpedo-boat destroyers have drawn together and are plowing up clouds of foam that sparkle like silver in the sun.

But what do we see over there? The Austrian lines open out, bend upon themselves, and their heads describe a wide curve. Is it possible? They are going away! They refuse to fight! With a raging anguish we all try to persuade ourselves that our eyes are deceiving us. It is a trick of the sunshine, a puff of wind that bends their smoke. * * * Not at all. They have completed their turning movement and show us their heels, looking like three railroad trains speeding away on rails of foam.

Oh! to have our eyes on our revenge for so many useless weeks, and to see it escape just at the limit beyond the reach of our guns! To feel that under our feet our gigantic machines, which, nevertheless, are not weakening, can no longer catch up with the prey whose legs are too long for us! To measure the distance, and to feel it growing greater, a little more each second, like an elastic that is being stretched! Fourteen thousand yards!

Fourteen thousand one hundred. Fourteen thousand two hundred. * * * Ah! we would fain command the waves, hurl a sudden hurricane into the air, churn the sea into foam and billows. Our potent keels would not slow down, but the destroyers would crash against each billow, would go slower, would exhaust their force, and our triumphant dash would overmatch their cowardice.

They flee toward the labyrinth of the Dalmatian Islands, which grow larger before us like a family of ocean monsters rising from the sea. We continue to pursue. Sixteen thousand—seventeen thousand yards. Perhaps the poltroons will be seized with remorse or indecision. But it is not so; their flight is a premeditated ruse. High up in the sky, slipping and gliding among the transparent clouds, a war plane swoops over the French warships, passes along them, and drops bombs that only our skillful dodging makes harmless; they burst opposite our ships. On the surface of the water one of the cruisers perceives the furrow of a periscope! Some lurking submarine has launched its torpedoes, perhaps; our speed has deceived it; no one is touched; we take a flying shot at the streak of foam, which instantly disappears. The submarine plunges into the depths, the aeroplane is already out of sight, and the destroyers are close to the channel of the archipelago. Eighteen thousand yards—nineteen thousand.

II—IN THE WAKE OF A TORPEDO

After a few hours of unquiet dozing I arose, made a summary toilet, ate I know not what food, swallowed hastily, before going on watch. In the middle of the day I found myself on the bridge again. A bright sun was silvering the distance. The three cruisers, deployed in loose order, continued their course toward the south of the Adriatic; behind, almost invisible, the smoke of the naval forces formed a black mane on the horizon. On board, every one who was not on duty was enjoying a siesta. Every one was finding consolation in dreams for the disappointments of the day before, but a few scores of eyes were watching the very calm sea. The *Ernest-Renan,* a few thousand yards away, was following a parallel course.

Something very white suddenly appeared in the furrows of foam. My binocular immediately followed this wrinkle on the water; you would have said a jet of steam, slipping along just under the surface. For a few seconds I hesitated. Perhaps the fin of a porpoise swimming close to the top deceived me. The remembrance of training in peace times brought back to my memory the track of a periscope, and I hesitated no longer.

"Quick! All on the left! Raise to eight hundred meters! Declination, forty! All engines at full speed ahead! Close the bulkheads! Begin firing!"

The cruiser bounds. In the hold the men of the watch close the bulkheads. The artillery fires. The shells fall around the white, moving streak. They burst like balls of dry snow on a blue wall. All the men, awakened from their siesta, all the officers come up on deck. A few meters from our hull passes the fleecy track of a torpedo launched against us. It has missed us, but a big 194 shell (7¾ inch), fired from one of our turrets bursts immediately above the periscope. It plows the water and splashes it up in the air; the stem of the periscope rises, falls, rises again, falls again, as a wounded animal tries to stand and falls again. Then nothing more is seen. The blue waves show only their habitual indolence. Across the void a storm of cheers comes to us from the *Ernest-Renan;* they have seen the shell tearing up the water, and they are certain that the explosions have crushed in the submarine.

We are going fast, so fast that in a few seconds the

cruiser is far from the place of death. The guns turn and follow it, ready to fire again, but nothing shows any more.

"Cease firing! As you were! Open the bulkheads! Resume your course! Engines at sixty revolutions!"

III—DIVINE SERVICE ON A WARSHIP

Every Sunday, divine service is celebrated on board—a serious, simple ceremony. Around the movable altar, flags stretched make stained-glass windows of bunting; the vault of the church is formed by the low whitewashed ceiling of the space between decks; to right and left, the partitions of the cabins, the white stems of the smokestacks, form the metal walls of the shrine; the parti-coloured tubes, steam pipes, well-polished cocks, cast red and yellow reflections; chairs for the officers, benches for the crew, are grouped to a depth of eight or ten yards. He comes who so desires. A bugle call announces services, and whoever is not on duty, either comes or stays away. While the priest is accomplishing the holy rites, you hear in the hold the breathing of the engines, the snoring of the ventilators; above your head, on deck, patter the sailors of the watch; the big Adriatic rollers slap against the hull and the quivering of the rapidly moving cruiser makes the altar tremble.

IV—THE BOOTY OF THE HIGH SEAS

Above the horizon appear the masts, smokestacks, and hull of a ship. Whether her conscience be troubled or at rest, she knows she cannot escape our speed, and does not try to fly. At 5,000 yards her flag informs us of her nationality. English or French, she may go ahead. If she is neutral we show her the international signal:

"Stop immediately!"

And stop she must. If she looks like going on, a blank cannon shot warns her not to play with fire. If she pretends not to understand the invitation, a shell falls just ahead of her, and lets her know we are not joking. If her screw continues to revolve a rap or two on the hull lets her know that the affair is serious. They always stop in time.

The cruiser comes to, within gun range of the suspect. In an instant one of our boats is lowered into the water, the crew seize the oars; the officer on duty, armed with a sword and a revolver, and with a big register under his arm, jumps into the boat, which pushes off.

"Captain, kindly range on deck all persons on board! Let each have his identification papers in his hand. I shall inspect them in five minutes!"

Stewardesses, stewards scatter through the cabins, which are filled with a sudden stir. In the midst of a concert of exclamations, murmurs, and laughter, feverish fingers dive into portfolios and bags. Travelers whose souls are white immediately find what is wanted; the ladies fix their hair, hastily dab a little powder on a suspicion of sunburn, and give themselves a finishing touch. The whole thing is tremendously amusing to them. Just as if it were on the stage! It would not take much to make them put on their prettiest dresses. But the officer is getting impatient, and the Captain is apologizing; one passenger cannot find his passport, which he thinks he has left in his trunk. Exactly! the story is an old one! But let this German quarry climb up, just as he is!

Finally, every one is drawn up in two or several lines— like a row of blind men holding out their trays, each one holds his passport. The men are extremely serious, almost indignant, and, behind their foreheads, you can divine silent tempests; they are on the watch for an imprudent word, in order to invoke their Consuls, their

Ambassadors, and the inviolable rights of neutrals. A vain hope. The officer sharply scans them, and turns over their papers with a careful finger. Stamps and paragraphs are in order, and also the description; the passports, the certificate of nationality, do not smell of trickery. But there is no touchstone like language; a few words, a few phrases, tell many secrets to expert ears, and hesitation shows guilt where the papers show innocence.

"Be so good as to tell me where you come from. Be so good as to tell me your name and your birthday. Have you been long abroad? Be so good as to answer in your own language. What is your profession?"

You must question pointblank, in different ways, and be careful not to carry on the conversation. No discussion, an instantaneous judgment, and you pass on.

The true prizes, the genuine booty, you recognize by sure symptoms—Germanic faces, Teutonic accents, harsh or honeyed answers, stammered explanations. In vain do they disguise their names and hand us forged writings, their Germanic race leaks through all their pores. They are hurrying to foment rebellion in Egypt or Tripoli; they are on their way to the Balkans to do their work; to burrow underground in India or China. Invariably they have Swiss or Dutch passports, but their certificate of nationality, brand new, is fresh from the printing press, and reminds you of false coins, too new and shiny. Suspects! The officer goes down to their cabins. Under the mattress, behind the washstand, in the folds of a counterpane, lie the incriminating papers. Enemies!

From this point, one must go on decisively, gracefully, in the French fashion. The officer halts in front of the German, addresses him by name, lays a light finger on his sleeve or shoulder, and says, without raising his voice:

"I arrest you. Follow my sailor, who will take your baggage and put you into the boat."

Cries, explosions of anger, insults must not disturb him. He must add nothing. What has been said has been said.

V—STORY OF THE WIRELESS AT SEA—THE SECRET LANGUAGE

We have on board an ear that never sleeps; it is the wireless telegraph. The apparatus is buried in the depths of the hold; a padded cabin isolates the operators from the noise of the machinery and the cross-currents of discord. From watch to watch the telegraphers pass over the receiver to each other, and the finest murmurs never escape their vigilance.

The air vibrates in an uninterrupted concert. Coming from stations near or far, from ships wandering on the Atlantic or close at hand, calls, conversations seek out their way; the ether transmits them instantaneously. The powerful antennae of the Eiffel Tower, of Ireland, of Germany, of Italy, or of Constantinople dominate with their noisy throats the feeble whispers. With their full force, to any distance, they launch the official news of the great ordeal. If some one talks too loudly, 500 or 1,000 kilometers away, (300 to 600 miles,) they raise their tones, throw more strength into their voices, until the interrupters become silent.

A tacit agreement alternates their messages. The German does not obstruct the Frenchman, the Turk waits until Malta has finished. Madrir, talking to Berlin, rests while London speaks. For these great stations, controlled by their Governments, send out only announcements of the first importance, such as the whole world should know, and they wish neither to confuse nor to be confused. Reports from the front, happenings at sea, diplomatic or financial transactions, plans or insults, circulate in all languages, and you can be certain that the newspapers will not publish them. If by chance the reader of newspapers finds them in his daily sheet, it will be a week or a fortnight later, in a garbled, unrecognizable form.

Sailors hear every bell and every sound; while the rest of the world must be content with the meagre, delayed communications authorized by the censorship, the sailor already knows. His griefs and joys precede the griefs and joys of the anxiously waiting millions. Ireland announces a simple movement of Russian strategy, but Norddeich—the German post—clamors to all the echoes of a German victory, an advance, the capture of thousands of prisoners. Norddeich laconically explains some event at sea, but Eiffel sets his biggest sparks cracking, announcing to Moscow, to Newfoundland, to the Sudan and the Red Sea the disaster at sea that has befallen some Teutonic force. In how many days, with how many changes, will the public read these bits of news? At every hour of the day and night we receive them brutal and imperious.

No illusions are permitted to us. Our enemies do not lie too grossly in these proclamations destined for their Ambassadors, their Consuls, the innumerable agents who uphold the prestige of Germany throughout the world; it is vital for Germany that these men should receive authentic information, which they will make the most of in their bargainings. There is nothing in common between the rhapsodies of her newspapers or of the Wolff Agency and her wireless announcements. At the most, in the case of defeats, she sends out statements made carefully vague. But this very vagueness makes us prick up our ears, and within a few hours London or Paris confirms the English or French victory.

Outside the Chancelleries and Governments, there are no day-to-day records of the war except on warships. We discuss squarely over flags placed exactly where they ought to be; our forecasts, our hopes are rarely deceived. And if the obligation of secrecy did not impose silence upon us we could tell our friends many a bit of news.

But underneath the great tenors of wireless telgraphy whisper the myriads of baritones, basses, members of the chorus. Thus in the tropical forest the roaring of lions by no means hinders the dialogues of insects and rodents; this network of lower voices gives the jungle its deep life. The slender tones of talking ships fill the atmosphere of the sea with a mysterious animation. A big liner, come from tropical seas, announces her passage of such and such a frequented cape. A torpedo-boat patrolling toward Gibraltar tells Port Said about the ships which it has sighted. This torpedo-boat has not got strong enough lungs to shout to the other end of the Mediterranean; it calls Bizerta or Toulon, who answers, takes its message, and relays it forward, like a rebounding ball, to the antennae of Malta, to the masts of a French cruiser in the Ionian Sea, to the wires of a Russian ship in the Ægean, and finally it reaches Port Said. A mailboat announces its position, a squadron asks for orders, a naval attaché or an ambassador sends out information gained by spies; the Resident General of Morocco is sending wheat to Montenegro; the main guards give warning that a submarine is in sight; colliers ask to be told exactly where they are to meet certain cruisers; the whole Mediterranean taps the antennae of the Commander in Chief as a swarm of subalterns tap at the door of military headquarters.

No disorder, no discord in these gusts of whisperings. Like the musicians in a well-drilled orchestra, all these talkers speak at the minute, at the second previously fixed for their turn; chronometer in hand, the telegraph operators watch for the instant allotted to them, and immediately send forth trills of short, brief notes; whether they have finished or not at the end of their period, they stop and wait, for immediately a distant voice begins its part, and would protest violently if any one prevented its speaking. The whole extent of the Mediterranean is divided into sectors, the time is cut up into fragments, and no one is allowed to break the silence if the pre-established table bids him keep still.

Besides, the guilty parties are quickly found out. Just as the fingers of a blind man acquire surprising sensitiveness, so the operators' ears distinguish the timbre, the tone, the musical value of the chatters whom they have never seen. For the initiated the electric radiations have a personality like human speech. Two posts, two ships have distinct voices, pronunciations. This one talks with a sputter, the other speaks with solemn slowness; the voice of one suggests a match scratched on sandpaper, another buzzes like a fly, another sings small, like the flight of mosquitoes. It is a concert almost magical. In his padded cabin the operator hears and distinguishes the whirr of the cricket, the squeak of the violin, the rasped wing-cover of the beetle, the hiss of frying, which the fantastic electricity is sending forth, hundreds of leagues away. It flickers, ceases, begins again; you would say a goblin symphony in some wide wilderness, and yet the least of these vibrations is a message of war, of life and of death.

And indeed they are careful not to talk without saying anything. They all use only secret languages. This perpetual chatter contains no word, no phrase which any one can understand unless he possesses the key on which rests the safety of ships. Cipher, cipher, cipher, nothing

OVER THE TOP WITH THE AMERICANS IN THE FOREIGN LEGION

Told by Donald R. Thăne, of the Foreign Legion of France

Back from the trenches, where he fought in the Foreign Legion of France, Donald R. Thane, an American boy, was wounded and "gassed" all in the same day. Mr. Thane has seen Mars in his blackest moods; he has seen him at play and laughs at some of the grim jests of the war god. His gossip of the trenches—or rather some of it—just as he told it, nervously, and coughing now and then, for his lungs are still raw from the gas, gives an American boy's view of the war and what is going on "out there."—Courtesy of the *New York Herald*.

I—STORY OF AN AMERICAN BOY IN FRANCE

I was walking through Belgium when the war started. Things began to get hot and I went over to Paris. It was there that I enlisted in the Foreign Legion.

Why did I do it?

Well, I'm not going to pull anything about wanting to rescue France, or being fired by the flame of liberty or anything like that. They asked a negro prizefighter—an American—the same thing. He ruefully regarded the many bandages that adorned his more or less mangled body, and said:

"Well, sah, I guess mah curiosity got de best ob mah good sense."

Looking back on it, he answered for me, too.

As soon as I enlisted I became a number. It was No. 38,606, and I think that when we started to fight there were about 65,000 men in the legion. I don't know how many there are now. I do know that regiments have been so decimated that they were consolidated. You must not think of a regiment of the legion, however, as you do of an American regiment with a fixed number of men. I have seen Zouave regiments with 43 companies and about 240 men in each company.

I was assigned to the First regiment of the legion, where there were a number of other Americans, about whom I will tell you later. If the Americans had all enlisted at about the same time probably they would have had a separate regiment, but as they came in separately they were scattered throughout the legion.

They sent us down to Lyons for about a month of training, which was a lot more than was given at first. Some of the men practically got uniforms and then went into the trenches. I knew a French sergeant whose brother enlisted and was killed ten days later.

At Lyons wounded officers and non-coms. taught us soldiering without an interpreter. All the commands were given in French, and the drill masters executed them as they gave them. Lots of the boys didn't know a word of French, but they soon learned to execute all the movements, commence firing, cease firing, rush and retire, to the French commands. That was all the officers cared about. All we needed was to be able to fight in French.

II—IN A LITTLE WOOD NEAR LASSIGNY

My regiment was stationed in a wood a little way south of Lassigny, and for a time everything was very pleasant. The Prussians couldn't see us, and we had to fear only an occasional shell which came our way. The Boches had a habit of combing the whole line once every morning and once or twice toward evening. I suppose it was just so we wouldn't get too "cocky."

The regiment was divided into three parts. One-third stayed up in the out-post trenches and did a little patrol work in the woods. A second part was in the second-line trenches, repairing them and ready to move up if an attack came, and the third part was in the rear washing up and resting.

The men on outpost had to be pretty careful, because sometimes at night the Boches would move up and throw a few grenades or take some pot shots at them, but on the whole we were pretty comfortable in the woods at Lassigny, getting used to the sound of shell fire and occasionally experiencing what it is like to have some one shoot at YOU, purposely—to kill you.

But this came to an end. One day the Prussians began to pay a great deal of unsolicited attention to our sector. Their artillery hammered at us incessantly all day and all night. We knew an attack would come when the artillery fire ceased, and more and more men were moved into our trenches all the time.

I was sorry for the outposts, who had little or no protection against this kind of fire, but who had to stay out in the front to see when the attack started. The French officers seemed to know about when the assault was due, and one night they moved us out of the woods into a more exposed position. Here we huddled in bombproofs about thirty feet below the surface of the earth.

Shells were bursting all around us. We could hear the earth and stones thrown up by the explosions come rattling down on the roof of our shelter, and we always looked up at the raftered ceiling and wondered if it was going to hold. To die here like rats in a trap was not what we expected. I had never been in an attack and I dreaded it, but I thought surely it must be better than this sitting here, waiting for the top of the ground to fall down and crush me.

The muffled roar of the cannon fire ceased. The assault was commencing.

We sprang to the entrance of the passage which leads to the world above. It was blocked by falling earth and rocks. With spades, with bayonets, with bleeding fingers and tattered nails we flew at the debris and clawed our way to the air, like sewer rats at bay and forced to fight.

We wanted to fight. It was not all courage on our part. If the Boches should win our trenches they would throw hand grenades in on us until all was silent in our self-made tomb, just as we would do if we reached their lines.

It is a rotten war!

We scrambled out just as the third wave of Prussians surged against the barbed wire entanglements and died away. It did not break back upon itself, like a water wave striking a breakwater. It simply melted, because our machine guns were rat-a-tat-tatting and our artillery was dropping a curtain of high explosives into a strip of No Man's Land about as wide as a city street.

It was horrible. Yet as every shell burst we felt exultation, because if those men passed the wire some of US would die. We wanted them killed right there. We did not want them to get among us, stabbing and shooting and clubbing.

It was my first fight. I could not help it—I was afraid. I wanted to get on my knees and pray that the gray waves should not pass the barrier, but my knees were too stiff. I prayed standing—prayed that more men would be killed!

For three hours this kept up. I stood there horrified, but for the first time in my life glad to see men die. No more waves were coming. Night was falling. The red in the sky seemed to be reflected in the narrow strip of ground before us, but it was not that. The guns spoke more slowly.

Great God, it was over! They had not passed. I was glad, but I was sick.

III—WE ATTACK THE PRUSSIAN TRENCHES

I spoke of the enemy coming over in waves. Many persons seem to think that this implies a weird and complicated formation. It does not. Nothing is simpler.

When they prepare for an assault the first line of trenches is filled with men. At the command they climb over the side and charge. Some run faster than others. This makes the onrushing edge of the mass of men thinner than the main body and irregular. It is like the tumbling crest of a white cap.

As these men charge the trenches are filled again. As soon as they are ready the second crowd starts over. Then the third, and the fourth and so on. There is no attempt to take cover, because there is no cover. It is a rush to get there. There is no regular formation. The trench spews forth a swarm of fighting demons and they come trampling and yelling across that terrible strip of earth as fast as they can come.

After our artillery annihilated the attack it began to shell their trenches. We knew that we would make a counter attack. Some of us may have slept that night. I didn't.

Early in the morning, when it was very cold and the impassive stars blinked dimly and more dimly, the "taraffia" was passed down the line. This is chiefly rum, and it makes one feel, "Why wait any longer? Let's get up and at them now." If it wasn't for this I think we would go crazy in those last twenty minutes before the attack.

Our artillery ceased.

"En avant, mes enfants! On les aura!" shouted the officers.

The first company mounted the side of the trench and dashed forward. Most of them were dangling in the barbed wire as we rushed past. The earth in front of us seemed to be whipped into a seething mass. They were sweeping low with their machine guns so as to hit us in the legs and drop us. With a shot through the stomach we might go on for minutes and maybe kill a Prussian before we died. But a hit in the legs drops a man and the artillery can blow him to pieces later, when the assault has been repulsed.

It is a scientific war.

A few of the first company reached the Prussian trenches before us. We clubbed and stabbed and slashed with the long knives they had given to us. The legion does not take any prisoners, because legionnaires are not taken prisoners. The Boches feel that we have no business in the war.

The trench was so narrow I could not use my bayonet, so I used the knife. I do not know how long we had been fighting, but the Boches cleared out. We tried to get our squads together and prepare for what we knew would be coming. The enemy simply had retired to their second-line trenches to let their artillery turn upon us in their first-line shelter. All morning they hammered us, but we hung on, lying flat upon our bellies and clinging to our mother, the earth, as if she would protect us. Showers of dirt almost buried us alive. Sometimes bits of metal found a soft billet, and there was one fewer of us to withstand the attack that would come as surely as death awaits us all.

Suddenly quiet struck us like a blow. The echo of the guns had scarcely died away when we heard the twitter and whistling of birds that had survived the terrific shocks of the explosions.

Then we heard a different sound. It was the yelling of the Boches. They were coming! Some rushed through the crooked communication trenches which we had blocked a little bit with earth and stones. Others swarmed over the top of the ground. Some seemed to rise from beneath our very feet.

Have you ever kicked into an ant hill? If you have you know how the Boches fell upon us. I saw some one climb over the rim of the trench and run back toward the French lines.

I followed him.

I could not feel my legs. I seemed to be flying. The strumming of a machine gun broke upon my consciousness. I leaped headlong into a shell hole. Dead men were around me and wounded lay thrashing there. Other men leaped on me and fell into the pit. We lay there until the sound of the machine gun stopped, then we started madly again for our own lines. A star shell burst and merciless light made everything stand out with terrifying plainness. It is cadaverous light, like that from a mercury tube.

We plunged into another shell hole. When the rest of the men came tearing past us we leaped out and followed them. I am not proud of my conduct in my first fight.

After this assault I gradually became accustomed to the noise and shock of artillery fire. We could hear the shells coming, passing over our heads and speeding away in the distance. It is a strange fact that after a few weeks of artillery fire one develops a sort of instinct which distinguishes between a shell coming toward him and one just sailing off somewhere else in space.

I got so that shells all around me did not bother me,

but let one come in my direction and this extra sense seemed to know it, and I would be flat on the ground before I had time to think about it.

It was at Belloy-en-Santerre, on the Somme, July 2, 1916, that I had a chance to ease my conscience for the way I had acted as a green recruit. Everything was made ready for an assault by our troops. The town had been literally knocked to pieces.

There was a wide strip of terrain between the trenches at this point, but all of us were by now accustomed to feel the breath of death against our cheeks, and when the big guns stopped roaring there came the familiar *"En avant, mes enfants! On les aura!"* We leaped over the parapets and tore across at them.

The artillery had made their first-line trenches almost untenable. The only men left in them were the machine gun operators in their heavily armored turrets and they kept spraying devastation among our legs until some of the boys got round behind and threw grenades into the turrets. After that the machine guns were quiet.

We reorganized when we had reached the first defences. I don't know how many of the boys were flattened out against the ground behind us, but I do know that several companies had to be consolidated to make one.

Then we swarmed over to the next defence line and stabbed and slashed and threw grenades. Parties of us ran to the bombproofs and threw in everything explosive that we had, and let me tell you that, all stories to the contrary notwithstanding, I never knew of anybody going down into a bombproof and being stabbed by Prussians who said they were wounded and needed help, because nobody ever goes into a bombproof to see until they have thrown grenades in and all is quiet. It would be foolish to do otherwise.

As I have said before, it is a rotten war any way you look at it.

IV—WHEN THE BOCHES THROW GAS BOMBS

Well, after the attack we held the first two lines of trenches. When I went off duty after being on outpost I simply lay down in the mud and mess of things and slept. I waked up coughing and wracking as if my body were going to burst.

The Boches had crept over and thrown gas bombs among us. Some of the men were too far gone to get out of it. Others had managed to get away. A few had gas masks, and one of these put his arms under my shoulders and dragged me with him to the rear. We all should have had our masks, and nowadays a soldier found without his is severely punished. I had mine then, but it was under my blanket and I couldn't get to it quickly enough.

They stuffed something under my nose, and it hurt almost as much as the gas, but it brought me to, and I was put in an ambulance. The body of it was filled with wounded men, so I sat with my legs dangling over the tailboard, propped up against a leather strap. The poor fellows inside groaned and grunted with every bump of the crazy vehicle. The road was pitted from shellfire, and I had to hang on for dear life to keep from being thrown off.

Presently the Boches began shelling the road. They were not purposely after the ambulances. They were just shelling that road. If ambulances were there they were likely to get hit.

I heard one coming. I knew she was headed toward us, but there was no place to duck to. Right behind us the road seemed suddenly to bow up like a steel band when the ends are sprung suddenly together. Then it settled back. I was so stunned by the shock of the explosion that I hardly felt anything else, but as the ambulance careened onward I began to feel a pain in my thigh. I put down my hand, and when I looked at it it was red. I had been hit.

A man lying on his back in the ambulance, with his feet beside me, had lost more than half of one of them as a result of the same explosion. There wasn't time to do anything for either of us. The driver went ahead like mad and got us to a dressing station, where dozens of men were waiting for treatment.

Some of them were serious. The surgeon looked at me and said, "You're easy. Can't waste much time on you. Lie on that table."

I lay down on my stomach and he probed for a second, then gave a yank. I thought he had pulled my leg out by the roots, but he thrust a pair of pincers in front of my eyes and said, "There it is. Want it?" and he dropped a bit of shell into my hand. I still have it.

Then a big ambulance, with seven other men in it, took me to Compiegne, where I lay in the dining saloon of a château for a few hours and then was sent to Paris.

The wound healed quickly and I was sent back to the trenches, but the gas had left my lungs bad, and I couldn't stand the cold and wet. It wasn't long before they invalided me out.

But I'm all right now, and I'm going back if they'll let me.

V—THE BOYS WHO ARE "GONE" FOREVER

A lot of the boys I knew in the legion are gone now. While I was in the hospital some of them got theirs. For instance, there was Allan Seeger. It was reported not long ago that he killed himself while lying in a shell hole, wounded. I don't believe that. I knew Seeger well, and it doesn't sound like him.

He enjoyed a close, strange friendship with a negro from the Barbadoes, whom we called Cafe-au-Lait because he was the color of coffee more than half milk. Cafe-au-Lait had Seeger's watch when I returned to the trenches, and he was in the shell hole with him when he lay there wounded. He had been shot through the stomach and some stretcher-bearers rescued him. He was put in an ambulance and sent to the rear, but he died before they could get him to a hospital, according to Cafe-au-Lait, who mourned his loss pitifully.

Then there was Christopher Charles, a dancer from New York, whom you'd never take for a fighter, but who could show the way to most of us. Another New York man in the legion was "Norri" Norritch. He was killed at Belloy-en-Santerre after they took me away with my lungs full of gas. They said he had made hundreds of thousands of dollars in New York real estate.

There was one Briton in the legion whose name was Longman. He had been discharged from the British army because he went to pieces after a girl had turned him down. His one idea was to get killed. He was always the first man over the top for an assault, and he never bothered about taking shelter from shell fire unless he was dragged into it. But he couldn't get hit.

Longman was reinstated in the British army for heroism and sent down to the Balkans. Newspapers all over the world have told his story. He went through the Serbian campaigns with all the fever, typhus and pestilence raging through the camps, and it never touched him. He wooed death and she passed him by.

Then the Turks took him prisoner. They never would

have done it had he known. Something knocked him on the head, and when he waked up he was in a Turkish hospital.

It would be hard to find a more conglomerate body of men than the legion. Spaniards, Italians, Greeks, Poles, who will not fight for Russia, but want to fight against Prussia; Americans and British, shoulder to shoulder, sharing blankets and little luxuries that filter into camp from time to time.

In my company were a Spaniard and a Chilian who had always been deadly enemies. The Spaniard had lost a fortune gambling, and then the Chilian won the girl the Spaniard was going to marry. They fought a duel, which the police interrupted. Both joined the legion and were assigned to the same squad.

VI—THE LEGIONAIRES IN THE BATTLE OF MONTLUEL

The discipline is very strict in a way, but the legionnaires have to be handled differently than any other troops. They still delight to tell about what was dubbed the "Battle of Montluel." Three pals from the legion were in the town on leave. One was an American civil engineer, one an Irishman of the school you read about —chivalrous, humorous, always ready to fight—and the third was an Englishman who had travelled so much that he belonged nowhere in particular.

They drank all the good wine in Montluel and refused to pay for any of it. At last they wandered into a tavern they had missed and demanded something to drink. The innkeeper refused them, having heard of their escapades.

The Irishman dashed at him. The proprietor floored him with a chair. The two others leaped upon the innkeeper. Peasants and townsmen rushed in with flails, sticks and anything handy and began beating the life out of the three legionaires, who yelled for the gendarmes. The gendarmes came, but they arrested the soldiers and returned them to their military commander. They were sentenced to twenty years of hard labor on the railroad in Algeria.

But they begged so hard to be allowed to fight as long as the war lasted that the commander agreed, saying they deserved to be shot anyway.

I don't believe they will ever serve their twenty years in prison, for if they are not killed they will have won their pardon. Already they have won "citations" and would have been decorated were they not technically prisoners.

I would just like to say one word about training men for fighting in Europe. I don't want to presume to give advice, but I fully believe that the only place to train men for this kind of fighting is right behind the lines, where they will hear the shells bursting. Then they can be moved up to the reserve trenches and used for repair and construction work until they are ready to be put into the fighting.

In this war every man must take care of himself. There has never been fighting like it. I don't care how well trained a soldier may be, he has got to see something of the war before he will be any good in a fight.

SECRET STORIES OF THE GERMAN SPY IN FRANCE

How Sixty Thousand Spies Prepared for the War

We have had a certain amount of experience of the German spy and his devious ways, but in France—the first country that the Huns had earmarked for destruction—the espionage system was even more fully developed. Ever since the beginning of the war the writer of this remarkable article has been engaged in collecting authentic information concerning German spies and their methods, and some of the results of his investigations are set forth. A startling light is thrown on the ramifications of a system that employed abroad more than sixty thousand men and women in every walk of life, and which is still far from having been eradicated.—Related in *Wide World Magazine*.

I—STORY OF A STARTLING DISCOVERY AT MONTE CARLO

IN THE early days of the war, when everything in the military and civilian life of France was still in a state of perturbation, certain undecipherable messages were picked up nightly by the wireless telegraphy station at Cros-de-Cagnes, a little fishing village on the French Riviera, some seven miles from Nice. Other stations in many other parts of the country and abroad likewise reecived those mysterious fragments from the unknown —partly in code, partly in unintelligible German—and transmitted them to military headquarters, where futile attempts were made to make head or tail of them. One thing, however, was certain: they emanated from an enemy source, a secret wireless installation somewhere, as the experts were convinced, either on the French or Italian Riviera. The problem of the whereabouts of the German or Austrian spies who thus dared to carry out their nefarious operations under the very noses of the French and Italian authorities at once became of intense interest to the police all the way between Marseilles and Genoa. But they searched for the culprits in vain.

Before the middle of August, 1914, however, thanks to a perspicacious English journalist, the mystery was elucidated.

Singularly well-inspired, he had gone to Monte Carlo to obtain war impressions. Had he searched all through France he could not have found a more fruitful subject for study than the little independent principality over which the Prince of Monaco and M. Camille Blanc et Cie. reign. For many years before the war the administrators of the gambling hall had done everything in their power to make Monte Carlo attractive to Germans and Austrians, in order to fill the void left by English visitors, a great many of whom had instinctively fled to Egypt or elsewhere, to get away from these ill-mannered or otherwise obnoxious guests. The Boches and their accomplices having been expelled from the principality on the second day of mobilization, our journalist found the authorities of the Casino still staggering under the blow which the cataclysm had dealt them. The Casino was closed, the palaces and villas and hotels on the hillside seemed to be sleeping more soundly than usual under the hot August sun, the Terrace overlooking the sea was deserted. Over everything was written, as it were, that stock phrase of the croupiers—who now sat, armed with fans in lieu of money-rakes, outside their own establishment—*"Rien ne va plus."*

With several pages of jottings in his notebook and his brain filled with impressions, the journalist, who intended to take an early afternoon train back to Nice, turned, on his way to the railway station, into the half-closed Café de Paris. Here, getting into conversation with a communicative *garçon*—a clearly well-informed Monagasque —he unexpectedly gleaned the most important item of intelligence he had yet come across, a piece of information so curious and so significant that he there and then decided to change his plans and spend the night at Monte Carlo.

"Yes, sir; it was high time they got rid of the Boches," said the waiter. "Monaco had become a veritable spies' nest. At any rate, they got hold of one—Kurz, the Austrian sub-director of the Casino. He was undoubtedly working for Francis Joseph, otherwise how can one explain the incriminating plans and documents which, *on dit,* were seized at his house? They got him early in the month, just after the Prince's notices to the Austro-Boches were posted up, and he's now at the island of Ste. Marguerite, where some others would be, too, if they weren't being protected."

As he reached the end of this last phrase the waiter lowered his voice to a confidential whisper, and after a quick glance in the direction of the *caissière's* desk, in order to assure himself that he was not observed, continued:

"The man with whom Kurz was naturally hand in glove we've still in our midst, though I don't suppose he'll have the face to stop here another twenty-four hours. Vicht, the Director-General of the Casino, is a German, and since the declaration of war he's done all he could to get the authorities to maintain his too-recent naturalization. He tries to make out he's a Monagasque. *Mais cela ne marche pas.* The wonder is that he's still here, for it's well known what he and Kurz have been up to for years past. Everybody acquainted with the position of affairs here knows that these two men had at their disposition a small army of detectives, whom they employed to shadow the *habitués* of the Casino, including certain well-known journalists, in order to ascertain the origin of information against Germany and the Germans which had been published in the press. Vicht and Kurz had become all-powerful here, and would have turned the principality into a German possession if they'd had the chance. They made a start last winter, it is said, by assisting in the publication of a German weekly newspaper run by an unsuspecting journalist. Ah, Vicht's a wily customer—a man to be watched, I think."

Thus put on the scent, the journalist decided, as I have said, to postpone his departure and await developments, which came much sooner than he expected.

Having dined at the Hôtel de Paris, he went out in the cool of the summer evening to stroll on the Terrace and smoke his cigar. It was a magnificent summer night, one of those *soirées d'été* when Monte Carlo and Monaco, with their soft-scented breezes from the hillsides and sea and the twinkling lights in the little harbour opposite the Condamine, were steeped in romance—a night for reflection. Thoughts of the war and the astounding fact that an enemy subject was still at liberty in the principality filled the journalist's mind as, at the end of a quarter of an hour's perambulation on the flower-adorned promenade, he stopped to rest and, leaning on the parapet, looked down on the harbour of the Bay of Hercules.

II—STORY OF THE MASTER SPY AND HIS YACHT AT MONACO

A good-sized yacht was moored there. Whose was it? It was not the *Princess Alice,* Prince Albert of Monaco's boat, which had been used for so many oceangraphic expeditions, and whose lines he knew well. Suddenly he remembered to whom it belonged—to Jellineck, the motor-car manufacturer, director of the Mercédès Company, and Austrian Consul at Monaco, and the whole story of that notorious spy's machinations flashed back to his mind. Strange that he had not thought of it before, when it was so recent!

Jellineck, an intimate friend of a French prefect of the Alpes-Maritimes, whose sister, it is said, had once been a governess to the children of the Austrian manufacturer, had suceeded in escaping when war was declared, and some of the blame had been laid by one of the Nice newspapers on the shoulders of the French official. Matters were made still worse when Jellineck's yacht, which had been sequestrated and taken to Cannes, was allowed, in most peculiar circumstances, to be removed clandestinely to Monaco, where presumably, it was in neutral waters. The affair created a great commotion locally, because Jellineck's *rôle* as a master-spy had long been suspected, supposition supported by the fact that a special messenger of his used to make the journey every week from Nice to Ventimiglia, to receive and dispatch his correspondence.

Whilst the journalist's eyes were fixed on the dark outline of Jellineck's yacht, on board of which there was not the slightest sign of life, his attention was attracked by a strange luminosity playing, like a will-o'-the wisp, over the masts. By jove—wireless! To his observant eye and well-trained technical mind there was not the slightest doubt about it; that light could be nothing else than radio-telegraphic sparks, the play of which can so often be seen around the antennae of wireless telegraphy stations.

This electric phenomenon furnished, as it were, the

missing link in a long chain of deductions which, subconsciously, his brain had been turning over and over days past—ever since, in fact, he had first heard from a friendly police-inspector at Nice of the mysterious messages picked up at Cros-de-Cagnes. The master-spy Jellineck—the removal of his yacht to Monaco—wireless messages dispatched or received there. With whom was he still communicating? Surely it must be Vicht!

No further time to be lost. The journalist left the Terrace immediately, walked swiftly down to the Condamine, and took a short cut to the police-commissary's office at Moneghetti. The little dark-eyed Italianesque official acted with commendable promptness and circumspection. Before the night was over two wireless installations were seized—one on board Jellineck's yacht; the other, traced in the same way, in a Monte Carlo villa residence, which, if it had not actually been occupied by Vicht or members of his family, had certainly been rented by an accomplice, who, like himself, clevery managed to slip through the fingers of the police. The flight of the Director-General of the Casino, first to Ventimiglia, afterwards to San Remo, and then to Diana Marina, coincided with the astute journalist's discovery —a tell-tale fact indeed.

It has now been proved beyond a shadow of a doubt that Monaco was, with Paris, Brussels, and Geneva, one of the Germans' chief spy centres, and the operations of their innumerable agents naturally spread to Nice, Cannes, Toulon, and other places along the Riviera. Even after Vicht's flight this dangerous man preserved sufficient influence in the principality to obtain his salary, which was brought to him from Ventimiglia, whilst his accomplice, Kurz, had the impudence to write to the gas company and order the gas to be laid on at his Monte Carlo villa, presumably in view of his triumphal return there after the victory of the Germans! A German millionaire, named Uhde, the owner of an important building rented by a big bank, situated just beyond the frontier line between Monaco and France, was arrested on the day after mobilization, just as he was trying to escape in his car. The owner of the chateau and estate of Almanarre, near Hyères, Uhde, who was formerly an officer in the Zieten Hussars, had chosen his property with true military foresight. It enjoys an extensive view over the Bay of Toulon, where he could follow at his ease all the movements of the French warships. His suspicious behaviour and frequent journeys to Germany led to a lawsuit, some time before the war, between him and M. Léon Daudet, whose *ante-bellum* revelations concerning espionage in France have been shown to be in a great measure correct. Uhde lost his action for libel before the Toulon court, which condemned him to pay the costs, and he met with little better results on appealing to Aix, where, having claimed four hundred pounds damages, he was awarded merely two pounds.

III—STORY OF THE MYSTERY OF THE MOTOR BOAT RACES

The German and Austrian agents at Monte Carlo, Nice, and elsewhere along the French Riviera hid their plans so carefully that the observation of direct spying was rare. Yet on other occasions than the one related above, as testified by M. Georges Prade, they were caught in the very act. The following striking instance came to the notice of this well-known sportsman in April, 1914, a few months before the war, when he was organizing the motor-boat races at Monaco.

An extremely powerful motor-glider, with an engine of four hundred horse-power, attained the enormous speed of sixty-two miles an hour in that year. Boat and motor were built by M. Despujols, a Paris manufacturer, and the glider was entered in the programme of events as piloted by a Spaniard named Soriano. On the last day of the races everybody heard with surprise that the boat would not take part in the trials, as the motor had already been taken to pieces and sent away. A little later it transpired that a buyer, name unknown, had paid no less than two thousand four hundred pounds for this specialized motor, and, though it was utilizable only for racing, had withdrawn it from the contest. The mystery deepened when it was further learnt that the motor had been sent first to Lyons, and thence to the well-known electrical and dirigible manufacturing firm of Siemens-Schuckert, at Biesdorf, near Berlin.

The whole truth came out in the course of an official inquiry conducted by M. Prade, to whom M. Despujols confided the details of the strange affair. The purchaser was an individual named Schmidt, who pretended he was a Russian, but who always steered German motor-boats and raced under the German flag. He was to have competed against M. Despujols' boat, but preferred to kill two birds with one stone and buy him out. Working in league with an engineer of the famous firm of Bosch, the magneto manufacturers, who represented the German house of Siemens, and with a workman who, although he was known to be earning only two pounds a week, was discovered to have distributed bank-notes very lavishly in return for information, Schmidt learnt that the motor in question was just what he was looking for. Sent to Berlin at the end of April, 1914, it was destined to form part of a curious motor-boat torpedo, filled with explosives, running automatically, and controlled from a distance by Hertzian waves. The value of such an engine as this in a naval engagement, had it been brought to perfection in all its parts, is self-evident.

Industrial espionage, of which this motor story is a typical example, was practised on a very large scale at Nice. The capital of the Riviera, where the Italian population is very numerous, was regarded by the Germans as one of the best centres for their operations when Italy came into the war on the side of the Entente Powers. Hence the completeness of their spy organization. Their principal meeting-place was at the bookshop of Hohberg, a vender of German "Kultur" in the Rue Maccarani. Hohberg was the publisher of a paper called *Deutsche in Nizza,* which had a circulation of twelve thousand copies weekly and contained articles with such titles as "In the Interests of Germanism." It heartily recommended its readers to patronize the Reichsadler-Apotheke, which masqueraded as an Anglo-Russian pharmacy, or the notorious spy Hübner, a florist of the Rue Masséna. It warmly upheld a campaign in favour of Riviera sanatoriums—run by German or Austrian doctors—such as the ones near Gorbio and Mentone, and which were admirably suitable as hiding-places for German officers, supposed to be convalescing but really spying. It contained a complete list of German doctors, tailors, etc., and frankly invited every Boche to pay a call at the Nice office, which thus served as a central organization for all the spies who, as tourists, naturalists, botanists, *masseuses,* chiropodists, and quacks overran that town and the whole of the beautiful Alpes-Maritimes.

"The man's topographical knowledge is extraordinary," said a Nice friend of mine one day, referring to a young Austrian, the tutor to the children of Jellineck-Mercédés, who used to spend every available holiday tramping about the lavender-covered hills near Breil and the

Franco-Italian frontier. "Although I've carried my beehives from place to place in these parts during more than twenty years, and pride myself on knowing every inch of the ground, yet he has often astonished me by his references to this or that mountain pathway or little-known landmark. These Austrians and Germans, almost without exception, possess a faculty for geographical surveying, linked with a strange liking for pedestrianism in the neighbourhood of frontiers and forts. Can that be merely a coincidence?"

This was some years before the war, and at the time my friend's declaration produced no more than a passing impression. But I have since come to see what an important truth and warning it contained, the very kernel of the thesis which another clear thinker and Alsatian patriot, the Abbé Wetterlé, developed with great skill at the general meeting of the Touring Club de France on December 5th, 1915.

IV—HOW EVERY GERMAN TOURIST BECAME A SPY

The Abbé Wetterlé showed in his lecture how every German, through his civil and military education, has become a potential spy; how, on going forth to spend his holidays in France or elsewhere abroad, he could not help being the active agent of those directors of his conscience, the Pan-Germanists.

"Recollect, everywhere and always, that you belong to the supreme race," they said to him, through their newspapers, pamphlets, and tracts. "Even if you know the language of the country where you are travelling, speak nothing but German. Never put up at any hotels but those kept by Germans, and amongst these choose only the ones kept by compatriots who you know have preserved all their attachment for the Fatherland. Insist in these establishments that they serve you with German products, and that the bill of fare is drawn up in your native tongue. Drink only beer imported from Germany. In the shops buy only those goods which bear the mark 'Made in Germany.' Praise wherever you go German industry, German methods, German science. To keep your feet on the right path, we will supply you with guides, in which you will find every needful address. Our good counsel will accompany you everywhere. And thus, whilst amusing and instructing yourself, you will render signal service to your country and will become a pioneer of Germanism in those countries which we wish, progressively, to dominate. Moreover, *never forget in the course of your travels that you can make a thousand useful observations. Note down what you see and send us the information you collect*. Details apparently the most insignificant may be of use to our industrial, commercial, and patriotic societies. Finally, strengthen the patriotic feeling with our compatriots established abroad. Tell them that Germany does not forget them, and that it is to their interest to remain in close relations with it. If you act in this way—and you cannot do otherwise, for we shall keep a sharp eye on you—you will contribute largely to the glory of Germany, which to-morrow will dominate the world."

This picture is in no way exaggerated. Identical language was addressed to German tourists by the Pan-Germanist Association and the Deutschtum im Ausland Society, and the guides they published inculcated the principles of the most barefaced espionage.

The information which these ambulatory amateur spies collected was undoubtedly precious. It assisted in the spread of German commerce and German ideas. Our enemies worked on the principle that every little helped, and that the observations of a spectacled professor tramping through France could be turned to almost as much use as those of a professional spy, working under cover of a bank or an insurance company like the Viktoria zu Berlin in Paris, which our friends and Allies the French very soon closed down. The sum-total of the efforts of all these amateur and professional spies was enormous, and would indeed have led to the domination of Europe by the Teuton but for his inborn crass stupidity.

I wonder when we shall really learn to know the true character of the German? French people, who long ago put a stop to Teuton tricks, are amazed to hear that we still allow the enemy to remain in our midst, and that we actually help them to carry on their businesses, just as though the war never existed. "Are you aware of the fact," I have often been asked by Parisian friends, "that these large German concerns were nothing more or less than gigantic spying organizations?"

V—REVELATIONS OF THE SPY SYSTEM

Those who have any doubt about this should read the remarkable revelations of M. Georges Prade anent the Viktoria zu Berlin Insurance Company, the premiums of which represented over eighty million pounds. In the Paris offices of this company, in the Avenue de l'Opéra, M. Prade discovered a peculiar organization called the Special Büro. The *employés* of this office were all Germans, between twenty-five and thirty years of age, and officers in the German reserve. They spent from five to six months in France, received forty pounds a month each, with an allowance for travelling expenses, and spent their time motoring all over France. Eastern France and the Alps was their favourite region. Naturally they all disappeared a few days before the German mobiliza-

tion in July, 1914. Whilst these men were spying out
the land, their colleagues in Paris were performing
equally useful work for the German Government, "establishing an exact estimate of the public fortune, a useful
element in assessing war taxation and indemnities," and
otherwise obtaining valuable information. The Viktoria,
for example, offered special terms to French officers. It
insured them, without extra charge, against war risks,
and, through the medium of visiting agents, advanced
money at very reasonable terms on their policies. The
Berlin offices of the Viktoria thus secured the names of
all the French officers who owed it money, an excellent
arrangement indeed on which to base an organization for
spying.

One of the most astounding institutions in Paris before
the war was a free German school, open to children of all
nationalities, where instruction was given entirely in German, and French was treated as a foreign tongue. Naturally history and geography were taught from the German standpoint, and a love of Germany and the Kaiser
was dinned into the pupils. Stranger still, none of the
professors held a French certificate, a *sine qua non* for a
French teacher, or were even naturalized. Yet in 1908
one of them was even decorated with the Legion of
Honour.

Side by side with this instance of "peaceful penetration" may be placed that of a commercial agency, the
Agence Schimmelpfeng, which existed in Paris for years,
and, under the guise of a society for giving confidential
information to commercial houses and their customers,
covered a most elaborate and minute spy system, with
central offices in Berlin. To give but one example of the
work of this agency, it knew the name of every baker in
the East of France, how many men he employed, and the
exact number of sacks of flour he used per week. Thus

the German military authorities knew almost to a loaf how much bread could be counted on for an invading army.

German spies were always particularly active in Eastern France. Another precaution they took was to secure all the contracts for coal for the frontier forts, in order to be able to withhold supplies at a critical moment and thus render them useless. On a par with this was the establishment of a German chemical works adjoining an airship factory, which they were ready to supply with hydrogen just as long as it suited them. The arrangement had this additional advantage: when any little hitch occurred with a machine, German workmen were always ready with their help. A French dirigible had thus no secrets for them.

Supplies and the methods by which as complete a control of them as possible could be obtained must have been made the study of a special section of the Secret Service department in Berlin. It is not curious that in 1912 a German firm should have succeeded in obtaining the contract for the exclusive furnishing of lubricating oil for the French army motor-cars? But this is nothing in comparison with the plans laid for getting possession of the iron-fields of Normandy and a certain part of the French Channel coast.

VI—STORY OF A "GERMAN GIBRALTAR" IN NORMANDY

Germany, lacking iron ore, obtained extensive concessions of land in Normandy and annually sent vast quantities of mineral to Krupp's, where it went to the making of munitions to be used against the Allies. In the extraction of this ore only German machinery, worked by German coal, was used. Simultaneously our arch-enemy got possession of a place called Diélette, eighteen miles west of Cherbourg, and constructed there a deep-water port, capable of accommodating vessels of fifty thousand tons. The ostensible purpose set forth by the *concessionnaires* was the shipping of ore and the working of a submarine iron-mine, but the real object was made clear when the German newspapers, in their bragging way, began to write about Diélette as the "German Gibraltar." And a German Gibraltar it would have become but for Great Britain's intervention in the war. For if France had not had our Navy behind her, nothing would have been easier than to land German troops at Diélette. The port and arsenal of Cherbourg would have been but a mouthful for the Huns, the western side of Cherbourg, owing to the natural disposition of the land, being undefended, as it has always been looked upon as impregnable. And so it was until the port of Diélette was constructed.

Diélette, the proposed German submarine base for the Channel, and adapted not only for military and naval purposes, but most conveniently situated for spying on Cherbourg, was used for the first time as a port only a week before the outbreak of war. On July 25th, 1914, the first big vessel arrived and was loaded in the record time of twenty-four hours. Under the superintendence of Raders, the chief spy, large quantities of explosives had been accumulated. The greater part was seized by the French Government, but when the authorities attempted to visit the mine it was discovered that many of the galleries had been wilfully flooded.

After all the arrangements had been made at Diélette, the Germans began to say that the carriage of iron ore thence to a German port had been found to be too costly, so they immediately began to acquire land and make arrangements for smelting on the spot. Furnaces were built at Caen, a railway line was constructed, the canal from that town to the sea was deepened, and things were so arranged that at any given moment Caen could be cut off from its natural port, Ouistreham. The electric cable transmitting the motive force for this port and for the opening and shutting of the bridges over the canal was aerial, and passed over land acquired by another of the prime movers of the Diélette and Caen schemes, a man named Thyssen, an intimate friend of the Kaiser. This cable was cut on August 12th, 1914.

The machinery and materials, directors and workmen of all these undertakings were German, so that, although some of the capital of the company was furnished by French shareholders, practically the whole of this part of Normandy was already, when war broke out, in the hands of the Huns. Normandy in their power, they set about getting Brittany. Private individuals bought up large tracts of land and islands, and there is no doubt that the splendid port of Brest would before long have been theirs. Was not one of the Kaiser's sons familiarly known in Berlin as the "Duke of Brittany?"

I have mentioned two of the chief spies connected with the Normandy plots, Raders and Thyssen. The former left the mine at Diélette on August 1st, but was arrested. Hefter, one of his subordinates, received a telegram that his brother had been run over by a train, and so got away on July 26th, whilst a third, a so-called Swiss, named Strobel, stayed in France for a month, and even returned to Diélette in January to destroy a trunk full of papers in a house which he had occupied.

Rheims, the cathedral city of saddened memories, was another of the great spy centres of France. More than seventy inhabitants, in every imaginable disguise, had to be shot, we are told by M. Léon Daudet, who before and since the war has thrown much light on German espionage. Every woollen mill in Rheims was known to the enemy, and at the time of the invasion they sent off to Germany more than a hundred wagon-loads of models and drawings of machines, and so on, together with multitudinous bales of merchandise. All account-books were soaked with paraffin and burnt, and all workmen's dwellings were systematically destroyed.

There is no doubt that as regards works, factories, and mills of all kinds, a systematic plan was followed wherever the German system of espionage operated. Those that could in any way be useful to the invaders during their occupation were carefully preserved, and those judged prejudicial to their future commercial prosperity were as ruthlessly destroyed. It was the same with private residences. Anything belonging to spies—many of them naturalized Frenchmen—was marked by advance guards in accordance with a carefully-prepared list, and was neither burnt nor pillaged when all around was destroyed.

Henkell, of Wiesbaden, had some years ago started a wine business at Rheims, and his warehouse was built between the barracks, the aviation ground, the military fodder stores, and other official buildings. From the windows of his establishment he and his *employés* could keep an eye on the movement of all military trains on the three lines leading from Rheims to Chalons, Charleville, and Laon.

VII—STORY OF HERMANN VON MUMM, "PRINCE OF CHAMPAGNE"

But this man Henkell was a mere underling compared with others. Hermann von Mumm, of champagne fame, was the high priest of the spies of Rheims. A multi-millionaire, he owned a splendid residence in that city, another in the Avenue du Bois de Boulogne in Paris, and a third in the Department of the Marne. He was served by a retinue of servants, most of whom were non-commissioned officers in the German army. Besides being an enthusiastic motorist, he kept a racing stable. Many German officers visited and stayed with him. Under cover of his wine business, the acquiring of vineyards or other land, these spies openly scoured the country until they knew it in its minutest details. Everything was thus foreseen and arranged for the German occupation—the position of trenches, good shelters, cemented platforms for heavy guns, and even stores of ammunition in disused quarries. It was entirely due to Mumm and his satellites that the Huns were able to establish themselves in Champagne so firmly. After the victory he was to have been Prince of Champagne.

Thanks to Hermann von Mumm's horse-dealings and the sumptuous fétes he was accustomed to give, he succeeded in establishing relations with innumerable people willing to uphold and help him in his nefarious work. At Chantilly, the racing centre, he had quite a little army of spies under his direction.

His brother, Walter von Mumm, a devotee of shooting, who with his friends was responsible for about four thousand head of game every year at Ville-aux-Bois, went to Germany in February, 1914, and on his return informed his keepers that he should preserve no game that year, *as he did not intend to shoot next season.* On July 25th, 1914, he left in one of his motor-cars, with his French chauffeur, for Frankfort, telling his servants he should be back in three weeks' time, between August 15th and 25th. Once over the frontier the chauffeur was astonished to see numbers of soldiers on the march, and was calmly informed by his master that it was *"la guerre."* On reaching Frankfort he was dismissed, and told to get back to France as best he could, which he did after a long and painful journey *viâ* Belgium.

In the district known as La Woevre, a great plain in the east, extending between the Meuse and the Moselle, all the large farms for years past gradually slipped into the hands of the Germans, who generally bought them much above their value, and then, as often as not, let them lie fallow. All the labourers were Germans, mostly not speaking French, whilst many others appeared to be much above their station—evidently spies who would be most useful to an invading army as knowing all the strategic points, pathways, bogs, and so on.

VIII—STORY OF A SECRET TELEPHONE SYSTEM

Much the same thing happened around Verdun. Many of these frontier towns had secret telephones installed in the cellars. A French ambulance worker, taken prisoner, was conducted into one of these farms to await the convoy she was to join. By accident she was hustled into a room full of telephonic apparatus, and was able, before she was hurriedly taken away again, to read the names of some twenty French villages inscribed over them. She had encountered by chance the central exchange of the spy farms.

In this manner did the Huns lay their plans for the hoped-for occupation of France. When the time came for the declaration of the war the majority of the spies of Germany made good their escape. But some, in accordance wth the orders of their superiors, remained behind to continue to assist in the conquest of the country.

When the German army was marching towards Paris signals were noticed at night on the heights of Meudon-

Bellevue, and these were answered by others along the river. Similar ones were noticed near the Gare du Nord and the Gare de l'Est, and it is a fact that at no matter what hour a train of stores left the former station bombs were always dropped upon it. This continued, I have been told by a person in authority, until certain spies, who had obtained employment with the railway company in order to signal the departure of the trains, were discovered and shot.

I have often been asked if I think that much spying still goes on, even in this third year of the war, and my invariable reply is, "Read the newspapers." Hardly a day passes without a case of espionage being recorded in the Press. Here are two typical examples which have come to my own particular notice quite recently.

The first is that of a certain Marie Liebendall, wife of Gimeno Sanches, born at Düsseldorf and twenty-eight years of age. Accused of espionage, she was sentenced to death by the Council of War of the Fifteenth Region. She gave herself out to be a countess, but in reality is the daughter of the manager of the Mannesmann works at Munich. After residing in Germany and the United States, she came to France, under the cloak of her Spanish husband, and devoted herself to spying. She was arrested at Cerbère, at the very moment she was escaping into Spain. Imprisoned at Marseilles, she attempted to poison herself.

The second case is that of Frido J. C. von Meyerem, who was sentenced to death on September 6th last by the First Court-Martial in Paris and then tried again in November by the Third Court-Martial, the first sentence having been quashed owing to a technical fault in the procedure. Meyerem was accused of concealing his German nationality at Nice in March, 1916, and also of entering the entrenched camp of Paris in the same month.

While at Nice he corresponded in invisible ink with an espionage agent, who sent him a cheque for about forty pounds. He was also charged with having furnished the enemy with information prejudicial to the operations of the army and compromising the security of the forts and other military establishments. Meyerem was again adjudged guilty and sentenced to death.

Thousands of these men and women, ready to risk their lives for the love of money and the German Fatherland, undoubtedly continue their dangerous work all over France to-day. The majority of them are women, either the German wives of French subjects or alleged "neutrals." They are thus free to go about under the protection of their borrowed or neutral flag, without let or hindrance. Some who are unmarried play, I am convinced, a more hazardous game by remaining in hiding until night, when they come forth like nocturnal birds of prey. This is by no means so difficult in a large city like Paris as one would think, as witness the case of an Austrian, Michel Augmeister, aged thirty-eight, a native of Martensdorf, who remained hidden away by his French wife in his apartment at 24, Rue Brey, for no less than twenty-six months. It was not until October 25th last that, as his health was suffering seriously from seclusion, his spouse considered it the wisest plan to give him up to the police.

IX—EXPOSURE OF THE "LONELY SOLDIER" TRICK

Among the multitudinous means employed by German female agents in France is the insertion of small advertisements in the Parisian papers proposing an exchange of correspondence with British officers at the Front. Until a stop was recently put to this practice, as the result of an inquiry at military headquarters, I frequently saw advertisements of this sort in a daily published in Paris. Here is a specimen of one announcement:—

"Refined Parisian lady wishes to exchange correspondence with cultured person at the Front, to improve knowledge."

A few days later the same advertiser varied the wording as follows:—

"Young Parisian widow, having greatly travelled, wants to exchange correspondence with cultured officer at the Front."

In a series of similar advertisements she became "an artist," "an actress," and "an independent lady." That a large number of "lonely" British officers were deceived and entered into correspondence with her is certain. It is satisfactory to be able to say that, through the vigilance of the authorities, she did not succeed in her object. A certain foolish young lieutenant had a narrow escape from falling into her clutches. He wrote—quite in good faith —that he would be glad not only to correspond, but also to meet her when he next came to Paris with his colonel, as he fairly frequently came to the capital, and put up at the Hôtel Continental. However, very fortunately for him, the meeting never came off, for before the letter had reached its destination the lady had received her warning and sailed for the United States.

X—TALES OF THE SPIES AT THE FRONT

Mr. W. Beach Thomas, the *Daily Mail* correspondent with the British Army, recounted on October 19th last a strange incident which occurred at Armentières, where the old and more regular method of warfare then prevailed. "Two days ago," he wrote, "a civilian was seen to leap over the parapet of our front trench and run for the German line, which is not far distant. He was shot dead before reaching it, *and in the evening the Germans recovered his body*. How had he reached our trench? Who was he? Was he spy or madman?" Few readers will hesitate over the answer.

There must indeed be numerous spies at the Front. I am told that in certain sectors the country people whose homes are still within the war area are frequently suspected, and wonder has often been expressed that the military authorities have not long ago ordered them to retire far to the rear.

I have heard of a ploughman who, for the guidance of Hun airmen, ploughed two converging furrows pointing directly to the position of a concealed battery, which was later severely shelled, and of a seemingly unsophisticated countrywoman who laid out a white sheet on the ground, wherein to pack her wares for market, hard by another important position that German planes were searching for. Both these people turned out to be disguised Boche agents.

The liberty of the *mercantis,* or itinerant merchants, who infest the rear and rob the French *poilu* or British "Tommy" by selling him wretched goods at an exorbitant price should likewise be curtailed.

Spies are to be divided into innumerable categories. Within the limits of a magazine article it is impossible to do more than touch on the fringe of this great topic. One could devote two or three chapters of a book merely to the subject of those spies who, from time to time, are carried at night-time within the French and British lines by German airmen, who pick them up again when dawn is about to break. This is the most perilous game which the spy is called upon to play. It leads to the most extraordinary adventures and hairbreadth escapes, and some of these I hope later on to have the opportunity of relating.

HOW STRONG MEN DIE — TALES OF THE WOUNDED

Experiences of a Scottish Minister

Told by Rev. Lauchlan Maclean Watt, Minister of St. Stephen's, Edinburgh

The courage of the Scots is one of the epics of the Great War. An insight into their strong character may be seen by this minister's story to *The Scotsman*, revealing the pathos and fortitude of men on their death-beds.

I—STORY OF THE MINISTER AT THE DEATH-BED

It is truly a great thing to see that the day of willing devotion to the noblest ideals is not yet gone from the life of our people. Suffering and death are faced without repining, and men say farewell to the promise of their youth ungrudgingly, feeling that the investment for the sake of the future of the world is worth the cost which they are paying. To the greatest life and death are very simple alternatives, lying easily to either hand, accepted without complaining.

One day I was going through a tent of suffering men just after a big "stunt." It was a day of much and great agony for those who were in actual bodily pain and for those of us who had to try to help them to endure it. I saw two men carried in and laid on beds side by side with each other. One was obviously very severely wounded. The other was swathed in bandages over his head and down over his face, apparently blinded. For a moment I hesitated, thinking it might be better to come back when, perhaps, the agonies of the one might be somewhat abated. But I put my hesitation aside. I found that the two men were brothers who, fighting in the same trench, had been struck down by the same shell. Late that evening an ambulance came for me as a man was dying, and I found it was the soldier I had spoken to earlier in the day.

The camp lay beautifully still, for the clouds were heavy and the stars were veiled. I stepped into the tent, into the breathing dark. The beds were swathed in shadow, only one red lamp hanging from a central post.

They had brought the brothers quite closely together, and the man with the bandaged eyes had a hand of the other in his own. The dying man took mine in a grip of ice.

"Padre," he whispered, "I am going home. And I wanted you to come again to me. Write tenderly to my people. This will break their hearts. And pray that my brother may be spared." There is no ritual for a moment like that. One could but ask Him who was broken also for others to be near this broken man whose body was pierced unto dying for the sake of those he loved. We whispered together there a few lines of "Jesus, Lover of My Soul," and a verse of the immortally wonderful "Lead, Kindly Light." And then he put his arm about my neck and drew me closer.

"I tried to do what was right," said he. "O Christ, receive my soul. Have mercy upon me." I heard a man near me, in the dark, say "Amen." And I knew the fellows were not sleeping. They were lying there, in their own pain, thinking of him who was passing that night into the great beyond. Then I said, very quietly, the last verse of the hymn he had whispered:

> So long Thy power hath blessed me, sure it still
>   Will lead me on,
> O'er moor and fen, o'er crag and torrent, till
>   The night is gone,
> And with the morn those angel faces smile
> Which I have loved long since and lost a while.

The silence lay between us for a little, till the dying man asked, "What o'clock is it?" And I told him.

"I'm so sorry for disturbing you so late," said he.

"Good-bye, padre, till we meet again." And with a sigh he passed away.

I heard a quiet step near me, and I looked around, with the dead man in my arms. I should not have been astonished if I had seen the very Christ, with His wounds shining there, behind me, in that quiet tent, now so terribly, infinitely still. It was only the woman with the red cross on her breast, the angel of the sick and weary in their pain, seeming always to us, in such a moment, the nearest we can get to Christ, for tenderness and help. And so I laid the dead man down upon his pillow; and had to turn immediately to the living one to comfort him.

II—LIFT YOUR HAT TO THE RED CROSS

As long as I live I shall lift my hat to the red cross. It is, of course, the symbol of the highest sacrifice earth's history ever knew; and it is still the mark of the tenderest devotion and most perfect self-surrender for the sake of others. Every man in khaki, and every man that has a soldier boy to love, should salute that symbol which speaks of love amid the hate and turmoil of war. For it means womanhood consecrated to gentle service, reckoning neither wage nor worry in aught it does, and it takes the sting from broken manhood that has ventured for the sake of honour and of duty, through comradeship in suffering, to the verge of life, and beyond it.

War takes a man in the splendid vigour of his full manhood and flings him out of trench and battlefield a bleeding thing. The devoted women of the hospital tent shrink from no duty when the suffering and mire-stained man is brought to them. There can be no greater self-mastery and no more sublime self-forgetfulness than the washing of the bodies of the stricken and the dressing of the terrible wounds that have broken their murderous way into the fair flesh of the soul's house. And how they work! It has to be seen to be understood, and once seen it can never be forgotten. Faithfulness, tenderness, and loving devotion are the marks of those ministering angels, "when pain and anguish wring the brow." There is no question of adherence to hours. It becomes a question of adherence to duty when a rush is on. There is no strike for shorter hours, or an increased wage, or a war bonus with them or the brave men whom they serve. The men, even to the roughest "grouser," appreciate it fully. "O sister! go to rest now," I have heard them say, pleadingly, to the tired woman with the red cross on her breast and the white cross in her heart.

III—THE LADS WHO DRIVE THE AMBULANCE CARS

So, also with the lads who drive the ambulance cars. I have felt my heart fill as I watched them bringing in the wounded. Gently as a mother carrying a sick child in her bosom, they creep with their agonized burdens over the rough roads, calculating every inequality, thinking through every stage of the journey. I remember, at midnight, standing by one that had just been brought in. The first to be lifted out on a stretcher was a fine fellow, an Irishman, with his right arm blown off. The doctor, with his lantern, leaned over and asked his name.

But the suffering man looked up in his face and said, "Sir, before we do anything, please thank the driver. He's a Christian and a gentleman."

The common sorrow of the allied nations binds them very tenderly together. I used to see a fine expression of this in the town where I was first stationed, where some women who had a garden, on the way to the cemetery, were wont to do a very beautiful thing. As, almost daily, the heavy lumbering wagons with the dead came rolling along, those kindly hearts came out and laid on each coffin, above the Union Jack, a bouquet of exquisite flowers. Then the wagons rumbled on toward the graves. It was a sweet tribute to the brave strangers who are fighting in France, so many of them giving their all in sacrifice for liberty, love, and home in this hideous uprising of all that was monstrous in the dark ages that are past.

One perhaps learns most by unlearning. I used to think of the spirit of pain as intensely, even immensely, vocal. I remember, especially, when I was young, a great gully in the north, beside the sea, up which the waves came dashing in perpetually recurrent warfare, the flood seeking ever higher, only to be drawn away down the sloping shingle again, shrieking, to the main. Often in the daytime I would listen, and, in the dark, would linger near, held by the awe of the unsleeping tragedy of that vast elemental grief which sways about the edges of the world. I told my heart, "This is the spirit of the world pain finding voice." But now I know otherwise. I have learned better in the school of suffering, in the land of war. The spirit of pain is silent—tholing, at its deepest. It looks at you out of those suffering eyes. There is no cry in it. For the mystery of duty is within its depths. The fifty-third chapter of Isaiah is its truest picture. So it comes to be that the nobility and manliness of the brave combine, with unforgettable splendour of ineffable beauty, the darkness of our times. When they do speak there is a majesty of stillness about their utterance, vast as the mid-deep, far away, out under the stars.

The lads are uplifted by the nearness of the Unseen. I have before me two genuine documents, letters of two fine boys who went godward up the highway of the sun—the way of sacrifice. They speak for themselves. No novelist's imagination could create so fine an utterance. One was scribbled in the trenches, the other in the hospital ward, to those who had the best claim on the best the writers had to give. Said one:

"I am in the trenches, and in half an hour we go over the top. Our artillery is going at it hammer and tongs, the biggest bombardment in English history. It is just like huge express trains rushing through the air in hundreds. All of us are happy in the prospect of a clean fight after so many weary months as passive spectators of anything but warfare, except on rare occasions. If I get through all right I shall add a postscript to this. If not, mother dear, I know you will not be beaten by a Spartan mother who had no heavenly Father revealed to her to look to for comfort, but yet could say, 'Come back with victory, or not at all.' With heaps of love. * * *"

The other is suffused with the same straightforward spirit of fearlessness and faith.

"I was so glad to see your answer this morning, but am sorry I have not enough strength to write much. A good few died of wounds in this hospital through weakness, but I am leaving all doubts with God, as He holds the key of all the Unknown, and I am glad. So if I die before long, and I cannot see anything more sure, I hope to meet you all in God's good time. My wound is numb. It is in my thigh, and I have no pain. * * * I am now at the balance, to live or die. So good day, and God bless all. * * *"

There was nothing really extraordinary about these boys among their fellows. But one is struck by the frequency with which the men, after a deep emotion, touch literature in their letters. Of course the secret of true style lies in a real experience. Some of them, it is true, tell absolutely false tales, and their letters are sentimental poses. But of the letters of dying men there can be no mistake, and these boys wrote these on the threshold of the eternal mystery. They are types of a large proportion of the army of today, fighting, suffering, and dying as those who have looked in the face of the Invisible, and are inheriting the promise, "Be thou faithful unto death and I will give thee a crown of life." It is surely an incentive to the people at home, for honour and remembrance.

THROUGH THE JAWS OF DEATH IN A SUNKEN SUBMARINE

Told by Emile Vedel in L'Illustration, Paris

Many a novelist and some dramatists have tried to imagine the last agonies of the crew of a submarine boat that has received a mortal wound and sunk. Here is a first-hand account of the dreadful reality, told by men who actually experienced the tragedy. How these men slipped out from the very jaws of death just as they were closing on them, even they cannot fully explain; but some strange freak of the machinery made their submarine bob back to the surface after the water pouring into it had sent the vessel down 200 feet. Emile Vedel, who is writing the story of the French naval operations in the Adriatic and publishing it serially, under governmental authority in *L'Illustration*, obtained the facts from the signed statements of two petty officers of the boat. Translated by Arthur Benington in the *New York World*. Copyright, 1917, Press Publishing Company.

I—STORY OF THE PRISONERS IN BOHEMIA

A COMPOSITE flotilla of French, British and Italian gunboats and submarines attacked an Austrian flotilla which had sneaked out from the Bocche di Cattaro, on the eastern shore of the Adriatic and shelled the port of Durazzo. The engagement resulted in the sinking of an Austrian destroyer. The following day the French picked up some sailors from another Austrian destroyer, the *Llka,* which had struck a mine and sunk. These sailors told them that in attacking the Austrian fleet the Allied boats had narrowly escaped killing the survivors of a French submarine that had been sunk and the crew of which had been rescued by Austrian gunboats.

What submarine it was they were at a loss to know,

but as time passed and nothing was heard from the *Monge,* they became convinced that it must have been she. This conviction was strengthened two months later, when Mme. Roland Morillot, wife of Lieut. Morillot, commander of that boat, received a letter signed "Crew of the *Monge,*" mailed from the concentration camp for prisoners at Deutsch Gabel, Bohemia, of which the following is a translation of a part:

"Notwithstanding the distance, we unite our grief with yours in weeping over the memory of him who in spite of all will ever remain our captain. Stricken by a blow of fate just when victory smiled most brightly, Commandant Morillot died like a hero, after having accomplished the almost impossible to save his vessel and his crew."

More months elapsed; then Chief Master Electrician Joffry and Quartermaster Mahe, both of the *Monge,* were returned to France from Austria in an exchange of prisoners. And they told the story.

II—STORY OF A COLLISION AT 30 KNOTS

The *Monge* belonged to the class of submarines that have to use a steam engine for recharging their diving accumulators. It had been scouting ahead of the rest of the flotilla and had crept close to the Bocche di Cattaro that night when the Austrian fleet came out. At 12.15 A. M. Commandant Morillot sighted the lights of the Austrian vessels. How many he couldn't tell, nor how far away they were. He submerged to 20 feet, leaving the night periscope above the surface. Suddenly he was aware of a rapidly approaching huge black mass, and was giving orders to fire a torpedo from the port tube when a hitherto unseen vessel passed at 30 knots right over the *Monge.* Its keel struck the submarine; the shock was terrific. The little boat rolled almost over.

The conning tower was smashed and the sea poured in through a gaping hole.

The crew of the *Monge* tumbled in heaps against the partitions of the compartments in which they happened to be. The stern dropped, the bows rose, and the boat began sinking stern foremost at an angle of 30 or 40 degrees. Abominable gases rose as the sea water flooded the tanks of sulphuric acid.

The electric lights went out. The *Monge* wabbled downwards in pitch darkness.

It is such moments as these that test master and men. How both were equal to the emergency, let Chief Electrician Joffry relate:

III—TWO HUNDRED FEET BENEATH THE SEA

"Clutching the periscope table," he said, "the Commandant faces this blow. He is a man whom nothing disconcerts. He orders that all submerging tanks be emptied. Several times he repeats the order to discharge the water. But the compressed air is not powerful enough to expel it, and we continue to sink. The hull creaks all over, but especially astern, for the stern, by reason of the angle at which we are going down, is sixty feet lower and under a pressure of two atmospheres greater than the bow. It is the steel heart of the *Monge* that is groaning. We must have at least 180 or 200 feet of water above us. Believing that this is the end, we sing the 'Marseillaise.'"

Quartermaster Mahe says the electric batteries were short-circuited by the crash and the inrush of water. The turbines stopped at the moment the lights went out.

"But if we see nothing, we can hear," adds the brave Mahe. "We hear everything, and every noise echoes like a knell: dull murmurs of surging water, nerve-wracking falls of men and things; questions anxiously spoken, crash of objects upon each other, sinister creakings of the hull under the terrible and ever increasing pressure. The smell of burning, the vile emanations of chlorine—forerunners of asphyxia—are inhaled everywhere, and grip our throats. Tango, the bob-tailed Arab dog, is stuck somewhere between the boilers."

IV—THE SONG OF DEATH—FROM DOWN BELOW

All at once in this antechamber of death there rises a song! To the steel heart of the *Monge* the even more highly tempered hearts of the French sailors are replying. They are singing! If the plates are springing, these hearts do not give way. Like their ancestors, the ancient Gauls, they fear nothing; and they prove it by intoning a hymn for France at 200 feet below the surface of the ocean. Yes, in their half overturned, flooded cage which threatens to crush like an eggshell, they sing! No audience is theirs and, so far as they know, none will ever know how they met their end. But no matter, it is for themselves they sing, possessed by the sublime exaltation that makes martyrs and heroes.

Groping about, they manage to make a lamp flash for a few seconds. This reveals the full gravity of the situation, for it shows the pointers of the manometers standing still at their limit, proving that they are far below the greatest depth permitted to the *Monge*.

Commandant Morillot's hand is upon the lever that controls the lead ballast, his last resource, but he hesitates to release it. If the leads be released the submarine will rise to the surface, but must be captured at once, for she will then be unable to submerge again. He looks at the men in the fitful light of the flashing lamp, questioning them with his eyes, as he thinks: If it is good to live it is also good to die for one's country. Their silence responding to his immobility expresses their acquiescence in the sacrifice.

But at last, under the direction of the Commander, the engineers get the turbines working again. The creaking diminishes, then it ceases. Ensign Appell strikes a match and holds it to the manometer. The pointer moves from its maximum (135 feet).

"Courage!" he cries, "we are rising!"

Quick to the periscopes! Alas, one of them has gone, and the other is blind!

Still they rise. Suddenly a crash above, and then another. Four shells explode right overhead. They are at the surface, and the Austrians are firing on them!

There is nothing for it but to submerge again, come what may. Scarcely has the Commandant given the order than a shell bursts right in the port periscope chamber, tearing a great hole in the hull. This time nothing can save the *Monge*. Only now does the captain let go the lead ballast. Since his vessel is lost, he will profit by the brief respite this lightening will give to save the crew. After closing the water valves he orders the forward hatchway opened and leads his men to it.

"Not that way, my boys," he says to those who take the wrong direction, "this way. As soon as you get out, leap overboard to show that the *Monge* is sinking and stop the enemy's fire."

V—GOOD-BY TO THE "MONGE"

Flashes from a lighthouse on shore show the men leaping overboard and the boat sinking lower and lower. The Austrians have ceased their fire.

"We marched forward singing the 'Marseillaise,'" said Joffry, "and with a cry of 'Vive la France!' we jumped. Then, nothing under our feet. Good-by *Monge!*"

We felt the shock of an explosion. The floating debris of the deck helped us to swim. Twelve of us clung to a floating gangway, swimming with our feet, for half an hour. Quartermasters Morel and Goulard were missing.

At last boats from the enemy destroyers came and picked us up.

And Morillot? He went down with the *Monge*. The details of his end are uncertain, but it is not difficult to reconstruct them. Joffry says: "He did not come up on deck. He remained at his post. Very calmly he stood watching the manometer reveal the gradual sinking of the vessel under him. He was surely saying in his heart 'If only my men can get away in time!' He told the last of us to hurry, and he helped us to find our way. What he did when he saw us all safe I do not know, but it seemed to me that the *Monge* sank more swiftly. He might have opened the water ballast valves to make her sink before the hand of the Boches could touch her. That is undoubtedly what he did, but I did not see him, nor did any one."

And Mahe, who was in the control chamber, says: "The captain told us: 'Our poor *Monge* is lost, but you have yet time. Come this way, my lads.' He opened the door and added: 'Au revoir, and courage, my lads!' I dared not tell him to come up with us, for I saw he had made up his mind to die with his ship, as he had already told some of us he would."

VI—THE LAST TORPEDO

The captain of the Austrian gunboat *Balaton* told the survivors that he had delayed launching boats to pick them up, because a torpedo had been fired at his boat from the *Monge* as she went down. He believed that Commandant Morillot, having seen all his men safely overboard, had gone below alone and deliberately fired a last torpedo. That is possible, or it may be that a torpedo was accidentally discharged from the sinking boat. Joffry spoke of feeling an explosion after getting into the water.

In an order of the day published as soon as the facts became known, Admiral the Duke of the Abruzzi paid tribute to the "heroic sacrifice in which Lieut. Morillot decided to remain on board his sinking boat," and added: "To do honor to this deed of the purest marine valor, his Majesty the King has deigned to confer upon him, *motu proprio,* the gold medal for valor." This was the first time this rare distinction had been conferred since the war began. In transmitting this notice to the French Admiral, Vice-Admiral Cutinelli-Rendina added:

"His memory will ever remain for us an object of admiration and worship."

ESCAPE OF THE RUSSIAN LEADER OF THE "TERRIBLE DIVISION"

True Story of How General Korniloff Escaped Across Hungary

Told by Ivan Novikoff

The story of how the famous Russian general, leader of the "Terrible Division," was captured by the Austrians, and how he escaped in an Austrian soldier's uniform, making his way right across Hungary, for a distance of over three hundred miles, until he regained the Russian lines. This is the first detailed narrative of the general's feat, as it is told in the *Wide World Magazine*.

I—STORY OF THE DREADED GENERAL— THE RUSSIAN TIGER

THE Forty-eighth Infantry Division of the Russian army had long been dreaded by the enemy. Their bravery and dash, their grim and almost desperate courage, had earned for them the name of the "Terrible Division."

Their leader was the redoubtable General Korniloff, a man of iron will and heroic courage. He was a worthy descendant of that other great Korniloff, whose dying words, "Lord, bless Russia and the Czar, save the fleet and Sebastopol!" are inscribed on his monument near the Malakhoff Hill, where he fell in the great assault of 1855. A tiger to his enemies was Korniloff, but very gentle where his own men were concerned, solicitous for their wants and comforts. Though they were among the bravest fighters in the Russian army, their leader never threw their lives away recklessly. As for him, they believed him to bear a charmed life. "Korniloff" was their war-cry, and they felt safe in his hands.

In those brave days when the Russians were attacking in the Carpathians, in the spring of 1915, Korniloff's men were ever foremost in the fighting. Mowed down repeatedly by the German and Austrian guns, which defended the ground yard by yard, they came back to the charge again and again with a furious *élan*.

The way of the Russians was barred by a commanding eminence held by two divisions of the enemy. From this height the fire had been devastating and unceasing, and the position seemed impregnable. Formidable defences of barbed wire guarded all the approaches, and mines and other murderous devices defied all their efforts to take the stronghold.

But Korniloff determined to accomplish the almost superhuman task. Deliberately he set about breaking down the defences. Two regiments were assigned to the task. Night by night they worked in as much secrecy as the darkness afforded, pressing on under a withering fire until at last the road was clear. Then they took the height by a furious assault, and were masters of the position that had galled them for so many months. Five thousand men had defeated twelve times their number. The Austrian general, with his staff, was taken prisoner, and when he learned of the numbers which had opposed his big army he broke down and wept with rage and grief. "Korniloff is not a man," he said; "he is an elemental force."

The Russians were now masters of this important strategical position. The town of Ivla lay in front of them, within reach of their guns, but it was strongly fortified; while in the neighbouring forests the enemy was concentrating in great numbers. The fighting continued with unabated fury.

It was in April, 1915, and the rugged slopes of the Carpathian hills and mountains were brightened with the new green shoots of the foliage, with the vivid splashes made by broom and poppy, anemone, and other variegated blooms.

The Austrian forces were receiving reinforcements rapidly, and the Russian general and his division, in their new position, were hard pressed. They were almost isolated, practically surrounded by sixty thousand fresh enemy troops. The Russians kept up a solid and heroic defence, but the enemy gave them no rest. Soon Korniloff's much-weakened force was in a desperate situation. All their bravery and sacrifice had been unavailing; the enemy was gradually gaining upon them.

Calm and self-possessed, General Korniloff viewed the situation. "We are too feeble to resist any longer," he told his officers; "we must attack." This was Korniloff's method. He called his men together and explained how things stood. A small force must attack the Austrians and thus cover the retreat of the main body. He called for volunteers, and from the serried ranks that presented themselves formed a small detachment pledged to make the supreme dash. It was a forlorn hope, this attack, but it might save the rest of the division, which was otherwise doomed to fall into the hands of the enemy.

II—MARCHING TO DEATH BEFORE THE HOLY IKON

Early on a beautiful spring morning the resolute band mustered, and were passed in a pathetic little review by their valiant chief, who knew that he should look upon but few of those faces again. As they bowed devoutly before the holy ikon raised above them, they cried, "For God, St. Nicholas, and the Czar!" Then they shouldered their rifles, and a moment later were on the move, headed by the commander himself.

The manœuvre surprised the enemy, as it was intended to do, but the advancing force was violently assailed by a triple fire from artillery, rifles, and machine-guns. Still, however, they stumbled on, singing a chant popular with the peasants on the banks of the Volga. Man after man fell around the intrepid Korniloff, but the survivors pressed on unheeding; they knew that every yard they advanced meant more chance for the Forty-eighth Division.

Steadily they ploughed their way onwards till they were close to the enemy's lines. By this time there was but a handful of them left. Korniloff himself was wounded, and his strength was fast failing him.

The Austrians looked on with astonishment. Would these madmen never surrender? The ground was strewn with their dead and wounded. What could the last few survivors hope to accomplish? At last a bullet brought down the indomitable general, and the one-sided fight was over.

III—THE GREAT KORNILOFF A PRISONER OF THE AUSTRIANS

When Korniloff came to himself, and was able to take account of his surroundings, he found himself in a hospital, being treated for his serious wounds. He was a prisoner of the Austrians, as were the few of his men who had been left alive when he himself was taken. But he breathed a sigh of relief, for the gallant Forty-eighth Division had been saved by his devotion and the sacrifice of his splendid little band.

Escape of the Russian Leader

Dreary months of illness and convalescence passed by. At last the general was well enough to be moved from the hospital, and his captors conveyed him to a safer and more suitable habitation. As a prisoner of mark, a residence was chosen for him at the château of Esterhazy, at Eisenstadt, in the Sopron Department in Hungary. This was the famous castle, built in 1683, where Haydn was *Kapell-meister* to the Prince Esterhazy of the time.

Korniloff made up his mind that Eisenstadt should not long have him as a guest, and with increasing health and strength he set about finding a means of escape. First of all he made friends with the men who acted as his guardians, and they were flattered at the notice taken of them by the redoubtable Russian general, whose fame had spread over the Empire. He took a great interest in these common soldiers; he talked to them of their lives, their homes, the fights they had been in; and learned from them a few words and expressions in Magyar.

Now, one of these Austrian soldiers (as General Korniloff afterwards related to the delegates of the Czech Brigade, when they welcomed him in Kiev and congratulated him on his escape) happened to be a Slovack. What more natural than that he should sympathize with the prisoner and agree to help him to regain his liberty? In exactly what way he did this, no one knows save Korniloff himself, and as regards such points he is naturally discretion itself. Anyway, one morning, as he was returning to his apartment from the park in which he was allowed to stroll, he passed a guardroom, the door of which was open. On a table just inside lay a private soldier's uniform, with forage cap and everything complete. No one was in sight, though he heard somewhere in the rear the voices of men at their morning tasks. It was the work of a second to slip in, snatch up the kit, hide it under his cloak, and hasten to his own room. Had it been placed there, by arrangement, by the Slovack? Presumably, considering what followed next.

For two days after that the general kept to his apartment, suffering from a fictitious cold. He feared that inquiries might be made as to the missing garments, but to his heartfelt relief he heard nothing further about the matter. As there was always a considerable coming and going of soldiers, he trusted that during the two days he remained invisible there might be some new arrivals who would not be familiar with his person when the time came for action.

IV—STORY OF KORNILOFF'S DARING ESCAPE

On the second evening Korniloff, who had already experimented with the borrowed uniform and found that it fitted him fairly well, dressed himself in it and shaved off his beard. For some time past he had practised to himself before a mirror his knowledge of the German language, which was fairly good, and its pronunciation with the soft Austrian accent.

At nightfall, arrayed in his disguise, he went down into the court-yard and across into the park, where, at a certain spot and hour, he had arranged to meet his Slovack friend.

Here he hung about near the gate for some time, talking to soldiers, smoking a cigar, and cursing in the best military slang. Nobody suspected him, and at a moment when the sentinel's back was turned he slipped out. At first he strolled along nonchalantly, hoping that if he had been observed the others would think he was only one of themselves going off for a spree without leave. As soon as he was out of sight, however, the general "put his best leg foremost" and made the utmost haste he could to-

Escape of the Russian Leader 349

wards a figure which he recognized to be that of the man who had promised to guide him towards Russia. They had provided themselves with a map and compass, and had also accumulated a little store of money. But Russia was a long way off, and their plans for the future were somewhat vague.

All that night and most of the next day Korniloff and his unknown friend (the general confessed that he never knew the name of his benefactor) walked in an easterly direction. They slept for some hours in a lonely field, and then got on the move again. Here and there peasants helped them on their way; they were offered food and drink and a rest. Though they avoided small towns, they were making their way to Budapest, thinking that something might happen in that great city to help them, and that they could easily pass unchallenged where so many races intermingled.

But before reaching the great city on the banks of the blue Danube an unexpected and most unhappy incident occurred. The plan of escape was almost entirely wrecked.

"We had noticed that wherever we went the gendarmes eyed us suspiciously," said the general to the already mentioned delegation. "In every village through which we passed, at every farm at which we called for bite or sup, on every plain which we crossed, there seemed to be eyes watching us. Soon our provisions became exhausted and we began to suffer the pangs of hunger. One day, after a long, hungry march, my Slovack guide—the faithful companion of the early part of my sufferings—decided, since he was on the point of exhaustion, to ask for food and water at an isolated farm. I warned him that it was dangerous, but hardly had the words passed my lips than he was gone. I saw him enter the farm and waited in vain—waited for ten long hours! At last I comprehended what had happened. I saw the gendarmes surround the house and heard the sound of gunshots. Flight, instant flight, was the only course open to me, and thus, alone for the remainder of my journey, I continued with all speed towards Budapest."

V—THE RUSSIAN GENERAL DISGUISED AS AN AUSTRIAN

On reaching the Hungarian city, General Korniloff found it, as he expected, full of troops. Reinforcements were coming in to be dispatched to the various fronts, while other men were on their way home on periods of furlough. Amid all these soldiers nobody took any notice of the disguised Russian in his simple Austrian uniform. Needless to say, he carefully avoided attracting attention to himself, always keeping where the crowds were thickest.

Feeling hungry, he went into a small eating-house frequented by working-class people and ordered beer, bread, and sausage. Most of the customers in the place spoke Hungarian, but two sitting at a table near him were talking in German, and he overheard what they said. One of them was a woman, who, to judge by her appearance, was engaged in munition-making.

"*Ach, du Guter!*" she exclaimed to her companion. "That Russian general they captured in the Carpathians last year—Korniloff—has escaped, and they are offering a reward for his capture."

The fugitive felt for a moment as if all eyes were bent upon him, but as a matter of fact nobody took any notice of him.

"Ugh!" growled the man addressed. "Why couldn't they keep him when they had him? How much are they offering?"

Escape of the Russian Leader

"Fifty thousand kronen."

"*Fui tausend!* Fifty thousand kronen for a *verdammten Russen!* And in these times, when the war costs so much!"

"*Ja, mein lieber,* but he's a general, you see," explained the woman. "I wish I could find him. It would be better than making munitions."

So there was a price of fifty thousand kronen on his head, reflected Korniloff, as he left the restaurant. He felt strangely elated at the thought that he was calmly passing among the enemy unknown and unsuspected with such a reward offered for his capture. He bought a newspaper to obtain confirmation of the woman's announcement, and there he found the notice in large type, with a curiously inaccurate portrait of himself.

The darkness was now falling, and he walked on until he found himself in the Franz Josefplatz. A large number of soldiers were camping in the square, lying upon the benches or on the ground, and evidently preparing to spend the night there. Artillery-wagons were lined up all round. A man he passed—an Austrian artillery man—looked up at him and smiled. He was fixing his haversack against the trunk of a tree to serve as a sort of pillow.

"As good here as anywhere else," said the man in German.

"To be sure," Korniloff replied. "Better than the trenches, anyway. Why is the regiment bivouacking here?"

"No room elsewhere, comrade," said the soldier. "Wounded and soldiers everywhere—all the barracks full; everything full. Well, it's a nice night. Have a smoke?"

He offered a cigar, which the disguised general accepted, sitting down beside his new-found friend.

"Where have you come from, and where are you going?" asked the Austrian.

"Rejoining my regiment after convalescence," replied Korniloff.

They sat and exchanged confidence for some time, the Austrian asking numerous questions which Korniloff parried as well as he could. The gunner confessed that he was heartily sick of the war, as were all his comrades. He heard nothing but complaints from his home, where conditions were getting harder and food was becoming scarcer.

"It's the same with you, eh, comrade?" he said. "I don't suppose you come from a part of the world that's any better off?"

The Austrian was a simple soul, and he told Korniloff many things that interested him. Finally, after he had babbled in this way for some time, both men fell asleep side by side.

VI—TRAMPING ACROSS HUNGARY WITH THE PEASANTS

Korniloff bade his chance host good-bye and was off on his journey again before the regiment was stirring. He decided that he must trust to his feet. He would march right across Hungary; and by means of his map and compass he hoped to make so straight a line that it would not take him more than a month. He was now in good health and in excellent trim generally, and he had no fear of the journey if he could only get enough food to keep him alive. He must not linger on the way, however, for every hour was now of importance to him.

Having taken a crust and a cup of coffee at a wayside tavern full of soldiers, he got out of the city while the day was still young. Then began a long and dreary tramp, mostly alone, for the peasants in this region were not communicative, for the simple reason that he could not speak their language. He tramped for whole days without passing anything bigger than small hamlets, and his conversation was limited to asking, most frequently at farmhouses, for *kruh* (bread) or *viz* (water).

Sometimes the peasants would look him up and down and ask him, *"Osztrak?"* ("Austrian?"), and he would nod his head.

Very rarely did he get anything without paying for it, and as he saw his small stock of heller gradually disappearing, he had to be as economical as possible with those that remained. He slept mostly in the open air, since the weather was fine and there was little danger; once he was given a "shake-down" in a loft, and once he paid a few heller for a bed at a country inn.

Eventually Korniloff was reduced to almost his last pieces of money, and he felt that he must husband these in case of a very pressing need. A day came when he got nothing to eat but some wild strawberries picked by the road-side. A woman whom he asked for a bit of bread chased him away from her door with an oath, calling him *"Verdammten Osztrak!"* The next morning he got some bread, but again a day passed with no food but wild berries and water from a brook.

Things were getting worse and worse, but Korniloff knew he was near the end of his journey, and would be safe in another three or four days if only he could hold out. He had now been walking for nearly twenty days.

VII—"HALT!"—HE SALUTES A GERMAN CAPTAIN

One of his narrowest escapes happened in the little town of Klausenburg, a quiet place ordinarily, but now the centre of great military activity. He was walking through the town, as it was the best way of keeping to the direct route. Suddenly, from behind him, he heard a harsh voice cry in German, *"Halte!"*

Looking round, he saw that it was he himself who was being addressed. He halted; there was nothing else to do.

"Why did you not stop and salute me?" asked an offensive-looking young Austrian officer.

Korniloff clinked his heels together and saluted.

"I did not see you, Herr Hauptmann!"

"Ah! you are blind, then? Who are you, and where are you going?"

"Johann Bach," said the Russian, affecting simplicity, "and I am going home to my wife."

"You will come with me first, so that we can make a few inquiries about you."

Disaster stared the fugitive in the face. His first impulse was to run, but he resisted it. To obey, however, would mean his immediate discovery.

"I beg your pardon, gracious Herr Captain," he said, as humbly as he could, though inwardly cursing. "I beg you not to detain me now, when I am so anxious to get to my dear wife."

"An hour longer from your wife won't hurt you," answered the officer. "Come with me."

His tone was so utterly offensive that, almost instinctively, Korniloff made a gesture of defiance. Quickly the officer called two men who were passing. "Take this man to the Kiraly barracks," he ordered. "I will meet you there in half an hour."

The two soldiers saluted, placed themselves on either side of Korniloff, and marched him off. He knew it was no good trying to escape, so he thought he would try friendliness. "Give me at least a smoke," he said; and very willing one of the men stopped, gave him a cigar, and lighted it. They asked him what he had done, or not done, to bring on himself this disciplinary measure.

"Oh, it's only because I don't know the way," said Korniloff. "Come and have a drink with me, comrades. There is no harm in that."

VIII—STORY OF A GIRL AND A SHEPHERD'S HUT

One soldier looked at the other, and they nodded—it was not far to the barracks—and then turned into a small beer-garden, where drinks were ordered. They were served by a comely young woman, who looked with interest at the captive, for soldiers are not reticent in talking to the opposite sex. Korniloff did not know how it came about, but presently his companions, who took a second glass of beer, began to feel the effects in a way that he would never have expected. Korniloff left the table with an excuse to his comrades, who paid little attention.

The girl, who had been watching him, beckoned to him from the side of the house, grasped his arm, and led him to the yard.

"Flee," she said, "across those fields. I will keep them in talk. I have put something in their beer. Flee!" she repeated, and thrust a piece of bread and meat into his hand.

By way of answer Korniloff seized her hand, kissed her, turned on his heel, and hastened away as quickly as he could. In a very short while the town of Klausenburg was miles behind him. He walked almost all through the night, fearful that a hue and cry might be raised.

The next day the general felt a new sympathy, as it were, in the air. This was Transylvania, where he would run much less risk of being discovered. He had seen a newspaper at the inn at Klausenburg which told him great news—that Roumania was on the point of joining the Allies.

He stopped two peasants and asked them where he was. They pointed out the directions of Russia and of Moldavai.

"You're a Russian," said one the peasants, speaking in a dialect known in the Bukovina.

Korniloff nodded, waiting to see what the result might be, but his confession evidently evoked sympathy.

"See!" said the man, taking him by the arm. "Follow yonder brook, cross the hill as straight as you can, and to-night you will find a shepherd's hut on the right of the road at the bottom of the hill. Go there and ask for Mathias Meltzer; he will help you."

With a cheery "good day" they left him, and Korniloff trudged on. After a stiff day's march he reached the hut and found the old shepherd, with a younger man. Korniloff repeated the message he had been told to give.

"And who are you? An escaped Russian?" asked the old man as he sat beside his wood fire and shaded his hand to look at the stranger. "The Russian outposts are half a day's march from here," he continued. "I often hear the guns. To-morrow the Roumanians come in on the side of the Allies. Soon the Russians and the Roumanians will join hands and all this land will be laid waste."

"Will you take me to the Russians?" asked Korniloff. "It will be worth your while."

The old man pondered for a time. "I don't mind helping a Russian," he said, at last. "They've always been decent to me. Lie you down now and get some sleep, for we must start before daybreak."

He handed his guest a little bread, coarse cheese, and some onions. Korniloff made a meal and was soon asleep.

They started on their journey next morning in wet and mist. Mathias covered the Russian with a discoloured piece of sackcloth to make him look like a shepherd, in case they met inquisitive strangers. They kept close to the bed of a river and a small forest, and, creeping forward stealthily, were by midday in sight of the Russian outposts.

Here Korniloff was safe with his own people, and great was their joy when they learned who he was. A few days later the general was able to send a trusty messenger to the shepherd, Mathias Meltzer, carrying a sum of money and a letter of thanks to tell him whom he had saved.

IX—SEQUEL: A SLOVACK SOLDIER AND A HANGMAN

The sequel to this stirring story remains to be told. Who was the noble Slovack soldier—true to his race and his duty towards a Slav in trouble—who assisted General Korniloff to escape, and what was his ultimate fate? For three months nothing was known. Only recently was the author of these lines able to read in the Hungarian papers the account of a court-martial, held at Presburg, which had condemned to death by hanging "a Slovack soldier, named Francis Mornyak, proved to have been guilty of having assisted General Korniloff to escape from the château of Esterhazy." The execution of this obscure hero took place immediately after the judgment.

THE AERIAL ATTACK ON RAVENNA

Told by Paolo Poletti

In *L'Illustrazione Italiana* this distinguished Italian author expresses his indignation at the bombardment of Ravenna by Austrian aviators, when the ancient Basilica of Sant' Apollinare narrowly escaped destruction. Translated for *Current History*.

I WRITE with a feeling of relief. My beautiful Sant' Apollinare is uninjured, or nearly so. A blind bomb may have furrowed the April sky of my city, in this marvellous foretaste of Spring; but the criminal attempt has been in vain. And, with me, innumerable citizens of Ravenna have breathed a sigh almost of content. It is true that there were human victims. But our pity for them is too deep for any comment to be adequate; the only way to commemorate them worthily is to avenge them. But it is not of this wrong we wish to speak today. We wish only to bring together and to distill into a brief comment the living essence of the spirit of Ravenna, as it has affirmed itself in this historic, solemn hour.

The people of Ravenna have felt a lightning flash of sudden revolt because of the outrage perpetrated on their monuments. The citizens of Ravenna, if they have not, for the antique glories of their city, the fully conscious veneration which we shall hardly expect to find among them, nevertheless do breathe in from these monuments a deep impression of exaltation and well-founded pride. Our readers will remember those "Monologues" which Gigi Easi wrote with such grace and such penetrating humour. In one, "The Art of Delivering a Monologue," he introduces as speakers the inhabitants of the various capital cities of Italy, each of whom magnifies the beauty of his own city.

So it happens that, along with the Florentine, the Neapolitan, the Venetian, and the rest, there is not lacking a good citizen of Ravenna who, with vibrant words and potent adjectives, in intense and enthusiastic exaltation, energetically affirms the supremacy of his mosaics and his basilicas. The scene is not only most exhilarating, but also, from the point of view of psychology, profoundly true. Our populace lives, and feels that it lives, with its mighty memories and with its great historic personages, whose moral significance at least it knows how to estimate, and whose remoter glory it understands by a kind of natural and traditional intuition, and respects it, I might almost say, by a distant residuum of atavistic suggestion.

Galla, daughter and sister of Emperors; Theodoric sleeping, sleeping, according to these humble fancies, a secular sleep under his heavy monolith; Justinian, upraiser of precious churches and reviser of the imperial idea and the laws of Rome; Theodora, the dancing girl become a Queen, speak a language incomprehensible to the rough minds of our people, yet a secret fascination emanates to them from the rich vaults, heavy with gold, of the antique basilicas; from those vaulted roofs toward which, in their time, rose the thunderous hosannas of triumphal victories, and the humble supplications of tragical misfortunes; those vaulted domes, dazzling with emerald and ruby, to which were raised hands wrung in despair and menace, or joined in the lowly adoration of prayer; toward which were raised foreheads tormented with gnawing hatred or consoled by illuminating love. . . .

The basilica of Theodoric, made the target of the iniquitous attempt of the Barbarians, ever speaks to the people in the mysterious tongue of days long gone. . . .

Oh, my beautiful Sant' Apollinare! we dreaded to see shattered thy gleaming mosaics; we dreaded to see cut in two and mutilated thy ten-centuries-old campanile, which sends forth joyful peals in the luminous evenings of May; we feared that the voice would be stilled, which arises from thee, to chant a profound poem of history and of art.

We recall your founder, Theodoric, and his reign in Ravenna; his wise and successful attempt to bring together in peaceful relations the conquerors and the conquered, engrafting into the ultimate stem of Latin civilization the young shoot of fresh barbaric energy; so that his terrible invasion did not interrupt the continuity of history, but proceeded to develop harmoniously in the integration of the old Roman elements with the new, blended in a single composed form of enduring life.

Of the art which reminds us, through the verses of Gabriel d'Annunzio, of the millenary of Ravenna, one might also speak: of the "Purple night, gleaming with gold"; of the Virgins of Sant' Apollinare, in Francesca's passionate speech:

"The Virgins of Sant' Apollinare burn not so bright in their heaven of gold"; and the prophecy:

"Oh, Prisca, another hero will draw the bow from thy desert toward the infinite. . . . Clad in armour, he awaits the new days; thy warrior awaits the certain dawn, when a voice through the desert paths shall call forth the ancestral valour!"

We fit the augury to the new times; and, to meet the new Barbarians, we invoke the sacred vengeance of Italy here, from this furthest bourne of our Garibaldian land!

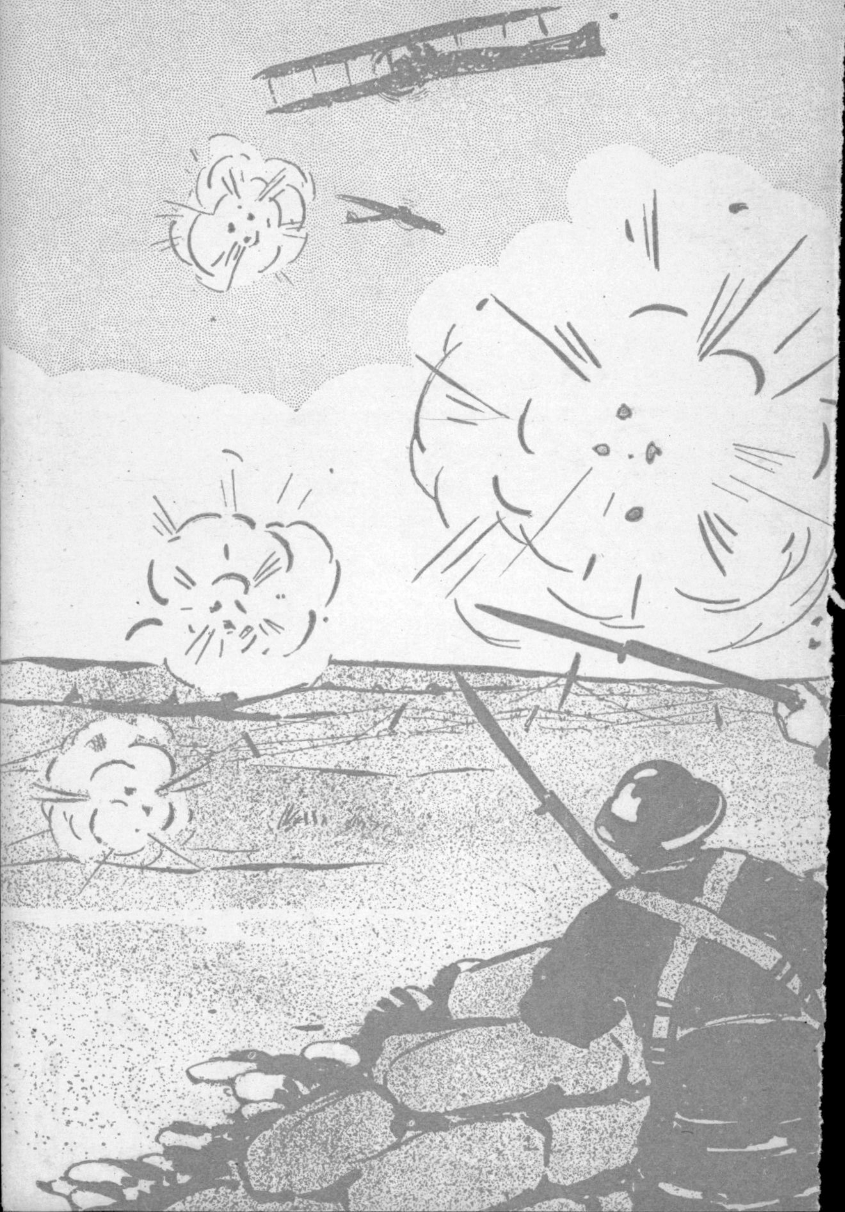